OLYMPIAD WORKBOOK

INTERNATIONAL MATHEMATICS OLYMPIAD

AF390168

01 **Learning Objectives**

02 **Multiple Choice Questions**

03 **HOTS (Achievers Section)**

04 **Model Test Paper**

05 **Answer Keys and Solutions**

06 **OMR Answer Sheet**

Published by:

V&S PUBLISHERS

F-2/16, Ansari road, Daryaganj, New Delhi-110002
☎ 23240026, 23240027 • *Fax:* 011-23240028
✉ info@vspublishers.com • ⊕ www.vspublishers.com

Online Brandstore: amazon.in/vspublishers

Regional Office : Hyderabad
5-1-707/1, Brij Bhawan (Beside Central Bank of India Lane)
Bank Street, Koti, Hyderabad - 500 095
☎ 040-24737290
✉ vspublishershyd@gmail.com

Follow us on:   

BUY OUR BOOKS FROM: AMAZON FLIPKART

© **Copyright:** *V&S PUBLISHERS*
ISBN 978-81-977325-3-9
New Edition

PUBLISHER'S NOTE

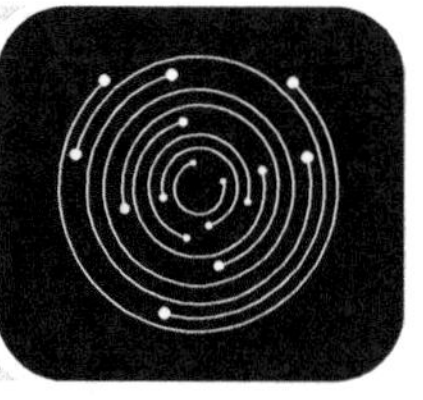

V&S Publishers has carved a significant niche in the publishing industry over the last decade, having successfully published more than 1000 titles across 9 languages spanning over 50 subject categories. Being known for the quality of content, we have built a reputation of excellence and reliability. We have consistently delivered **"Value & Substance"** to our readers, through a wide range of titles across a variety of genres covering school books, fiction and non-fiction that caters to different people from every section of the society.

The **Olympiad Guidebooks for classes 1-10** across all subjects, launched almost a decade ago, under the **GEN X Imprint**, became a go-to-source for the school students in no time, owing to their invaluable and substantive content written in a guidebook pattern,.

Having successfully sold a million copies of the same and in response to demand by both students as well as shopkeepers nationwide; we now present before you our newly launched **Olympiad Workbook Series**, designed for **classes 1-10 across 4 subjects**.

The workbooks are meticulously curated by a team of experienced educators, researchers and subject matter experts, edited by professionals and peer reviewed by teachers. The team has poured its efforts and expertise into creating a crisp and concise workbook which will help and guide the students to the path of success in Olympiad exams. The **MCQs** identified will not only help in scoring top marks in Olympiads but also inculcate a sense of deeper understanding of the subject, by way of solving **HOTS** and referring to complete solutions at the end of the book.

Here we present our new release– **OLYMPIAD WORKBOOK (IMO) CLASS–9** having following features:

- ☞ Based on the latest syllabi
- ☞ MCQs with comprehensive coverage of topics
- ☞ HOTS Questions liberally included
- ☞ A dedicated chapter on logical reasoning
- ☞ Model test paper for thorough practice
- ☞ Sample OMR sheet for real time simulation

We have made sure through our best efforts, that this workbook strictly follows the latest syllabi and patterns of the Olympiad Examination.

As **V&S Publishers** continuously strive to enhance the readability and maintain the credibility of our academic publications, we seek the support of our valuable readers in influencing and enriching the lives of future generations of students.

P.S. While every care has been taken to ensure the correctness of the content, if you come across any error, howsoever minor, do not hesitate to discuss with teachers while pointing that out to us in no uncertain terms.

We wish you all the best for your exams!

DISTINCTIVE FEATURES

WHY OLYMPIADS?

Olympiads are just like competitive exams; conducted by various bodies at national and international levels. The aim is to experience a competitive examination at the school level and also to help students to discover their interest across subjects like English, Mathematics, Science and General Knowledge.

COMPLEMENTS SCHOOL SYLLABI

The syllabi across all Olympiad examination closely follow the pattern of academic books. Hence, they not only provide a competitive examination experience, but also help to revise topics for school examinations as well, while strengthening conceptual precision.

01 Learning Objectives

They list the whole chapter as subtopics, helping the teachers to guide children in a step-by-step manner.

02 Multiple Choice Questions

MCQs act as an excellent learning aid, helping you to understand and work on your mistakes.

03 HOTS (Achievers Section)

The High Order Thinking Questions aim to help the student to solve Application-based questions and gain practical understanding of the subject.

04 Model Test Paper

Model test paper are provided at the end of each book, which help the student to test the knowledge which they have gained after thorough reading of all chapters.

05 Answer Key

Detailed Answer Key along with explanations aid the pupil to indentify, understand the mistakes they make during the course of Olympiad preparation.

WHY V&S OLYMPIADS?

We at V&S Publishers aim to build an avid-reading student audience. Hence, our resolve is to follow an innovative pedagogic pattern which would help students to navigate through the book with utmost ease and comfort. Crisp theory, practical examples and illustrations keep our book interactive and comprehensive.

ANALYTICAL & LOGICAL REASONING

Practicing analytical ability questions, not only helps in developing intellectual ability but also plays a vital role in building critical thinking ability which helps an individual to think about a question or a crisis like situation in day to day life; from all aspects and directions.

CONTENTS

1

LEARNING OBJECTIVES

- ➤ Natural numbers
- ➤ Whole numbers
- ➤ Rational numbers
- ➤ Irrational numbers and real numbers

MULTIPLE CHOICE QUESTIONS

1. Which of the following number is rational?

   (A) π

   (B) $\dfrac{22}{7}$

   (C) $\sqrt{7}+2$

   (D) $0.141141114...$

2. If $\dfrac{\sqrt{3}+1}{2-\sqrt{3}} = x + y\sqrt{3}$, then x, y have values equal to

   (A) 3,5

   (B) 5,3

   (C) 3,4

   (D) 3,6

3. $\left(\dfrac{\sqrt{3}+\sqrt{2}}{\sqrt{3}-\sqrt{2}} + \dfrac{\sqrt{3}-\sqrt{2}}{\sqrt{3}+\sqrt{2}} \right) \times 50$ equals

   (A) 1000

   (B) 200

   (C) 500

   (D) 1500

4. If $x = 2 + \sqrt{3}$, then $x + \dfrac{1}{x}$ is equal to :

   (A) $2\sqrt{3}$

   (B) 4

   (C) 14

   (D) 7

5. The value of the expression

   $\dfrac{16 \times 2^{n+1} - 4 \times 2^{n}}{16 \times 2^{n+2} - 2 \times 2^{n+2}}$ is

   (A) 2

   (B) 2^{n}

   (C) $\dfrac{1}{2}$

   (D) 4

6. Find the value of $x^3 - 2x^2 - 7x + 5$, if $x = \dfrac{1}{2-\sqrt{3}}$.

   (A) 1

   (B) 0

   (C) 2

   (D) 3

7. If $\dfrac{\left(x^{a+b}\right)^2 \left(x^{b+c}\right)^2 \left(x^{c+a}\right)^2}{\left(x^a x^b x^c\right)^4} = y$ then y is equal to

   (A) x^{a+b+c}

   (B) 1

   (C) x^{c+a}

   (D) 2

8. If $5^{x-3} \times 3^{2x-8} = 225$, then $x = ?$

   (A) 4

   (B) 3

   (C) 5

   (D) 6

9. $\sqrt{13 - m\sqrt{10}} = \sqrt{8} + \sqrt{5}$, then $m =$

   (A) -2

   (B) -5

   (C) -6

   (D) -4

10. $\left[2 - 3(2-3)^3 \right]^3 = x$ then the value of $x = ?$

    (A) 125

    (B) -125

    (C) 25

    (D) 625

POLYNOMIALS

LEARNING OBJECTIVES

➤ Polynomials and their types

➤ Factors of polynomials

MULTIPLE CHOICE QUESTIONS

1. Number of terms in the expand form of $(x - y - z)^2$ will be
   (A) 6
   (B) 9
   (C) 12
   (D) 3

2. Square root of $a^2 + 4b^2 + 9c^2 + 6ac + 4ab + 12bc$ will be
   (A) $a + 2b + 3c$
   (B) $a + 3b + 2c$
   (C) $a + 2b - 3c$
   (D) $a - 2b + 3c$

3. If $a^2 + b^2 + c^2 = 16$ and $ab + bc + ca = 10$, then the value of $(a + b + c)$ will be
   (A) ± 7
   (B) ± 8
   (C) ± 4
   (D) ± 6

4. The value of $9a^2 + 4b^2 + 16c^2 + 12ab - 24ac - 16bc$ for $a = 2$, $b = 1$, $c = -2$ will be
   (A) 0
   (B) 64
   (C) 256
   (D) 32

5. If $x^4 + \dfrac{1}{x^4} = 47$ then the value of $x^3 + \dfrac{1}{x^3} =$
   (A) 18
   (B) 27
   (C) 25
   (D) 16

6. If $x + \dfrac{1}{x} = -3$, then the value of $x^3 + \dfrac{1}{x^3}$ is
   (A) −54
   (B) −9
   (C) −27
   (D) −18

7. Cube root of $\dfrac{27}{x^3} - \dfrac{8}{x^6} - \dfrac{54}{x^4} + \dfrac{36}{x^5}$ will be,
   (A) $\dfrac{3}{x} - \dfrac{2}{x^2}$
   (B) $\dfrac{3}{x} - \dfrac{2}{x}$
   (C) $\dfrac{3}{x} + \dfrac{2}{x^2}$
   (D) $\dfrac{-3}{x} + \dfrac{2}{x^2}$

8. If $(x + k)^3 + (x - k)^3 = 2x^3 + 54x$, then k will be,
   (A) 3, −3
   (B) 4
   (C) −4
   (D) 6, −6

9. If $x^3 - \dfrac{1}{x^3} = 108 + 76\sqrt{2}$, then $x - \dfrac{1}{x}$
   (A) $3 + \sqrt{2}$
   (B) $3 + 2\sqrt{2}$
   (C) $3 - 2\sqrt{2}$
   (D) $\sqrt{3} + 2\sqrt{2}$

10. If $3x + 2y = 13$ and $xy = 6$, then $27x^3 + 8y^3$ will be equal to
    (A) 1859
    (B) 729
    (C) 793
    (D) 891

11. If $x + y = 4$, $xy = 4$, then $2x^3 + y^3$ will be equal to
    (A) 15
    (B) 17
    (C) 16
    (D) 24

12. If $a + b = 6$, and $ab = 8$, then value of $(a^2 + b^2 - ab)$ will be
    (A) 6
    (B) 8
    (C) 12
    (D) 16

13. The value of $(x - 1)(x^2 + 1 + x)(x^6 + x^3 + 1)$, will be equal to

(A) $x^9 + 1$ (B) $x^6 + 1$
(C) x^6 (D) $x^9 - 1$

14. If $a + b + c = 15$ and $a^2 + b^2 + c^2 = 83$ then the value of $(ab + bc + ca)$ will be equal to
(A) 71   (B) 74
(C) 72   (D) 116

15. If $a + b + c = 15$, and $a^2 + b^2 + c^2 = 83$, then the value of $a^3 + b^3 + c^3 - 3abc$ will be
(A) 105   (B) 90
(C) 108   (D) 180

16. If $\dfrac{x}{y} + \dfrac{y}{x} = -1$ then $x^3 - y^3 =$
(A) -8 (B) 0
(C) 1   (D) -1

17. $30^3 + 20^3 - 50^3 =$
(A) 11500   (B) -90000
(C) 0   (D) 9000

18. If $a + b + c = 6$ and $a^3 + b^3 + c^3 = 6\left(3 + \dfrac{abc}{2}\right)$ then $ab + bc + ca$ will have the value equal to
(A) 16   (B) -11
(C) 11   (D) 12

19. The volume of a cuboid is $3x^2 - 27$, its possible dimensions are
(A) $3, x^2, -27x$ (B) $3, x - 3, x + 3$
(C) $3, x^2, 27n$ (D) $3, 3, 3$

20. If $a^2 + b^2 + c^2 = ab + bc + ca$, then the value of $(a + b + c)$ will be
(A) 0   (B) 1
(C) -1 (D) 2

HOTS (ACHIEVERS SECTION)

21. If $a = \dfrac{2^{x-1}}{2^{x-2}};\ b = \dfrac{2^{-x}}{2^{x+1}};$ and $a - b = 0$ then what is the value of x?
(A) -2 (B) 1
(C) -1 (D) 2

22. If $\dfrac{x}{y} = \dfrac{2}{3}$ then what is the value of $\dfrac{4}{5} + \dfrac{y-x}{y+x}$?
(A) 3   (B) 2
(C) 1   (D) -1

23. If $x^3 + \dfrac{1}{x^3} = 110$ then what is the value of $x + \dfrac{1}{x}$?
(A) 5   (B) 6
(C) 7   (D) 9

24. If $f(x) = x^4 - 2x^3 + 3x^2 - ax + b$ is a polynomial such that when it is divided by $(x - 1)$ and $(x + 1)$, the remainders are 5 and 19 respectively. What is the remainder when $f(x)$ is divided by $(x - 2)$?
(A) 8   (B) 10
(C) 12   (D) 14

25. If $\dfrac{3 + \sqrt{7}}{3 - \sqrt{7}} = a + b\sqrt{7}$ then what is the difference between a and b?
(A) 3   (B) 5
(C) 8   (D) 11

—Darken Your Choice with HB Pencil—

1.	Ⓐ Ⓑ Ⓒ Ⓓ	6.	Ⓐ Ⓑ Ⓒ Ⓓ	11.	Ⓐ Ⓑ Ⓒ Ⓓ	16	Ⓐ Ⓑ Ⓒ Ⓓ	21.	Ⓐ Ⓑ Ⓒ Ⓓ
2.	Ⓐ Ⓑ Ⓒ Ⓓ	7.	Ⓐ Ⓑ Ⓒ Ⓓ	12.	Ⓐ Ⓑ Ⓒ Ⓓ	17.	Ⓐ Ⓑ Ⓒ Ⓓ	22.	Ⓐ Ⓑ Ⓒ Ⓓ
3.	Ⓐ Ⓑ Ⓒ Ⓓ	8.	Ⓐ Ⓑ Ⓒ Ⓓ	13.	Ⓐ Ⓑ Ⓒ Ⓓ	18.	Ⓐ Ⓑ Ⓒ Ⓓ	23.	Ⓐ Ⓑ Ⓒ Ⓓ
4.	Ⓐ Ⓑ Ⓒ Ⓓ	9.	Ⓐ Ⓑ Ⓒ Ⓓ	14.	Ⓐ Ⓑ Ⓒ Ⓓ	19.	Ⓐ Ⓑ Ⓒ Ⓓ	24.	Ⓐ Ⓑ Ⓒ Ⓓ
5.	Ⓐ Ⓑ Ⓒ Ⓓ	10.	Ⓐ Ⓑ Ⓒ Ⓓ	15.	Ⓐ Ⓑ Ⓒ Ⓓ	20.	Ⓐ Ⓑ Ⓒ Ⓓ	25.	Ⓐ Ⓑ Ⓒ Ⓓ

CO-ORDINATE GEOMETRY 

3

LEARNING OBJECTIVES

➤ Cartesian Co-ordinate Axes
➤ Quadrants

➤ Cartesian Co-ordinates of a Point
➤ Convention of Signs

MULTIPLE CHOICE QUESTIONS

1. Minimum distance of point $(4, 6)$ from x-axis will be
   (A) 4
   (B) 6
   (C) 8
   (D) $\sqrt{52}$

2. If a circle is such that x-axis is tangent to it, and the coordinate of centre of circle is $(2, 3)$, then the point of tangency will have ordinate equal to
   (A) 2
   (B) 0
   (C) –3
   (D) –4

3. A square is constructed parallel to the coordinate axis. If the perimeter of square is equal to 24 units and the coordinate of a vertex is $(5, 3)$ then the point on square which is at a distance 6 units from the point $(5, 3)$ can have ordinate :
   (A) 9, –3, 3
   (B) 5, 9, 3
   (C) 3, –3, 5
   (D) 5, 3, –9

4. The perpendicular distance of point $(-11, -2)$ from y-axis will be :
   (A) 11
   (B) 2
   (C) $\sqrt{125}$
   (D) –11

5. Point $P(4, -3)$ will lie in :
   (A) I quadrant
   (B) II quadrant
   (C) III quadrant
   (D) IV quadrant

6. A point on line $y = 3x + 2$ has equal ordinate and abscissa, then the point will lie in
   (A) I quadrant
   (B) II quadrant
   (C) III quadrant
   (D) IV quadrant

7. Suppose two points M and N lie on y-axis, and have same absolute value of abscissa but different signs. If the abscissa of point M is K, then the distance between M and N is equal to:
   (A) $|K|$
   (B) $|2K| = 2|K|$
   (C) $2K$
   (D) $4|K|$

8. If P, Q and R are the vertices of a triangle and coordinates of the points are $(0,4)$ $(0,0)$ and $(3, 0)$ respectively then the perimeter of ΔPQR will be :
   (A) 12 units
   (B) 10 units
   (C) 5 units
   (D) 13 units

9. Area of ΔPQR in problem 13 will be :
   (A) 12 sq. units
   (B) 6 sq. units
   (C) 5 sq. units
   (D) 8 sq. units

10. $A(2, 3)$, $B(3, 0)$ and $C(14, 13)$ are vertices of triangle ABC. Then the centroid of this triangle will lie in :
    (A) I[st] quadrant
    (B) IInd quadrant
    (C) IIIrd quadrant
    (D) IVth quadrant

11. Point $(-3, -2)$ will lie in :

(A) 1st (B) 2nd

(C) 3rd (D) 4th quadrant

12. The mirror image of point $(4, 3)$ about x-axis will be

(A) $(4, -3)$ (B) $(-4, -3)$

(C) $(-4, -3)$ (D) $(5, -3)$

13. The mirror image of point $(-4, -2)$ about x-axis will lie in :

(A) I^{st} quadrant   (B) IInd quadrant

(C) IIIrd quadrant   (D) IVth quadrant

14. A point P on line $2x + 3y = 5$, has equal value of both ordinate and abscissa, then the mirror image of point P about y-axis will be :

(A) $(1, -1)$ (B) $(-1, 1)$

(C) $(-1, -1)$ (D) $(-2, 1)$

15. A point 'A' in I^{st} quadrant with coordinates $(3, 2)$ is reflected about x-axis. The image of point A about x-axis is point Q, and, then the point Q is reflected about y-axis The coordinates of final point will be :

(A) $(-3, -2)$ (B) $(-3, 2)$

(C) $(3, -2)$ (D) $(-2, -3)$

16. The distance between $(12, 5)$ and origin is

(A) 13   (B) 12

(C) 5   (D) 17

17. The area of triangle formed by the points $A(2, 0)$, $B(6, 0)$, $C(4, 6)$ is

(A) 10 sq. units   (B) 6 sq. units

(C) 12 sq. units   (D) 24 sq. units

18. Equation of y–axis will be

(A) $y = 0$ (B) $y = x$

(C) $x = 0$ (D) $x = 5$

19. A line which makes $60°$ with x-axis in anticlockwise sense has equation :

(A) $y - \sqrt{3}x = 0$ (B) $y + \sqrt{3}x = 0$

(C) $\sqrt{3}y + x = 0$ (D) $\sqrt{3}y - x = 0$

20. A line makes equal angle with x and y-axis and pass through first quadrant has equation :

(A) $x = 2y$ (B) $x = y$

(C) $x + y = 0$ (D) $x + \sqrt{3}y = 0$

HOTS (ACHIEVERS SECTION)

21. In the adjoining Diagram, $PQ = ?$

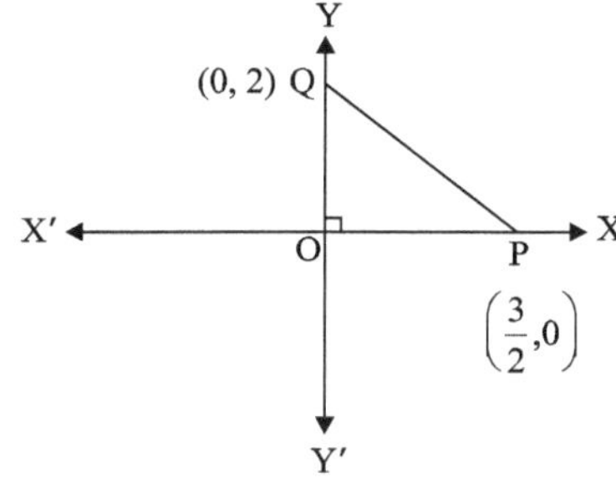

(A) 4 cm   (B) 2.5 cm

(C) 2 cm   (D) 5 cm

22. In the given figure, what is the length of AB?

(A) 13 units

(B) 9 units

(C) 12 units

(D) 18 units

23. In the adjoining figure, what is the area of ΔABC?

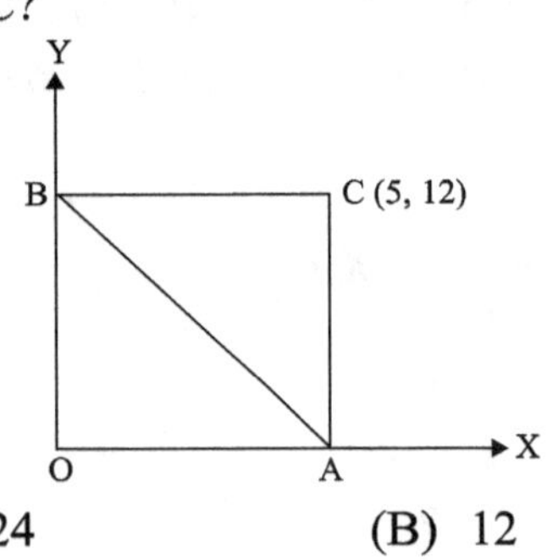

(A) 24   (B) 12
(C) 30   (D) 3

24. In the given figure Area of ΔABC

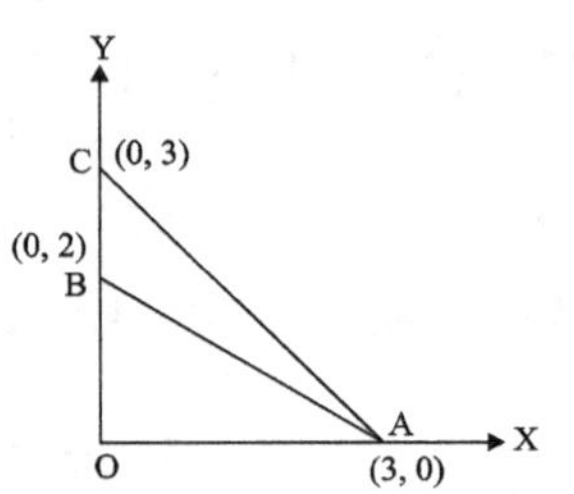

(A) 3 unit   (B) 4 (1/2) unit
(C) 1(1/2) unit   (D) 1 unit

25. If $(2, 2p + 2)$ is the mid-point of $(3p, 4)$ and $(-2, 2q)$, then the value of p and q are
(A) 2, 4   (B) 3, 6
(C) 7, 9   (D) 8, 10

LINEAR EQUATIONS IN TWO VARIABLES

LEARNING OBJECTIVES

➤ Linear equation
➤ How to solve linear equation

➤ Graph of Linear equation

MULTIPLE CHOICE QUESTIONS

1. If $x = k^2$ and $y = k$ are solutions of equation $x - 5y = -6$ then $k =$
   (A) 2, 3   (B) 3, -2
   (C) $-3, 2$ (D) $-2, -3$

2. The equation $x - y + 1 = 0$ is satisfied by $x = a^2$ and $y = a$ then $a =$
   (A) Can't be determined
   (B) 2
   (C) -1
   (D) -2

3. The solution of equation $x - y + 8 = 0$ is $x = k^3$ and $y = 0$, then $k =$
   (A) 2   (B) -2
   (C) -3 (D) $-\dfrac{1}{2}$

4. If the equation $x + 3y + 4k = 6$ is satisfied by $(2, 3)$ then the value of k is :
   (A) $\dfrac{5}{4}$ (B) $-\dfrac{5}{4}$
   (C) $\dfrac{3}{4}$ (D) $-\dfrac{3}{4}$

5. If the equation $(x + 3y) - (3x + y) + (x - y) = (a - b)$, then which of the following is a solution for the above equation ?
   (A) (a, b) (B) (b, a)
   (C) $(-b, -a)$ (D) $(b, -a)$

6. If the equation $k(x^3 - y^3) = (x^2 + y^2 + xy)$ and $y = \dfrac{1}{k}$, then the value of x is
   (A) $\dfrac{1}{2k}$ (B) $-\dfrac{1}{2k}$
   (C) $\dfrac{2}{k}$ (D) $-\dfrac{2}{k}$

7. If the equation, $x - y + \left(\sqrt{x} + \sqrt{y}\right) = 10$ and the value of x is 9, then value of y will be
   (A) 4   (B) -4
   (C) 9   (D) 16

8. The equation, $(x + y) + \left(x^{\frac{2}{3}} - y^{\frac{2}{3}} - (xy)^{\frac{1}{3}}\right) = 12$, then what will be the value of y if $x = 8$
   (A) 2   (B) 1
   (C) -8 (D) 27

9. If $(2k - 3, k)$ is a solution of the equation $6x + 2y = k - 5$, then $k =$
   (A) -1 (B) -2
   (C) 1   (D) 2

10. Arun and Kajol together contributed 100 rupees for the Prime Minister Relief fund. If the money donated by Arun is ₹ 80 less than twice the money donated by Kajol then the money donated by Arun is :

(A) ₹ 40   (B) ₹ 60

(C) ₹ 80   (D) ₹ 20

11. A number is 27 more than the number obtained by revising its digits. If one of the digits is 3, then the other digit is

(A) 5   (B) 6

(C) 3   (D) 9

12. If the point $(4, 5)$ lies on the graph $3y = ax + 3$, then $a =$

(A) 2   (B) 3

(C) -3 (D) 4

13. If the point $A(3, 5)$ and $B(1, 4)$ lie on the graph of line $ax + by - 7 = 0$, then (a, b) will be :

(A) $(1, 2)$ (B) $(1, -2)$

(C) $(-1, 2)$ (D) $(-1, -2)$

14. If $C = \dfrac{(F - 32) \times 5}{9}$, where C denotes the temperature in Celsius and F denotes the temperature in Fahrenheit, then temperature (in Celsius) at which the numerical value on both scales is same will be

(A) $-30°C$ (B) $-20°C$

(C) $-40°C$ (D) $-80°C$

15. The area bounded by the graph of the equation $\dfrac{x}{4} + \dfrac{y}{5} = 1$ and the coordinate axes will be

(A) 20 sq. units   (B) 10 sq. units

(C) 5 sq. units   (D) 15 sq. units

16. The point of intersection of graphs of the equations $3x + 4y = 12$ and $6x + 8y = 48$ is

(A) $(3, 4)$

(B) $(4, 3)$

(C) $(5, 3)$

(D) The graphs will not intersect

17. The point of intersection of $3x + 4y = 15$ and x-axis will be

(A) $(0, 5)$ (B) $(5, 0)$

(C) $(-5, 0)$ (D) $(0, 3)$

18. The graph of the equation $15x + 36y = 108$ will cut the y- axis at :

(A) $(0, -3)$ (B) $(0, 5)$

(C) $(0, 6)$ (D) $(0, 3)$

19. The distance between the graphs of the equations $x = 3$ and $x = -3$ is

(A) 5   (B) 8

(C) 6   (D) 4

20. The equation $3x + 2y = 8$ has :

(A) Unique solution   (B) No solution

(C) Infinite solutions   (D) Two solutions

HOTS (ACHIEVERS SECTION)

21. If $9^{x+2} = 240 + 9^x$ then what is the value of x?

(A) 0.1   (B) 0.2

(C) 0.4   (D) 0.5

22. If $a + b + c = 9$ and $a^2 + b^2 + c^2 = 35$ what is the value of $a^3 + b^3 + c^3 - 3abc$?

(A) 92   (B) 98

(C) 108   (D) 112

23. What is the remainder when $x^{51} + 51$ is divided by $x + 1$?

(A) 50   (B) 51

(C) -51 (D) 52

24. How many kilograms of tea at 50 per kg should be mixed with 35kg of tea costing Rs.60 per kg so as to sell the mixture at Rs.57 per kg without gaining or losing anything in the transaction?

(A) 5kg   (B) 7kg

(C) 25kg   (D) 15kg

25. Mega city High School earned Rs.5100 on tickets sales for a play. The cost per ticket was Rs.12. If t represents the number of tickets sold to the play, which of the following equations could be used to determine the number of tickets sold for the play?

(A) $12 = 5100t$ (B) $12t = 5100$

(C) $t = 5100 - 12$ (D) $t = 5100.12$

1.	Ⓐ Ⓑ Ⓒ Ⓓ	6.	Ⓐ Ⓑ Ⓒ Ⓓ	11.	Ⓐ Ⓑ Ⓒ Ⓓ	16	Ⓐ Ⓑ Ⓒ Ⓓ	21.	Ⓐ Ⓑ Ⓒ Ⓓ
2.	Ⓐ Ⓑ Ⓒ Ⓓ	7.	Ⓐ Ⓑ Ⓒ Ⓓ	12.	Ⓐ Ⓑ Ⓒ Ⓓ	17.	Ⓐ Ⓑ Ⓒ Ⓓ	22.	Ⓐ Ⓑ Ⓒ Ⓓ
3.	Ⓐ Ⓑ Ⓒ Ⓓ	8.	Ⓐ Ⓑ Ⓒ Ⓓ	13.	Ⓐ Ⓑ Ⓒ Ⓓ	18.	Ⓐ Ⓑ Ⓒ Ⓓ	23.	Ⓐ Ⓑ Ⓒ Ⓓ
4.	Ⓐ Ⓑ Ⓒ Ⓓ	9.	Ⓐ Ⓑ Ⓒ Ⓓ	14.	Ⓐ Ⓑ Ⓒ Ⓓ	19.	Ⓐ Ⓑ Ⓒ Ⓓ	24.	Ⓐ Ⓑ Ⓒ Ⓓ
5.	Ⓐ Ⓑ Ⓒ Ⓓ	10.	Ⓐ Ⓑ Ⓒ Ⓓ	15.	Ⓐ Ⓑ Ⓒ Ⓓ	20.	Ⓐ Ⓑ Ⓒ Ⓓ	25.	Ⓐ Ⓑ Ⓒ Ⓓ

INTRODUCTION TO EUCLID'S GEOMETRY

LEARNING OBJECTIVES

➤ Axioms or postulates
➤ Euclid's geometry

➤ Important terms related to geometry

MULTIPLE CHOICE QUESTIONS

1. The number of planes passing through three non-collinear points is :
   (A) 1   (B) 2
   (C) 3   (D) 4

2. Which of the following does not need a proof ?
   (A) Axiom   (B) Theorem
   (C) Statement   (D) Definition

3. How many lines can pass through 2 given points ?
   (A) 1   (B) 2
   (C) 3   (D) Infinite

4. How many lines can be drawn parallel to a given line L and passing through a fixed point P ?
   (A) 0   (B) Infinite
   (C) 2   (D) 1

5. If 4 lines pass through a point these are said to be
   (A) Unique lines
   (B) Parallel line
   (C) Concurrent lines
   (D) Perpendicular.

6. $\overleftrightarrow{AB}$ has how many end points ?
   (A) None   (B) 2
   (C) 3   (D) Infinite

7. Two circles are said to be congruent, if and only if :
   (A) They have equal radius
   (B) They are intersecting,
   (C) They have common chord of equal length
   (D) They are non-intersecting.

8. If $AB \parallel CD$ and $CD \parallel PQ$ then AB and PQ are
   (A) Parallel to each other
   (B) Perpendicular to each other
   (C) Intersecting but not perpendicular
   (D) Collinear points (A, B, and Q)

9. Two straight lines can intersect in how many points (maximum) ?
   (A) 2   (B) 3
   (C) 4   (D) 1

10. For determination of a plane, how many unique lines are required (minimum) ?
    (A) 2   (B) 3
    (C) 4   (D) 1

11. A point has
    (A) 1 dimension   (B) 2 dimension
    (C) 3 dimension   (D) 0 dimension

12. A surface has
    (A) 2 dimension   (B) 3 dimension
    (C) 1 dimension   (D) 0 dimension

13. A surface has
    (A) Definite end points
    (B) Indefinite end points
    (C) 1 end point
    (D) 2 end points

14. If two planes intersect each other, then the minimum point of intersection will be
    (A) 2   (B) 3
    (C) 1   (D) 0

15. If an angle is such that its complementary angle is 20°, the*n* angle is
(A) 50°   (B) 70°
(C) 20°   (D) 160°

16. The measure of an angle if five times its complement is 12° less than twice its supplement
(A) 32°   (B) 36°
(C) 34°   (D) 42°

17. Boundaries of surfaces and solids are :
(A) Curved, solids
(B) Curved, surfaces
(C) Linear, point
(D) Dimensionless curved respectively

18. If line $AB \perp CD$ and $CD \perp PQ$, then AB and PQ are
(A) Perpendicular
(B) Parallel
(C) Intersecting
(D) Skew if the points A, B, C, D. P and Q are in same plane.

19. The number of lines that can be drawn through 4 distinct points in a plane if no three points are collinear
(A) 12   (B) 6
(C) 8   (D) 4

20. In problem 24 number of lines that can be drawn if 3 of the 4 points are collinear will be
(A) 4   (B) 6
(C) 8   (D) 12

HOTS (ACHIEVERS SECTION)

21. In the figure given, if A and B are the centres of the two intersecting circles, what type of a triangle is $\triangle ABC$?

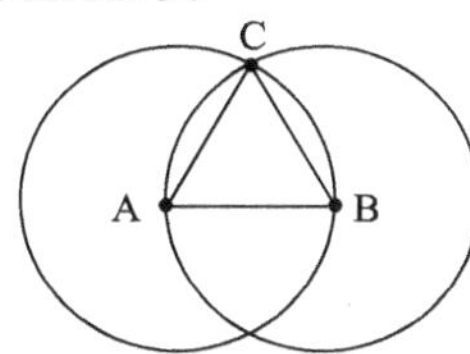

(A) A scalene triangle
(B) A right triangle
(C) An isosceles triangle
(D) An equilateral triangle

22. In Indus Valley Civilisation (about 300 B.C.), what were the dimensions of the bricks used for construction work?
(A) 1:3:4   (B) 4:2:1
(C) 4:4:1   (D) 4:3:2

23. Identify the incorrect statement
(a) Only one line can pass through a single point.
(B) Only one line can pass through two distinct points.
(C) A terminated line can be produced indefinitely on both the sides.
(D) If two circles are equal, their radii are equal.

24. If X, Y, Z are the three points on a line and Y lies between X and Z, which of the following is true?
(A) XY + YZ = XZ
(B) XY + XZ = YZ
(C) XZ + YZ = XY
(D) 12(XY + YZ) = XZ

25. ABCD are the four points on a line.
A   C   D   B If AD = BC, which of the following has its length the same as BD?
(A) AD   (B) BC
(C) AC   (D) CD

1.	Ⓐ Ⓑ Ⓒ Ⓓ	6.	Ⓐ Ⓑ Ⓒ Ⓓ	11.	Ⓐ Ⓑ Ⓒ Ⓓ	16	Ⓐ Ⓑ Ⓒ Ⓓ	21.	Ⓐ Ⓑ Ⓒ Ⓓ
2.	Ⓐ Ⓑ Ⓒ Ⓓ	7.	Ⓐ Ⓑ Ⓒ Ⓓ	12.	Ⓐ Ⓑ Ⓒ Ⓓ	17.	Ⓐ Ⓑ Ⓒ Ⓓ	22.	Ⓐ Ⓑ Ⓒ Ⓓ
3.	Ⓐ Ⓑ Ⓒ Ⓓ	8.	Ⓐ Ⓑ Ⓒ Ⓓ	13.	Ⓐ Ⓑ Ⓒ Ⓓ	18.	Ⓐ Ⓑ Ⓒ Ⓓ	23.	Ⓐ Ⓑ Ⓒ Ⓓ
4.	Ⓐ Ⓑ Ⓒ Ⓓ	9.	Ⓐ Ⓑ Ⓒ Ⓓ	14.	Ⓐ Ⓑ Ⓒ Ⓓ	19.	Ⓐ Ⓑ Ⓒ Ⓓ	24.	Ⓐ Ⓑ Ⓒ Ⓓ
5.	Ⓐ Ⓑ Ⓒ Ⓓ	10.	Ⓐ Ⓑ Ⓒ Ⓓ	15.	Ⓐ Ⓑ Ⓒ Ⓓ	20.	Ⓐ Ⓑ Ⓒ Ⓓ	25.	Ⓐ Ⓑ Ⓒ Ⓓ

LINES AND ANGLES

LEARNING OBJECTIVES

➤ Angles, Types of Angles
➤ Properties of angles and lines

➤ Angles Made by a Transversal with Two Lines

MULTIPLE CHOICE QUESTIONS

1. Determine the value of x from the given figure;

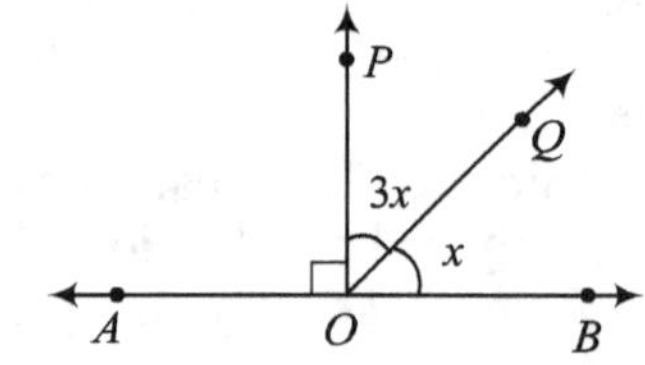

(A) 45° (B) 22.5°
(C) 25.5° (D) 25°

2. If $y - x = 10°$, then $y =$

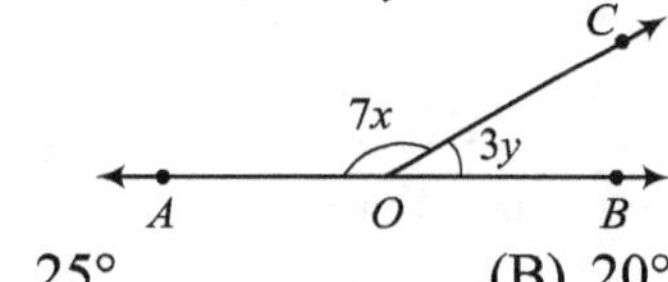

(A) 25° (B) 20°
(C) 15° (D) 10°

3. If $b = a + 20°$, then $a =$

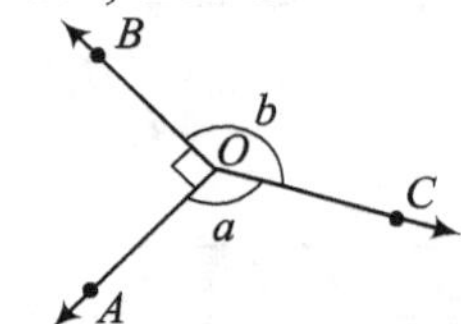

(A) 145° (B) 125°
(C) 130° (D) 135°

4. POQ is a line. Ray OR is perpendicular to line PQ. OS is another ray lying between rays OP and OR, then $\angle POS$ is equal to :

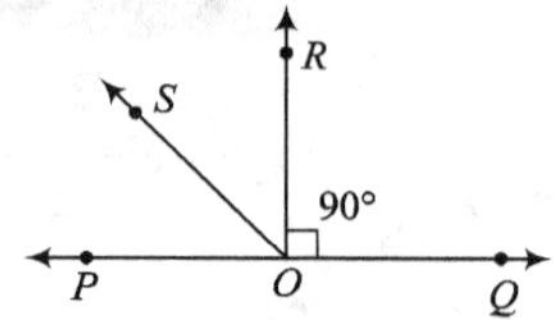

(A) $\angle ROS - \angle QOS$
(B) $\angle QOS - 2\angle ROS$
(C) $\angle QOS + 2\angle ROS$
(D) $2\angle ROS - \angle QOS$

5. The value of m is

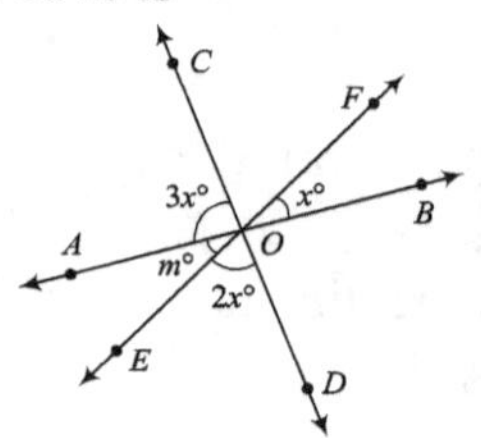

(A) 60° (B) 30°
(C) 45° (D) 20°

6. If $\dfrac{q}{p} = 5$, $\dfrac{r}{p} = 3$, then $r + p =$

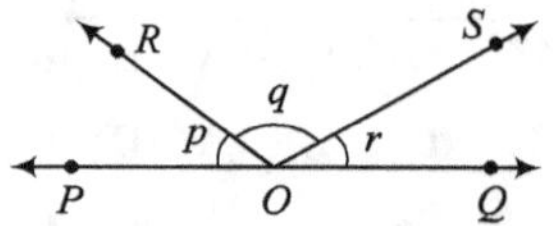

(A) 80° (B) 120°
(C) 160° (D) 100°

7. Find x from the figure.

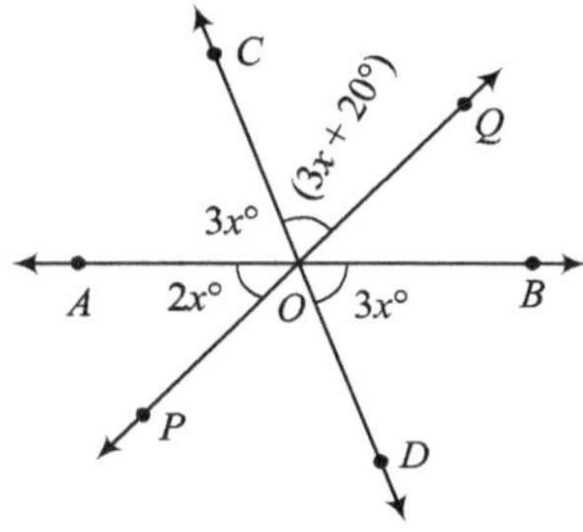

(A) 20° (B) 25°
(C) 10° (D)15°

8. In the adjoining figure, $\angle AOQ : \angle AOP = 5 : 7$, then measure of $\angle BOQ$ is :

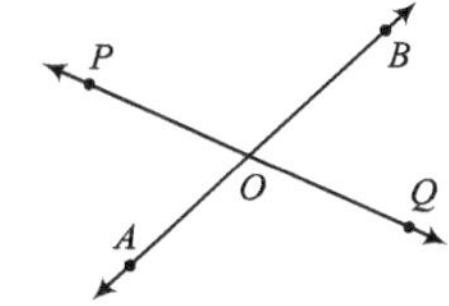

(A) 75° (B) 105°
(C) 60° (D)120°

9. If $x = 3y = \dfrac{6}{7}z$ then, find the value of y.

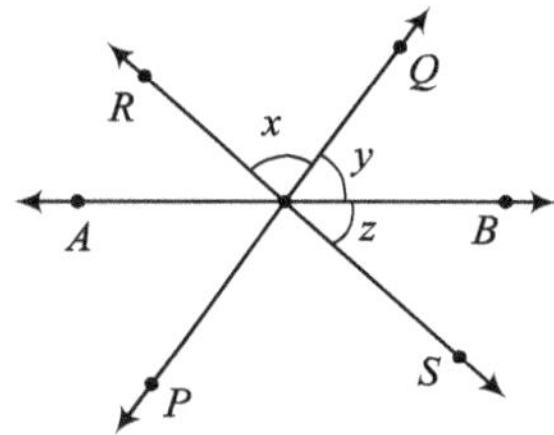

(A) 36° (B) 24°
(C) 72° (D) 84°

10. In the adjoining figure, $\angle AOC + \angle BOE = 70°$ and $\angle BOD = 40°$, then measure of reflex $\angle BOE$ is

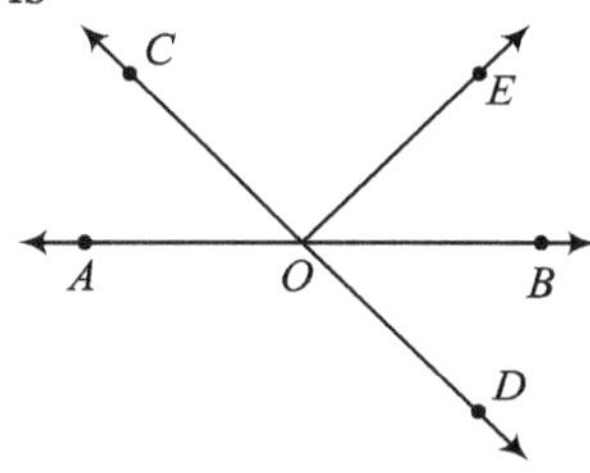

(A) 320° (B) 330°
(C) 290° (D) 250°

11. Find x from the adjoining figure :

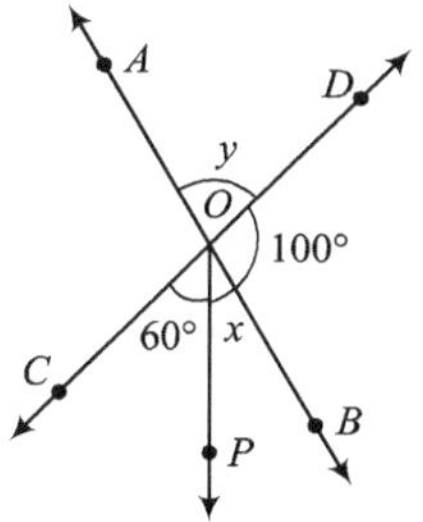

(A) 30° (B) 20°
(C) 40° (D)80°

12. Find the value of $x - y + z$

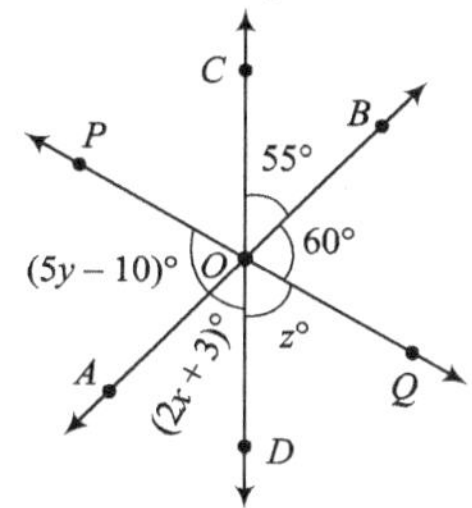

(A) 77° (B) 85°
(C) 127° (D) 137°

13. In the figure if $l \parallel m$, find x.

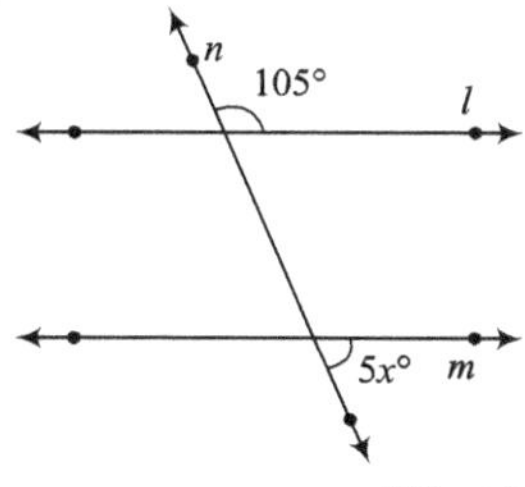

(A) 21° (B) 15°
(C) 25° (D) 23°

14. In the adjoining figure, $AB \parallel CD$ and, $PQ \perp AB$, find the measure of $\angle PCM$.

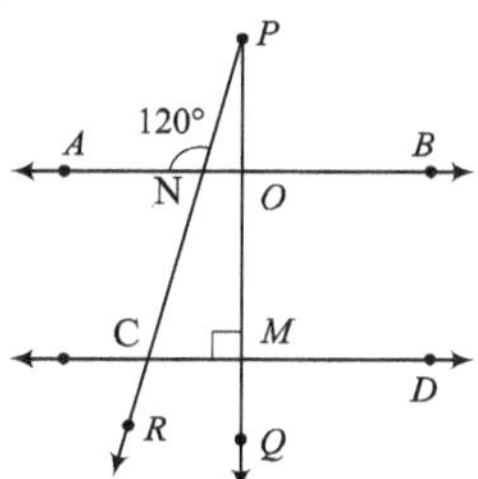

(A) 120° (B) 60°
(C) 30° (D) 90°

15. $AB \parallel CD$, and $\angle RQB = 115°$, and $\angle PRQ = 30°$. The measure of $\angle APC$ is :

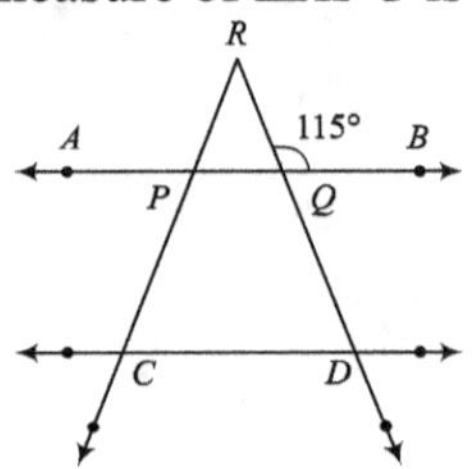

(A) 115°
(B) 45°
(C) 85°
(D) 30°

16. PQ and PN trisects $\angle APL$, then the measure of $\angle LPQ$ is :

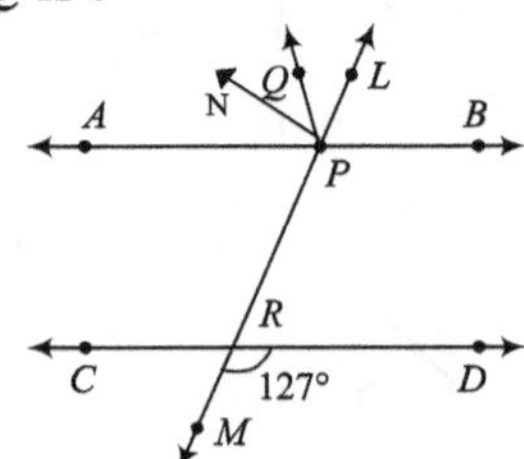

(A) $\left(42\dfrac{1}{3}\right)°$

(B) $\left(48\dfrac{2}{3}\right)°$

(C) $\left(47\dfrac{2}{3}\right)°$

(D) $\left(19\dfrac{1}{3}\right)°$

17. If $x : y = 2:3$, then the value of y is equal to :

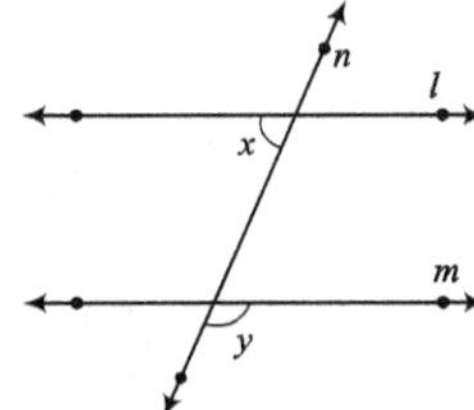

18. $AB \parallel CD \parallel EF$ and $GH \parallel KL$. The measure of $\angle HKL$ is

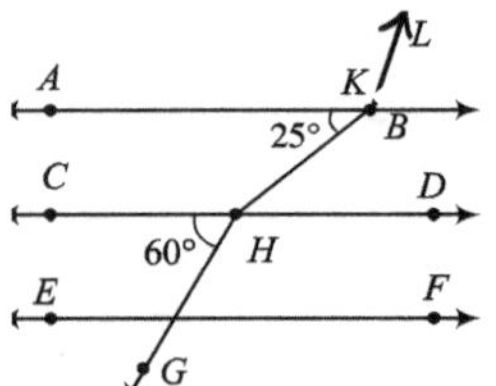

(A) 85
(B) 135°
(C) 215°
(D) 145°

19. $AB \parallel CD$ and $PQ \parallel RS$, then the measure of $\angle A_1MB_1$ is (Here $\therefore$ A_1M and B_1M are the bisectors of $\angle C_1A_1B_1$ and $\angle D_1B_1A_1$ respectively)

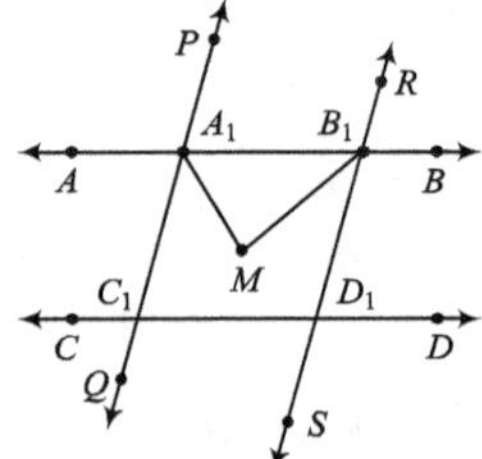

(A) 70°
(B) 85°
(C) 90°
(D) 12°

20. Find x from the given figure ($CP \parallel BQ$) :

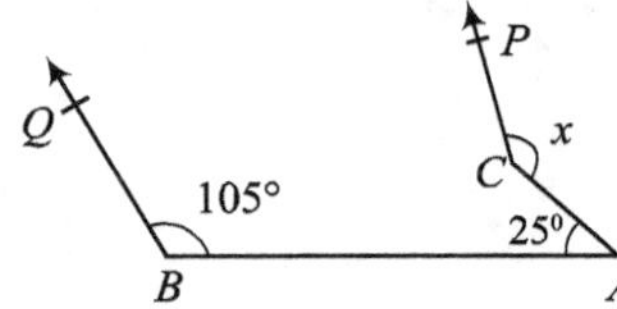

(A) 105°
(B) 130°
(C) 125°
(D) 175°

21. In the given figure, what is the value of x?

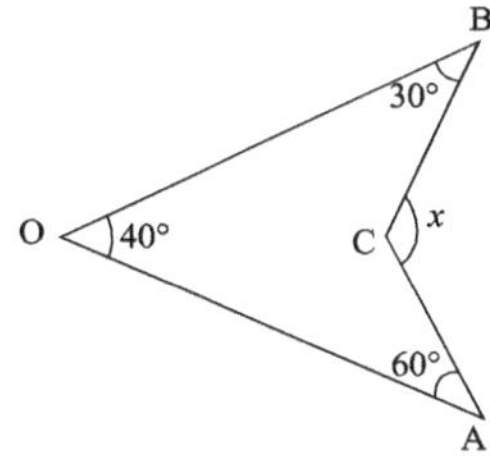

(A) 70°
(B) 100°
(C) 90°
(D) 130°

22. In the given figure BD = DC and ∠DBC = 25°. What is the measure of ∠BAC?

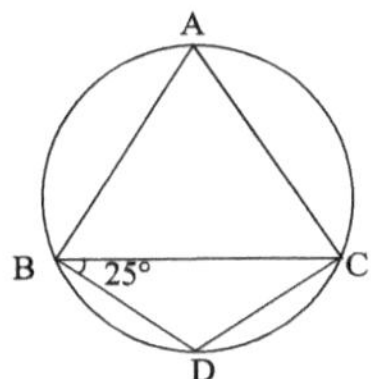

(A) 70°
(B) 50°
(C) 90°
(D) 130°

23. In the above figure O is the centre and PQ is diameter. If ∠ROS = 40°, what is the measure of ∠RTS?

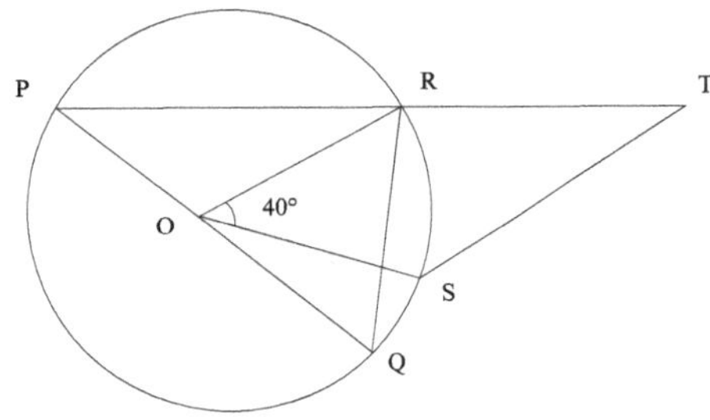

(A) 40°
(B) 50°
(C) 60°
(D) 70°

24. If O is the centre of the circle, ∠AOC = 100°, what is the measure of ∠ABC?

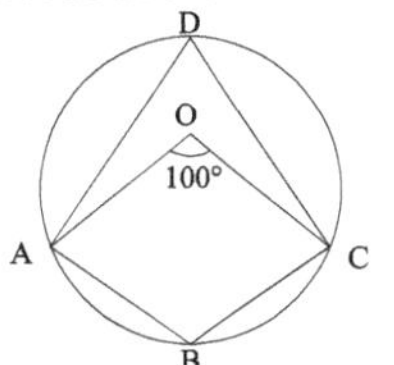

(A) 50°   (B) 100°
(C) 120°   (D) 130°

25. If $2∠A = 3∠B = 6∠C$, then what is the difference between ∠B and ∠C?

(A) 20°   (B) 30°
(C) 40°   (D) 60°

TRIANGLES 

LEARNING OBJECTIVES

➤ Triangles, Types of Triangles
➤ Congruence of Triangles

➤ Rules of Congruence
➤ Properties of Triangles and Inequalities in a Triangle

MULTIPLE CHOICE QUESTIONS

1. The sum of all the exterior angles of a triangle is
   (A) 180°
   (B) 360°
   (C) 540°
   (D) 270°

2. Find x if BO and CO are the bisectors of exterior angles at B and C respectively.

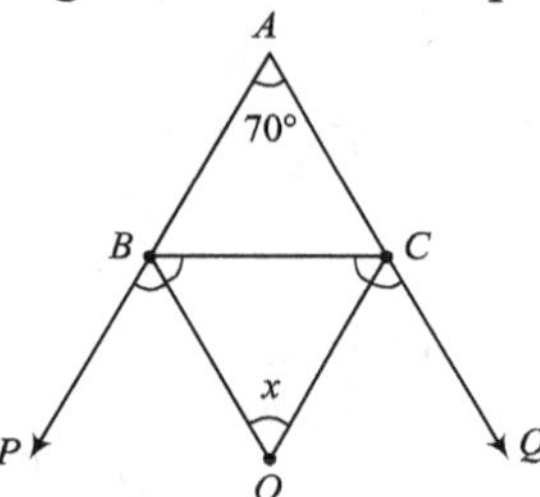

   (A) 115°
   (B) 125°
   (C) 65°
   (D) 55°

3. In an isosceles triangle $AB = AC$. Side AB is extended to P such that $\angle CAP = 108°$. The measure of $\angle ABC$ is :
   (A) 30°
   (B) 126°
   (C) 108°
   (D) 54°

4. The value of x from the adjoining figure will be

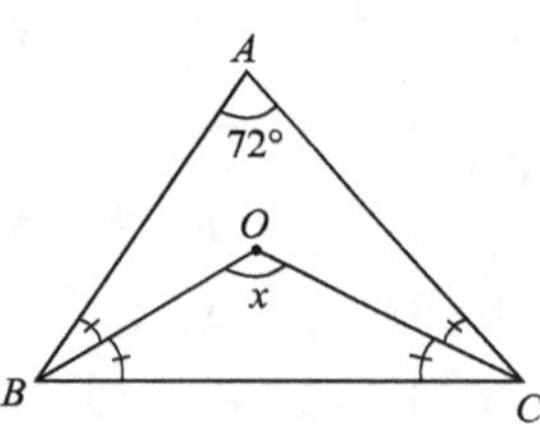

   (A) 116°
   (B) 126°
   (C) 108°
   (D) 132°

5. Side QR of a triangle PQR is produced both ways and the measures of exterior angles formed are 86° and 124°. The measure of $\angle P$ is :
   (A) 30°
   (B) 40°
   (C) 60°
   (D) 80°

6. AB and CD are parallel lines and transversal EF intersects them at P and Q respectively. If $\angle APR = 25°$, $\angle RQC = 30°$ and $\angle CQF = 65°$ then

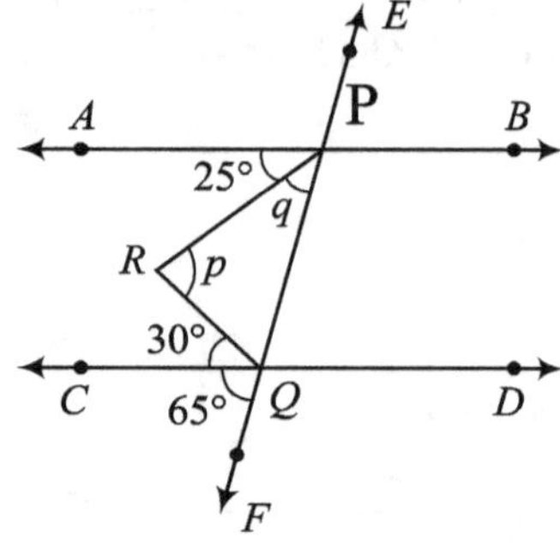

   (A) $p = 55°, q = 40°$
   (B) $p = 50°, q = 45°$
   (C) $p = 35°, q = 60°$
   (D) $p = 60°, q = 35°$

7. The value of x in the adjoining figure will be :

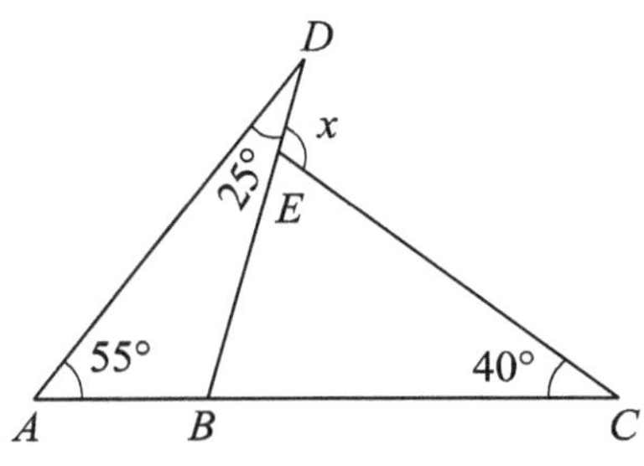

(A) 120°   (B) 90°
(C) 65°   (D) 80°

8. The value of x from the adjoining figure will be :

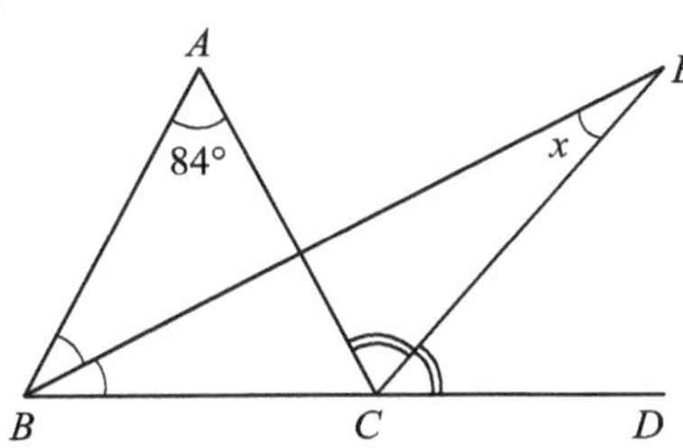

(A) 41°   (B) 45°
(C) 42°   (D) 48°

9. ABC is an isosceles such that $AB = AC$ and AD is the median to base BC. Then, $\angle BAD =$

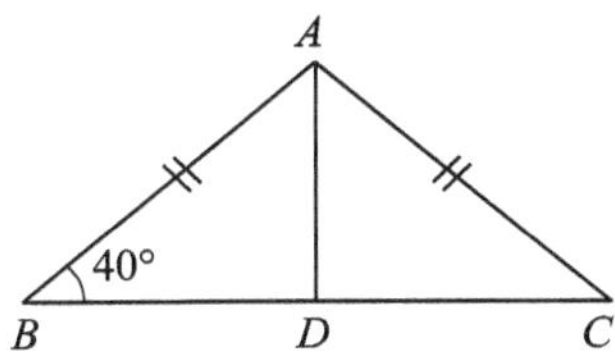

(A) 40°   (B) 50°
(C) 60°   (D) 100°

10. ABC is a triangle in which $\angle B = 2\angle C$. D is a point on BC such that AD bisects $\angle BAC$ and $AB = CD$ .BE is the bisector of $\angle B$. The measure of $\angle BAC$ is

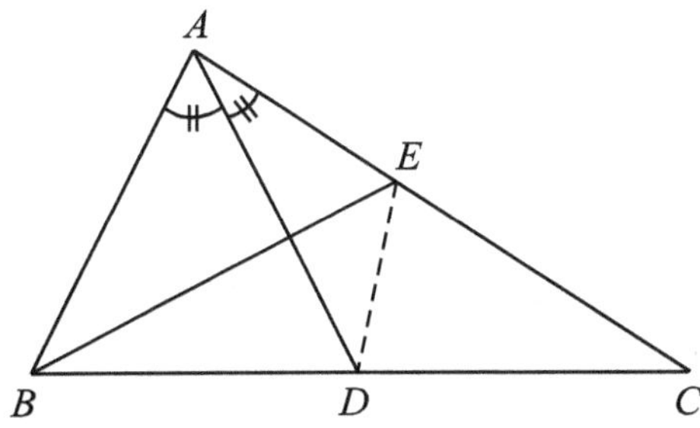

(A) 74°   (B) 73°
(C) 72°   (D) 95°

11. O is any point in the interior of $\triangle ABC$, then
(A) $AB + AC = OB + OC$
(B) $AB + AC < OB + OC$
(C) $AB + AC > OB + OC$
(D) $AB + BC + AC < OA + OB + OC$

12. $ABCD$ is a quadrilateral having AC as a diagonal, then
(A) $CD + DC+ AB + BC < 2AC$
(B) $CD + AD+ AB + BC = 2AC$
(C) $CD + AD+ AB + BC > 2AC$
(D) $CD + DA +AB < BC$

13. In $\triangle PQR$, S is any point on the side QR. Then
(A) $PQ + QR + PR > 2PS$
(B) $PQ + QR + RP < 2PS$
(C) $PQ + QR + RP = 2PS$
(D) $PQ + QR + RP < PS$

14. In $\triangle ABC$, $AC > AB$ and AD is the bisector of $\angle A$. Then
(A) $\angle ADC < 2\angle ADB$
(B) $\angle ADC < \angle ADB$
(C) $\angle ADC > \angle ADB$
(D) $\angle ADC = \angle ADB$

15. In a $\triangle ABC$, $\angle A = 50°$, $\angle B = 60°$. The longest side of the triangle will be
(A) AB (B) BC
(C) CA (D) None of these

16. If $QT \perp PR$, $\angle TQR = 40°$ and $\angle SPR = 30°$. The value of $x + y$ is :

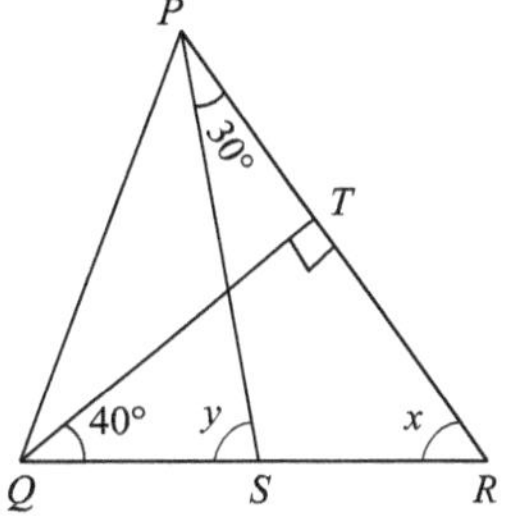

(A) 120°   (B) 130°
(C) 110°   (D) 100°

17. In a right angled triangle, one acute angle is double the other. If the length of hypotenuse of the triangle be x, then the length of the smallest side is :

(A) $\dfrac{x}{3}$ (B) $\dfrac{x}{2}$

(C) $\dfrac{x}{4}$ (D) $\dfrac{2x}{3}$

18. If two isosceles triangles have a common base, then the line joining their vertices will
(A) Bisect them at acute angle
(B) Bisect them at obtuse angle
(C) Bisect them at right angle
(D) None of these

19. If the length of the three altitudes of a triangle are equal, then the triangle must be a/an
(A) Isosceles triangle
(B) Equilateral triangle
(C) Scalene triangle
(D) Right triangle

20.

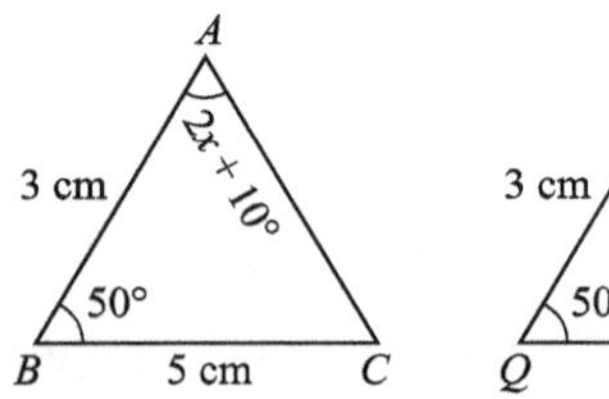

The value of x will be :

(A) 20°   (B) 40°

(C) 30°   (D) 60°

HOTS (ACHIEVERS SECTION)

21. Difference between the semi-perimeter and the sides of a ∆ABC are 8 cm, 7 cm and 5 cm respectively. What is the area of triangle?

(A) 20 cm²   (B) $14\sqrt{20}$ cm²

(C) $20\sqrt{14}$ cm²   (D) $12\sqrt{10}$ cm²

22. In ∆ABC, ∠B = 2∠C. D is a point on BC such that AD bisects, ∠BAC. It is given that AB = CD. BE is the bisector of ∠B. What is the measure of ∠BAC?

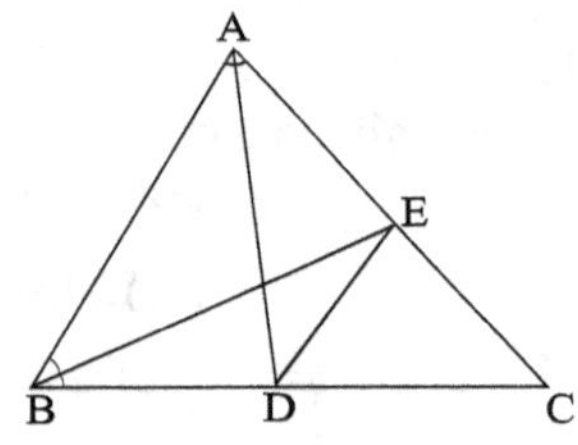

(A) 72°   (B) 73°
(C) 95°   (D) 75°

23. If each side of a triangle is doubled, then what is the percentage increase in its area?
(A) 200%   (B) 250%
(C) 300%   (D) 400%

24. Given 'p' is the exterior angle of ∆PQR and 'q + r' is the sum of interior angles opposite to 'p'. Which of the following is true?
(A) $p + r = q$ (B) $p = q + r$
(C) $p + q = r$ (D) $r = q - p$

25. Identify the interior opposite angles of the exterior angle ∠ACD of ∆ABC.

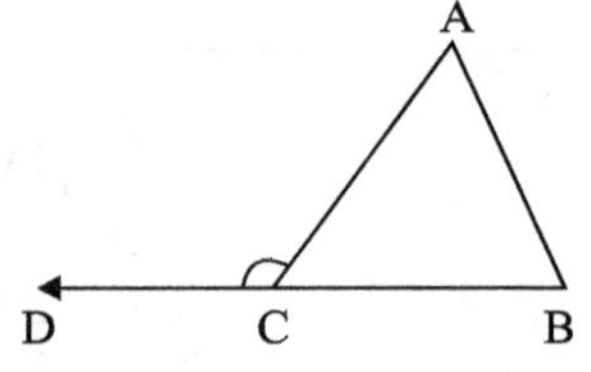

(A) ∠B, ∠C   (B) ∠A, ∠C
(C) ∠A, ∠B   (D) ∠B, ∠D

---Darken Your Choice with HB Pencil---

1.	Ⓐ Ⓑ Ⓒ Ⓓ	6.	Ⓐ Ⓑ Ⓒ Ⓓ	11.	Ⓐ Ⓑ Ⓒ Ⓓ	16	Ⓐ Ⓑ Ⓒ Ⓓ	21.	Ⓐ Ⓑ Ⓒ Ⓓ
2.	Ⓐ Ⓑ Ⓒ Ⓓ	7.	Ⓐ Ⓑ Ⓒ Ⓓ	12.	Ⓐ Ⓑ Ⓒ Ⓓ	17.	Ⓐ Ⓑ Ⓒ Ⓓ	22.	Ⓐ Ⓑ Ⓒ Ⓓ
3.	Ⓐ Ⓑ Ⓒ Ⓓ	8.	Ⓐ Ⓑ Ⓒ Ⓓ	13.	Ⓐ Ⓑ Ⓒ Ⓓ	18.	Ⓐ Ⓑ Ⓒ Ⓓ	23.	Ⓐ Ⓑ Ⓒ Ⓓ
4.	Ⓐ Ⓑ Ⓒ Ⓓ	9.	Ⓐ Ⓑ Ⓒ Ⓓ	14.	Ⓐ Ⓑ Ⓒ Ⓓ	19.	Ⓐ Ⓑ Ⓒ Ⓓ	24.	Ⓐ Ⓑ Ⓒ Ⓓ
5.	Ⓐ Ⓑ Ⓒ Ⓓ	10.	Ⓐ Ⓑ Ⓒ Ⓓ	15.	Ⓐ Ⓑ Ⓒ Ⓓ	20.	Ⓐ Ⓑ Ⓒ Ⓓ	25.	Ⓐ Ⓑ Ⓒ Ⓓ

LEARNING OBJECTIVES

➤ Quadrilaterals

➤ Types of Quadrilaterals

➤ Properties of Quadrilateral

MULTIPLE CHOICE QUESTIONS

1. The diagonals of a rectangle $PQRS$ meet at O. If $\angle QOR = 64°$ then Find $\angle OPS$?

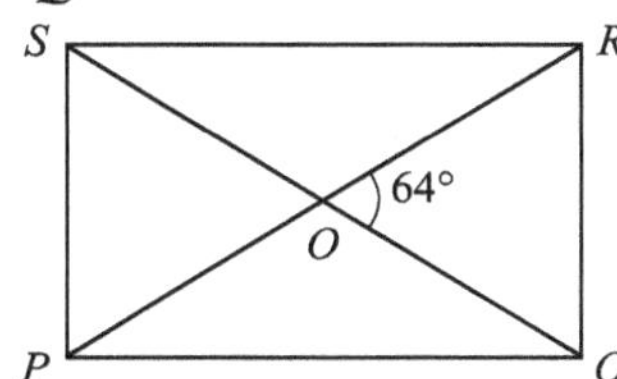

   (A) 60° (B) 58°
   (C) 62° (D) 64°

2. The figure formed by joining the mid-points of consecutive sides of a quadrilateral is a
   (A) Parallelogram (B) Trapezium
   (C) Rectangle (D) None of these

3. Three angles of a quadrilateral are 98°, 92°, 70° respectively. What is the measure of 4th angle?
   (A) 92° (B) 98°
   (C) 100° (D) None of these

4. The angles of a quadrilateral are in the ratio 2:4:5:7. What is the difference between largest and smallest angle?
   (A) 80° (B) 100°
   (C) 60° (D) 90°

5. If the length of each side of rhombus is 15 cm and one of its diagonals is 24 cm what is length of other diagonal?

   (A) 16 cm (B) 14 cm
   (C) 18 cm (D) 12 cm

6. If an angle of a parallelogram is two third of its adjacent angle what is the measure of smallest angle of parallelogram?
   (A) 81° (B) 72°
   (C) 54° (D) 108°

7. In which of the following figures are the diagonals equal?
   (A) Rectangle (B) Parallelogram
   (C) Rhombus (D) Trapezium

8. If $\angle P$, $\angle Q$, $\angle R$, $\angle S$ of a quadrilateral $PQRS$ taken in order are in the ratio $3 : 7 : 6 : 4$, then $PQRS$ is a
   (A) Kite (B) Trapezium
   (C) Rhombus (D) Parallelogram

9. The angles of a quadrilateral are in the ratio $3 : 5 : 9 : 13$. What is the sum of largest and smallest angle of quadrilateral?
   (A) 168° (B) 192°
   (C) 144° (D) None of these

10. The figure formed by joining the mid-points of the adjacent sides of a square is
    (A) Parallelogram
    (B) Rectangle
    (C) Rhombus
    (D) Square

11. *ABCD* is a parallelogram in which W, X, Y, Z are mid = points of sides AB, BC, CD and DA respectively. AC is the diagonal, then which of the following is correct?

(A) $YZ = AC$

(B) $YZ = \dfrac{1}{2} AC$

(C) $YZ = \dfrac{1}{2} AB$

(D) None of these

12. *P* is the mid-point of side *AB* of a parallelogram *ABCD*. A line through *B* parallel to *PD* meets *DC* at *Q* and *AD* produced at *R*, then which of the following is correct?

(A) $AR = BC$

(B) $AR = \dfrac{1}{2} BC$

(C) $AR = 2BC$

(D) $AR = 3BC$

13. If consecutive sides of a parallelogram are equal then it is a (none of the angle $\neq 90°$)

(A) Kite

(B) Rectangle

(C) Rhombus

(D) Square

14. If *ABCD* is a square then what is the measure of $\angle DCA$?

(A) 45°

(B) 90°

(C) 55°

(D) None of these

15. The diagonals of a rectangle *PQRS* meet at *O*. If $\angle QOR = 44°$ Then what is the measure of $\angle OPS$?

(A) 22°

(B) 68°

(C) 44°

(D) 64°

16. *ABCD* is a rhombus with $\angle ABC = 56°$. What is the measure of $\angle ACD$?

(A) 42°

(B) 62°

(C) 52°

(D) 48°

17. In $\triangle ABC$, AD is the median through A and E is the mid-point of AD. BE produced meets AC in F, then which of the following is correct?

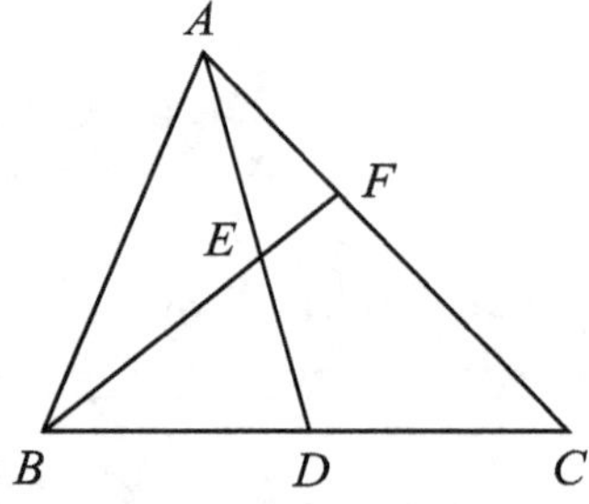

(A) $AF = \dfrac{1}{2} AC$

(B) $AF = \dfrac{2}{3} AC$

(C) $AF = \dfrac{1}{3} AC$

(D) None of these

18. The resulting figure obtained by joining the consecutive midpoint of sides of a rhombus will be *a* :

(A) Parallelogram having unequal diagonals.

(B) Square

(C) Rectangle

(D) rhombus

19. The resulting figure obtained from joining the consecutive mid points of sides of a square is

(A) Rectangle

(B) Square

(C) Trapezium

(D) Rhombus

20. Select the correct statement

(A) Every rectangle is a square

(B) Every square is a rhombus

(C) Every rhombus is a parallelogram

(D) Every parallelogram is a rhombus

21. A wooden log is first cut in the form of a cuboid of length 2.3 m, width 0.75 m and of a certain thickness. Its volume is 1.104 m³. How many rectangular planks of size 2.3 m × 0.75 m × 0.04 m can be cut from the cuboid?

    (A) 12   (B) 14

    (C) 16   (D) 24

22. In the parallelogram ABCD, AP and BP are bisectors of $\angle A$ and $\angle B$ which meet at P.

    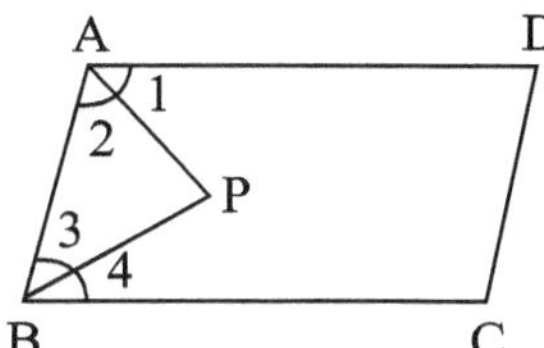

    What is $2\angle APB$ equivalent to?

    (A) $\angle A + \angle B$ (B) $\angle A + \angle C$

    (C) $\angle B + \angle D$ (D) $\angle A - \angle D$

23. In the given figure, AO and DO are the bisectors of $\angle A$ and $\angle D$ of the quadrilateral ABCD. Find $\angle AOD$.

    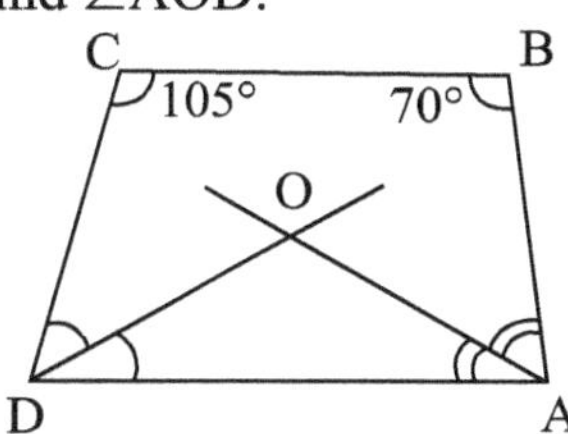

(A) 67.5°   (B) 77.5°

(C) 87.5°   (D) 99.75°

24. In the parallelogram ABCD, what are the measures of the angles x and y?

    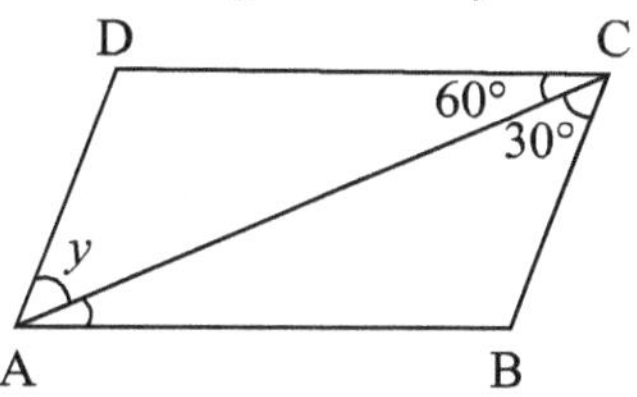

    (A) 60°, 30°   (B) 30°, 60°

    (C) 45°, 45°   (D) 90°, 90°

25. In parallelogram PQRS, what are the values of $\angle QSP$ and $\angle SPQ$?

    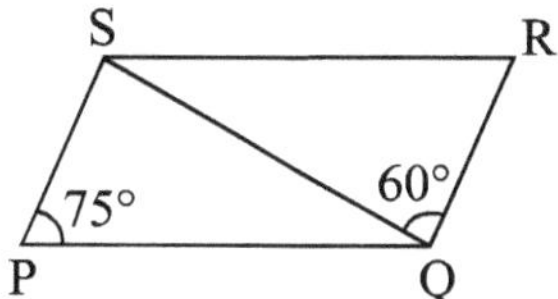

    (A) 45°, 60°   (B) 60°, 45°

    (C) 70°, 35°   (D) 35°, 70°

Darken Your Choice with HB Pencil

1.	Ⓐ	Ⓑ	Ⓒ	Ⓓ	6.	Ⓐ	Ⓑ	Ⓒ	Ⓓ	11.	Ⓐ	Ⓑ	Ⓒ	Ⓓ	16	Ⓐ	Ⓑ	Ⓒ	Ⓓ	21.	Ⓐ	Ⓑ	Ⓒ	Ⓓ
2.	Ⓐ	Ⓑ	Ⓒ	Ⓓ	7.	Ⓐ	Ⓑ	Ⓒ	Ⓓ	12.	Ⓐ	Ⓑ	Ⓒ	Ⓓ	17.	Ⓐ	Ⓑ	Ⓒ	Ⓓ	22.	Ⓐ	Ⓑ	Ⓒ	Ⓓ
3.	Ⓐ	Ⓑ	Ⓒ	Ⓓ	8.	Ⓐ	Ⓑ	Ⓒ	Ⓓ	13.	Ⓐ	Ⓑ	Ⓒ	Ⓓ	18.	Ⓐ	Ⓑ	Ⓒ	Ⓓ	23.	Ⓐ	Ⓑ	Ⓒ	Ⓓ
4.	Ⓐ	Ⓑ	Ⓒ	Ⓓ	9.	Ⓐ	Ⓑ	Ⓒ	Ⓓ	14.	Ⓐ	Ⓑ	Ⓒ	Ⓓ	19.	Ⓐ	Ⓑ	Ⓒ	Ⓓ	24.	Ⓐ	Ⓑ	Ⓒ	Ⓓ
5.	Ⓐ	Ⓑ	Ⓒ	Ⓓ	10.	Ⓐ	Ⓑ	Ⓒ	Ⓓ	15.	Ⓐ	Ⓑ	Ⓒ	Ⓓ	20.	Ⓐ	Ⓑ	Ⓒ	Ⓓ	25.	Ⓐ	Ⓑ	Ⓒ	Ⓓ

AREAS OF PARALLELOGRAMS AND TRIANGLES

9

LEARNING OBJECTIVES

➤ Polygonal Regions
➤ Area Axioms

➤ Important Formulae and Facts

MULTIPLE CHOICE QUESTIONS

1. Let ABCD be a parallelogram and P, Q, R and S be the midpoints of DC, BC, AB and AD respectively. Area of parallelogram $PQRS$ is

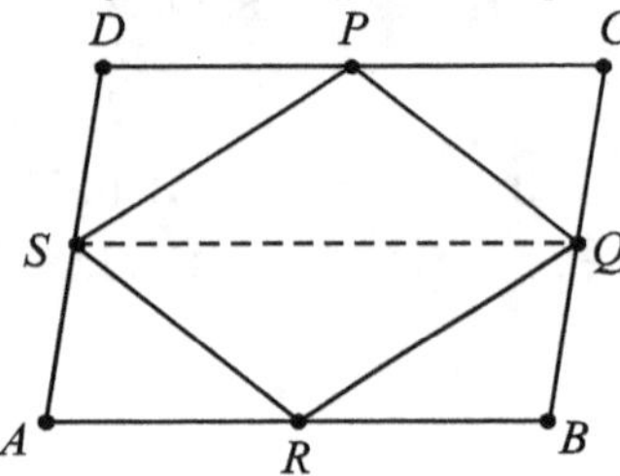

(A) $\dfrac{1}{2}$ ar $(ABCD)$

(B) 2 ar $(ABCD)$

(C) $\dfrac{1}{4}$ ar $(ABCD)$

(D) $\dfrac{2}{3}$ ar $(ABCD)$

2. P and Q are the points on AB and BC respectively of ‖gm $ABCD$, then

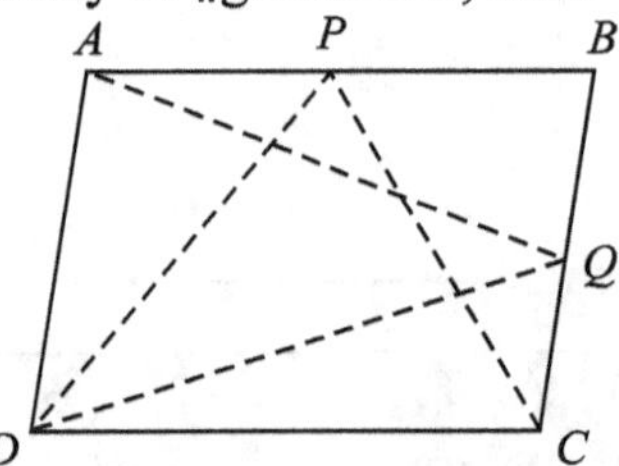

(A) ar $(\triangle PDC) = \dfrac{1}{2}$ ar $(\triangle AQD)$

(B) ar$(\triangle PDC)$ = ar $(\triangle AQD)$
$= \dfrac{1}{2}$ ar (parallelogram $ABCD$)

(C) ar$(\triangle PDC)$ = ar $(\triangle AQD)$
$= \dfrac{1}{3}$ ar(parallelogram $ABCD$)

(D) ar $(\triangle PDC) = \dfrac{2}{3}$ ar$(\triangle AQD)$

3. The median of a triangle divides it into two:
(A) Similar $\triangle$s
(B) Congruent $\triangle$s
(C) Isosceles $\triangle$s
(D) $\triangle$s with same areas

4. In $\triangle ABC$, P, Q, R are the midpoints of sides BC, CA, AB respectively, then ar$(\triangle PQR)$ =

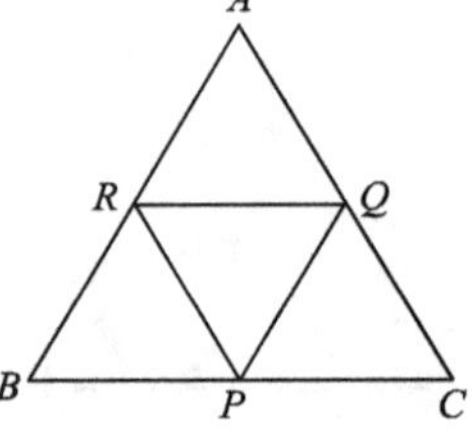

(A) $\dfrac{1}{2}$ ar$(\triangle ABC)$

(B) $\dfrac{1}{4}$ ar$(\triangle ABC)$

(C) $\dfrac{1}{8}$ ar$(\triangle ABC)$

(D) $\dfrac{1}{3}$ ar$(\triangle ABC)$

5. With reference to Q9, ar(trapezium RQCB) =
   (A) $\dfrac{1}{3}$ ar(ΔABC)   (B) $\dfrac{3}{4}$ ar(ΔABC)

   (C) $\dfrac{1}{4}$ ar(ΔABC)   (D) $\dfrac{1}{2}$ ar(ΔABC)

6. If P, Q, R and S are midpoints of AB, BC, CD and DA of parallelogram $ABCD$ and ar($ABCD$) = 26 m², then ar($PQRS$) =
   (A) 13 m²   (B) 6.5 m²
   (C) 6.75 m²   (D) 19.5 m²

7. If AD is median of ΔABC and P is a point on AC such that ar(ΔADP) : ar(ΔABD) = 2 : 3, then ar (ΔPDC) : ar (ΔABC) is
   (A) 1 : 5   (B) 1 : 6
   (C) 5 : 1   (D) 3 : 5

8. ABC is a right angled Δ at A, $BCED$, $ACFG$ and $ABMN$ are squares on sides BC, AC, AB respectively. $AX \perp DE$ meets BC at Y then,

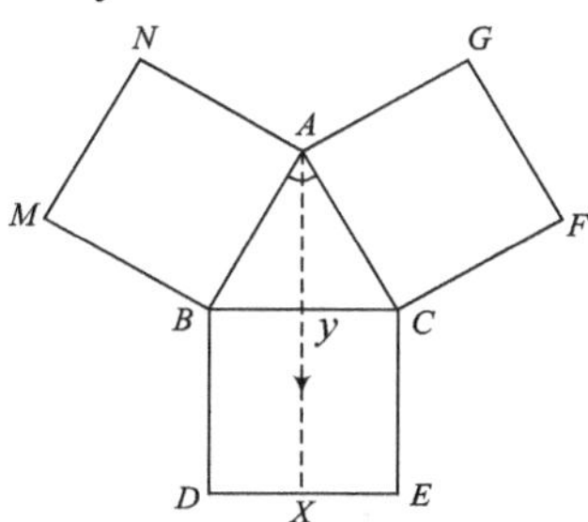

   (A) ar ($BCED$) = ar ($ABMN$) + ar ($ACFG$)
   (B) ar ($CYXE$) = 2ar (ΔABC)
   (C) ar ($BCED$) = ar($ABMN$) + ar(ABC)
   (D) ar(ΔABC) = ar($BCDE$)

9. $ABCD$ is a trapezium in which $AB \parallel CD$ and $CD = 40$ cm, and $AB = 60$ cm. If X and Y are, respectively, the mid points of AD and BC, then $XY =$
   (A) 45 cm   (B) 50 cm
   (C) 60 cm   (D) 55 cm

10. In Qn.14, ar(trap. $DCYX$) = K ar($XYBA$), then $K =$
   (A) $\dfrac{9}{11}$ (B) $\dfrac{10}{11}$

   (C) $\dfrac{1}{11}$ (D) $\dfrac{3}{11}$

11. area of trapezium, $PQRS$ in the given figure is :

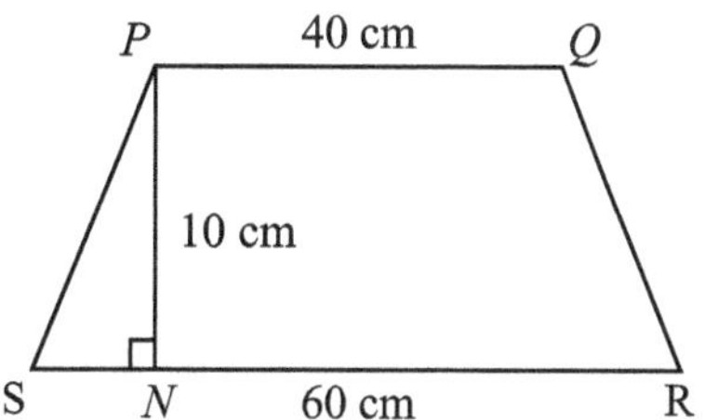

   (A) 500 cm²   (B) 250 cm²
   (C) 125 cm²   (D) 375 cm²

12. $ABCD$ is a trapezium in which $AB \parallel DC$, then

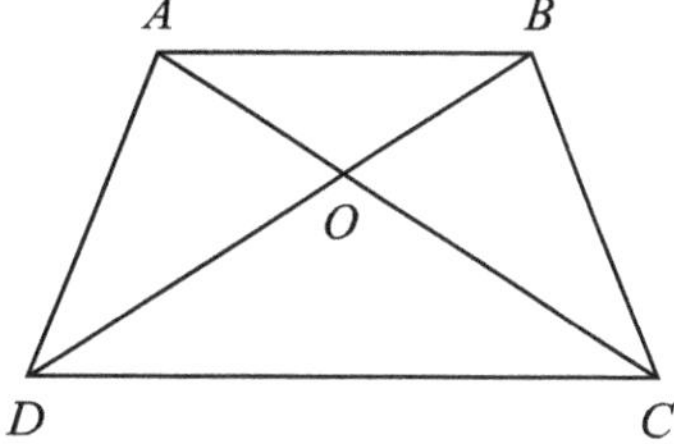

   (A) ar (ΔAOB) = ar (ΔDOC)

   (B) ar (ΔAOB) = $\dfrac{3}{4}$ ar (ΔDOC)

   (C) ar (ΔAOD) = ar (ΔBOC)
   (D) ar (ΔAOD) $\neq$ ar (ΔBOC)

13. Find the area of quadrilateral $ABCD$,

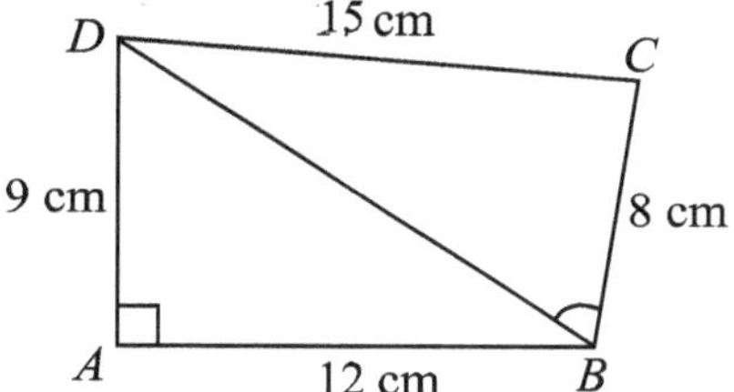

   (A) 114 cm²   (B) 112 cm²
   (C) 102 cm²   (D) 97 cm²

14. $ABCD$ is a rectangle with O as any point in its interior. If ar (ΔAOD) = 3 cm², and ar(ΔBOC) = 6cm², then ar($ABCD$) =
   (A) 9 cm²   (B) 27 cm²
   (C) 18 cm²   (D) 6 cm²

15. *ABCD* is a parallelogram in which *BC* is produced to *E* such that *CE* = *BC*. *AE* intersects *CD* at *F*. If area Δ*DFB* = 3 cm², area of parallelogram *ABCD* is:
   (A) 6 cm²   (B) 12 cm²
   (C) 18 cm²   (D) 9 cm²

16. The area of trapezium is :

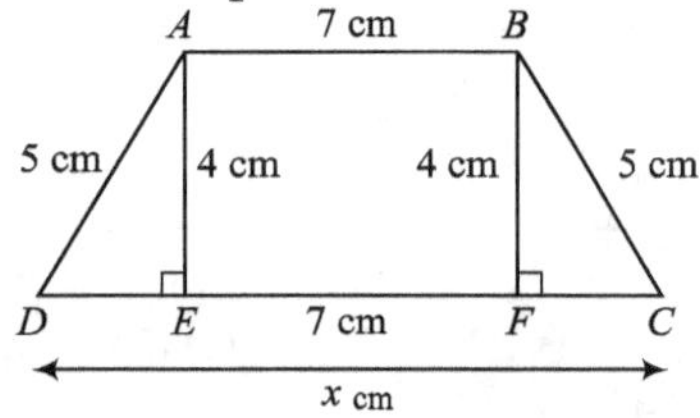

   (A) 40 cm²   (B) 20 cm²
   (C) 30 cm²   (D) 35 cm²

17. *ABCD* and *FECG* are parallelograms equal in area. If ar(Δ*AQE*) = 12cm², then ar(parallelogram *FGBQ*) =

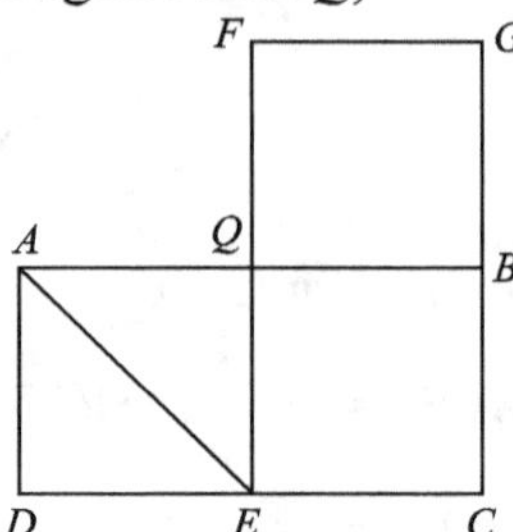

18. *PQRS* is a rectangle inscribed in a quadrant of a circle of radius 13 cm. *A* is any point on *PQ*. If *PS* = 5cm, then find ar(Δ*ARS*).
   (A) 15 cm²
   (B) 20 cm²
   (C) 25 cm²
   (D) 30 cm²

19. *ABCD* is a parallelogram. *P* is the midpoint of *AB*. *BD* and *CP* intersect at *Q* such that *QC* : *QP* = 3 : 1. If the ar(Δ*PBQ*) = 10 cm², then area of parallelogram *ABCD* is :
   (A) 80 cm²
   (B) 40 cm²
   (C) 160 cm²
   (D) 120 cm²

20. A rhombus has diagonals of length 8cm and 6cm. The ratio of area of rhombus and its side length is:
   (A) 6 : 12
   (B) 24 : 5
   (C) 5 : 6
   (D) 3 : 5

HOTS (ACHIEVERS SECTION)

21. In the figure, AB ∥ CD. What is the value of *x*?

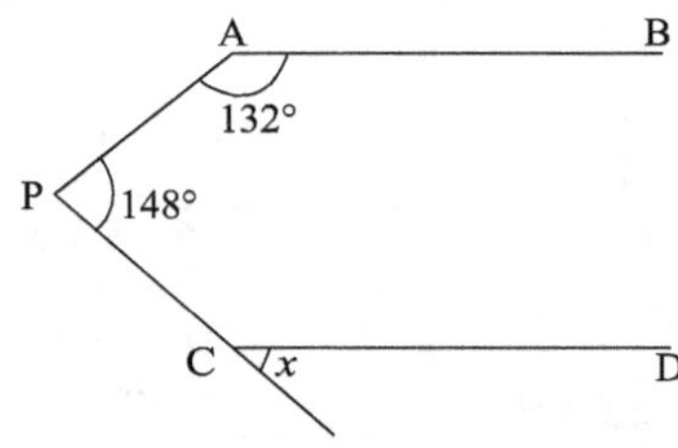

   (A) 115°   (B) 100°
   (C) 95°   (D) 105°

22. What is the perpendicular distance of point A(4, 3) from Y – ax*is*?
   (A) 6   (B) 5

   (C) 4   (D) 3

23. The radius of the internal and external surface of a hollow spherical shell are 3 cm and 5 cm respectively. If it is melted and recast into a solid cylinder of height $\frac{8}{3}$ cm, then what is the diameter of cylinder?
   (A) 7 cm   (B) 10.5 cm
   (C) 14 cm   (D) 21 cm

24. If the diagonal of a cuboid is $\sqrt{251}$ cm, its breadth is 9 cm and height is 7 cm, then what is its length?
   (A) 8 cm   (B) 10 cm
   (C) 11 cm   (D) 12 cm

25. In $\triangle XYZ$, P and Q are two points on side XZ such that XP = PQ = QZ.

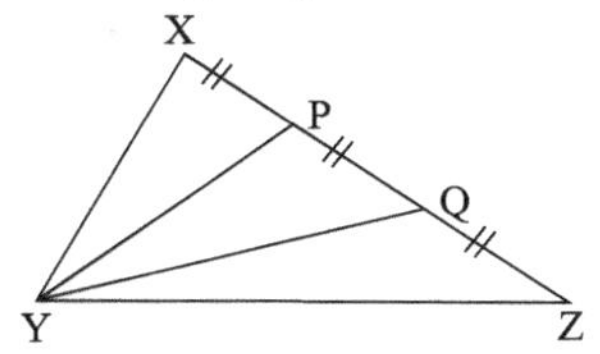

Which of the following is correct?
(A) ar($\triangle PXY$) = ar($\triangle PYZ$)
(B) ar($\triangle PXY$) = ar($\triangle PYQ$) = ar($\triangle QYZ$)
(C) ar($\triangle PYQ$) = ar($\triangle XYQ$)
(D) ar($\triangle QYZ$) = ar($\triangle XYQ$)

1. Ⓐ Ⓑ Ⓒ Ⓓ	6. Ⓐ Ⓑ Ⓒ Ⓓ	11. Ⓐ Ⓑ Ⓒ Ⓓ	16 Ⓐ Ⓑ Ⓒ Ⓓ	21. Ⓐ Ⓑ Ⓒ Ⓓ
2. Ⓐ Ⓑ Ⓒ Ⓓ	7. Ⓐ Ⓑ Ⓒ Ⓓ	12. Ⓐ Ⓑ Ⓒ Ⓓ	17. Ⓐ Ⓑ Ⓒ Ⓓ	22. Ⓐ Ⓑ Ⓒ Ⓓ
3. Ⓐ Ⓑ Ⓒ Ⓓ	8. Ⓐ Ⓑ Ⓒ Ⓓ	13. Ⓐ Ⓑ Ⓒ Ⓓ	18. Ⓐ Ⓑ Ⓒ Ⓓ	23. Ⓐ Ⓑ Ⓒ Ⓓ
4. Ⓐ Ⓑ Ⓒ Ⓓ	9. Ⓐ Ⓑ Ⓒ Ⓓ	14. Ⓐ Ⓑ Ⓒ Ⓓ	19. Ⓐ Ⓑ Ⓒ Ⓓ	24. Ⓐ Ⓑ Ⓒ Ⓓ
5. Ⓐ Ⓑ Ⓒ Ⓓ	10. Ⓐ Ⓑ Ⓒ Ⓓ	15. Ⓐ Ⓑ Ⓒ Ⓓ	20. Ⓐ Ⓑ Ⓒ Ⓓ	25. Ⓐ Ⓑ Ⓒ Ⓓ

CIRCLES

LEARNING OBJECTIVES

- ➤ Circle
- ➤ Terms Related to Circle
- ➤ Central Angle
- ➤ Important Theorems

MULTIPLE CHOICE QUESTIONS

1. $AB = AC$ and O is the centre of the circle, then,

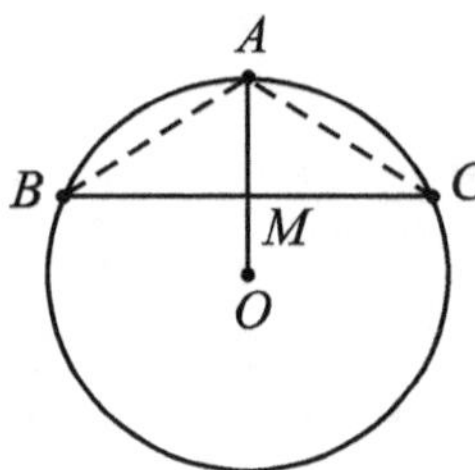

   (A) $BM = MC$
   (B) $BM \neq MC$
   (C) OM is not perpendicular to BC
   (D) None of these

2. Bisector AD of $\angle BAC$ of $\triangle ABC$ passes through the centre of the circumcircle of $\triangle ABC$, then,
   (A) $AB \neq AC$
   (B) $AB = AC$
   (C) $BC = AC$
   (D) $BC = AB$

3. AB and AC are two equal chords of a circle whose centre is O. If $AB \perp OD$ and $OE \perp AC$, then,
   (A) $\triangle ABE$ is an isosceles triangle
   (B) $\triangle ADE$ is an equilateral triangle
   (C) $\triangle ADC$ is an isosceles triangle
   (D) $\triangle ADE$ is an isosceles triangle

4. Find the measure of $\angle ABC$.

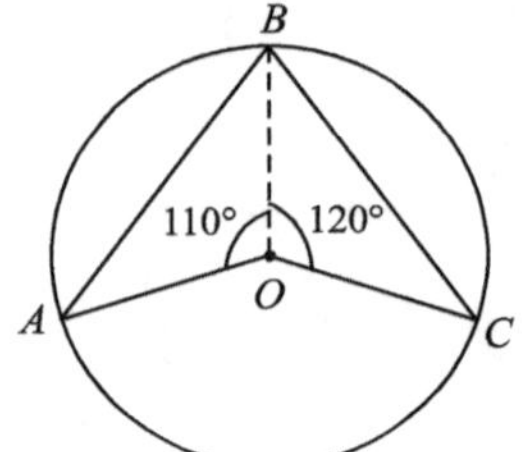

   (A) $85°$ (B) $70°$
   (C) $75°$ (D) $65°$

5. Any cyclic parallelogram is a:
   (A) rhombus   (B) rectangle
   (C) square   (D) trapezium

6. The measure of $\angle BOC$ is

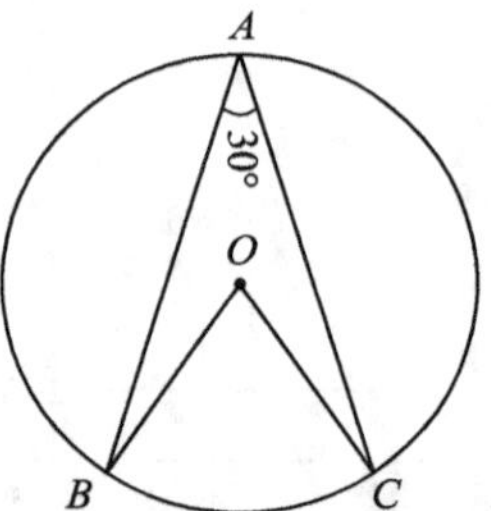

   (A) $90°$ (B) $75°$
   (C) $60°$ (D) $120°$

7. In the adjoining figure, $AB = AC$ and $\angle ACB = 40°$, then $\angle BDC = $?

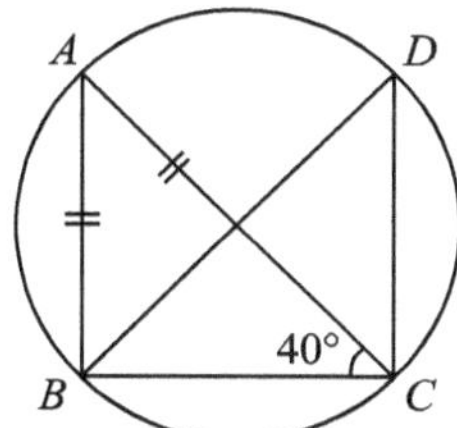

(A) 40°   (B) 80°

(C) 90°   (D) 100°

8. P is the centre of the circle, and $\angle XPZ = 120°$, $\angle XZY = 35°$, then the measure of $\angle YXZ$ is :

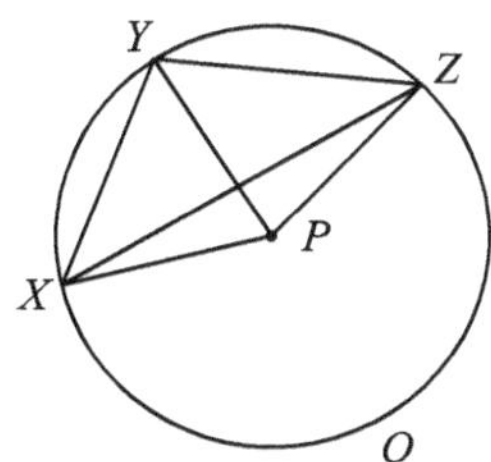

(A) 50°   (B) 25°

(C) 35°   (D) 60°

9. Chords AD and BC intersects each other at right angles at point P. If $\angle DAB = 44°$, then $\angle ADC = $?

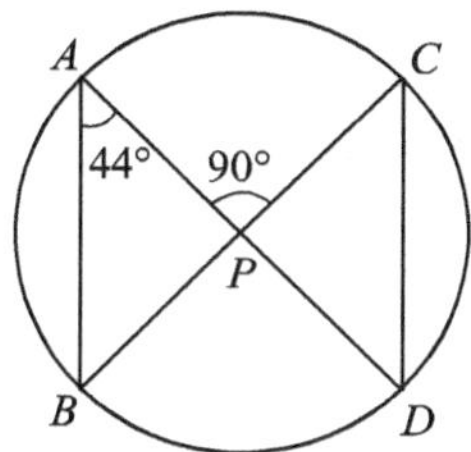

(A) 44°   (B) 88°

(C) 46°   (D) 54°

10. $PQRS$ is a cyclic quadrilateral such that PR is a diameter of circle. If $\angle QPR = 64°$ and $\angle SPR = 31°$, then, $\angle R = $?

(A) 95°   (B) 64°

(C) 85°   (D) 31°

11. If the length of an arc of a circle is proportional to angle subtended by it at the centre then, the ratio of ABC : circumference = ?

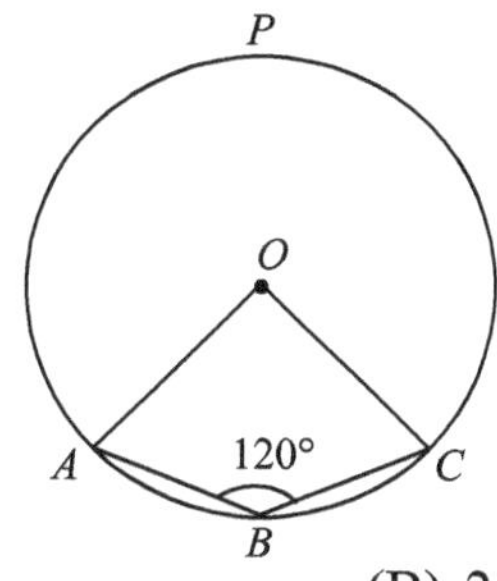

(A) 1 : 3   (B) 2 : 3

(C) 1 : 2   (D) 3 : 4

12. If A, B, C are three points on a circle with centre O such that $\angle AOB = 90°$ and $\angle BOC = 120°$, then $\angle ABC = $?

(A) 60°   (B) 90°

(C) 135°   (D) 75°

13. The chord of a circle is equal to its radius. The angle subtended by this chord at the mid arc of the circle is

(A) 60°   (B) 120°

(C) 150°   (D) 75°

14. O is the centre of circle, with $AC = 30$ cm and $DA = 10\sqrt{5}$ cm, then the measure of DC is

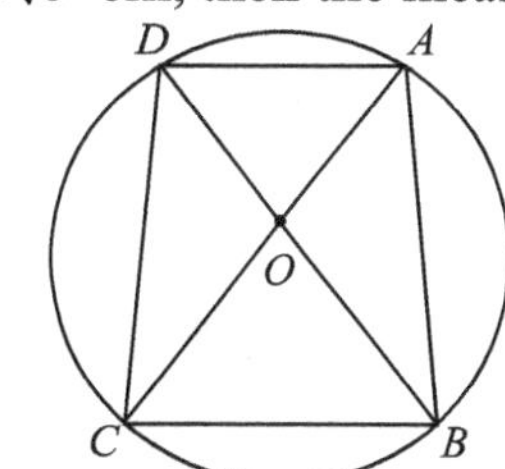

(A) $10\sqrt{5}$ cm   (B) 20 cm

(C) $20\sqrt{5}$ cm   (D) 25 cm

15. In the adjoining figure, O is the circumcentre of $\triangle ABC$, then the value of $\angle OBC + \angle BAC$ is

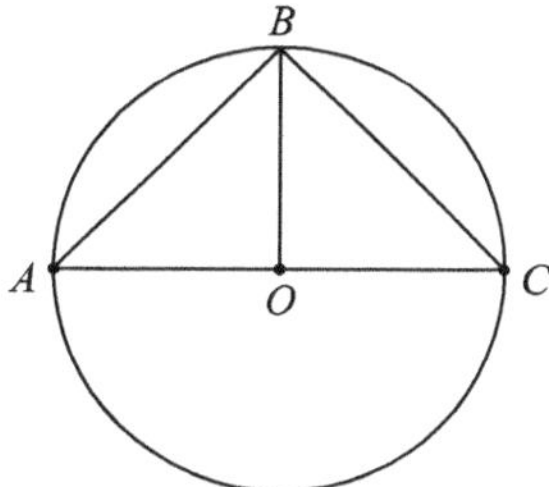

(A) 60°   (B) 90°

(C) 120°   (D) 150°

16. Find the value of $(x + y)$.

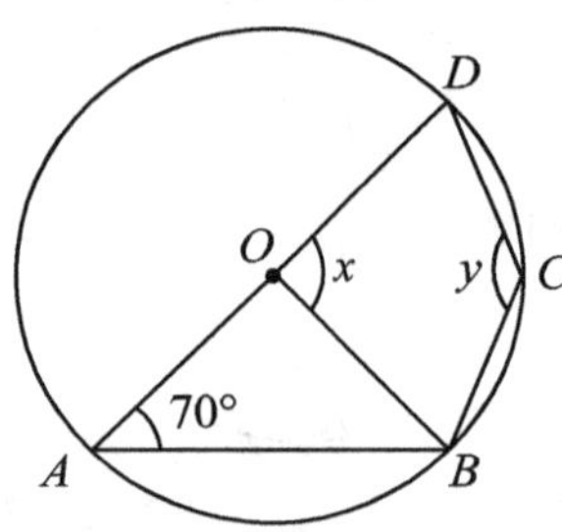

    (A) 230°   (B) 240°
    (C) 235°   (D) 250°

17. In the adjoining figure, $AB = AC$, and $\angle ACB = 64°$, then $\angle BEC = $?

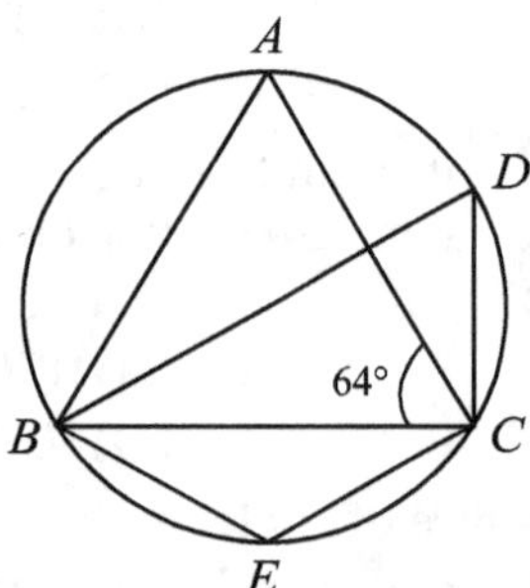

    (A) 130°   (B) 128°
    (C) 122°   (D) 120°

18. The sum of the angles in the 4 segments exterior to a cyclic quadrilateral
    (A) 360°   (B) 450°
    (C) 540°   (D) 720°

19. $AB \parallel CD$, and $\angle B = 65°$ and $\angle DAC = 30°$
    The measure of $\angle CAB = $?

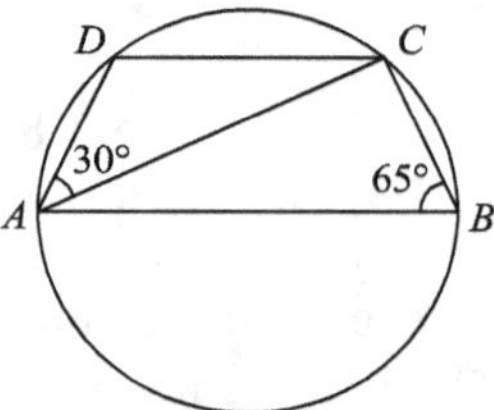

    (A) 25°   (B) 30°
    (C) 40°   (D) 35°

20. In the given figure $\angle A = 60°$, $\angle ABC = 80°$, then the measure of $\angle BQC$ is

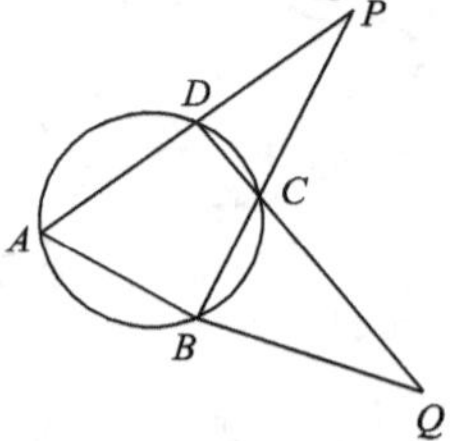

    (A) 40°   (B) 25°
    (C) 30°   (D) 20°

HOTS (ACHIEVERS SECTION)

21. If AB and CD are two chords of a circle intersecting at point E, as per the given figure. Then:

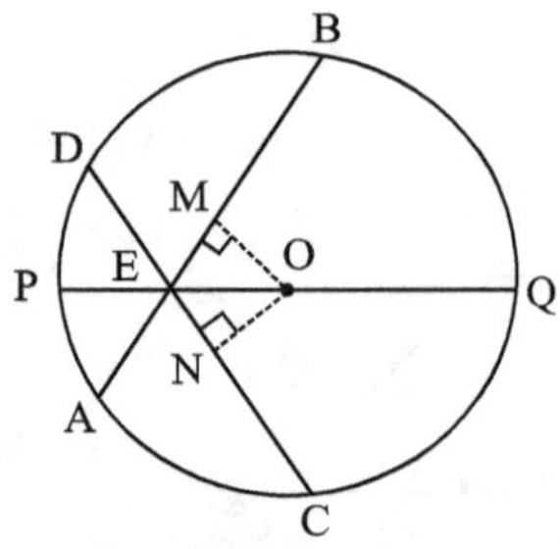

    (A) $\angle BEQ > \angle CEQ$
    (B) $\angle BEQ = \angle CEQ$
    (C) $\angle BEQ < \angle CEQ$
    (D) None of the above

22. If a line intersects two concentric circles with centre O at A, B, C and D, then:
    (A) AB = CD
    (B) AB > CD
    (C) AB < CD
    (D) None of the above

23. In the below figure, the value of $\angle ADC$ is:

(A) 60°   (B) 30°
(C) 45°   (D) 55°

24. In the given figure, find angle OPR.

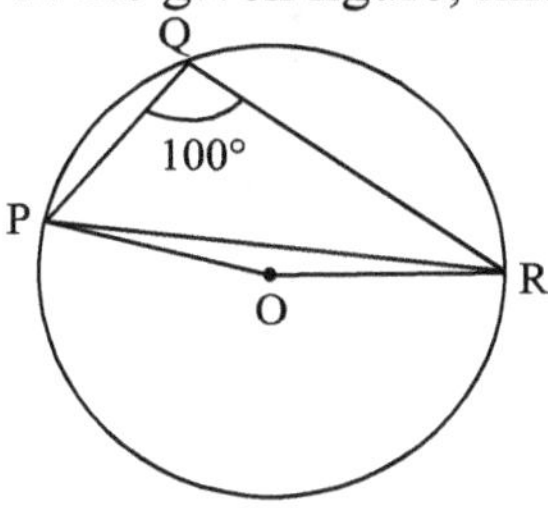

(A) 20°
(B) 15°
(C) 12°

(D) 10°

25. In the given figure, $\angle AOB = 90°$ and $\angle ABC = 30°$, then $\angle CAO$ is equal to:

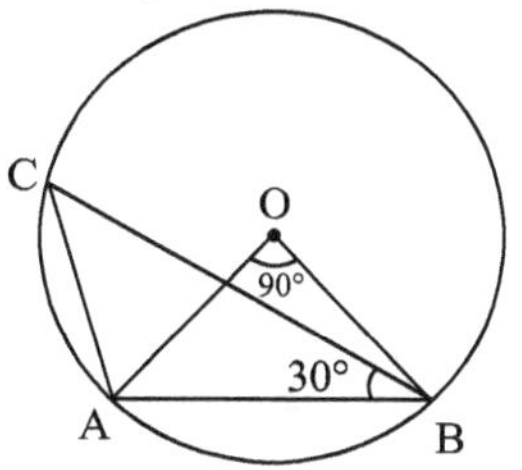

(A) 30°
(B) 45°
(C) 60°
(D) 90°

1.	Ⓐ Ⓑ Ⓒ Ⓓ	6.	Ⓐ Ⓑ Ⓒ Ⓓ	11.	Ⓐ Ⓑ Ⓒ Ⓓ	16	Ⓐ Ⓑ Ⓒ Ⓓ	21.	Ⓐ Ⓑ Ⓒ Ⓓ
2.	Ⓐ Ⓑ Ⓒ Ⓓ	7.	Ⓐ Ⓑ Ⓒ Ⓓ	12.	Ⓐ Ⓑ Ⓒ Ⓓ	17.	Ⓐ Ⓑ Ⓒ Ⓓ	22.	Ⓐ Ⓑ Ⓒ Ⓓ
3.	Ⓐ Ⓑ Ⓒ Ⓓ	8.	Ⓐ Ⓑ Ⓒ Ⓓ	13.	Ⓐ Ⓑ Ⓒ Ⓓ	18.	Ⓐ Ⓑ Ⓒ Ⓓ	23.	Ⓐ Ⓑ Ⓒ Ⓓ
4.	Ⓐ Ⓑ Ⓒ Ⓓ	9.	Ⓐ Ⓑ Ⓒ Ⓓ	14.	Ⓐ Ⓑ Ⓒ Ⓓ	19.	Ⓐ Ⓑ Ⓒ Ⓓ	24.	Ⓐ Ⓑ Ⓒ Ⓓ
5.	Ⓐ Ⓑ Ⓒ Ⓓ	10.	Ⓐ Ⓑ Ⓒ Ⓓ	15.	Ⓐ Ⓑ Ⓒ Ⓓ	20.	Ⓐ Ⓑ Ⓒ Ⓓ	25.	Ⓐ Ⓑ Ⓒ Ⓓ

CONSTRUCTIONS

LEARNING OBJECTIVES

➤ Basics of Construction
➤ Construction Steps

MULTIPLE CHOICE QUESTIONS

1. Which of the following angles can be constructed using a ruler and compass?
   (A) 35° (B) 40°
   (C) 90° (D) 50°

2. Which of the following angles can be constructed using a ruler and compasses?
   (A) 35° (B) 45°
   (C) 95° (D) 55°

3. Which of these angles we cannot construct it using a ruler and compasses?
   (A) 120°
   (B) 70°
   (C) 60°
   (D) All can be constructed

4. Which of these angles cannot be constructed using a ruler and compasses?
   (A) 120° (B) 60°
   (C) 140° (D) 135°

5. If a, b and c are the lengths of three sides of a triangle, then:
   (A) $a + b > c$ (B) $a - b > c$
   (C) $a + b = c$ (D) $a - b = c$

6. Which of the following set of lengths can be the sides of a triangle?
   (A) 2 cm, 4 cm, 1.9 cm
   (B) 1.6 cm, 3.7 cm. 5.3 cm
   (C) 5.5 cm, 6.5 cm, 8.9 cm
   (D) None of the above

7. The side lengths 4 cm, 4 cm and 4 cm can be sides of:
   (A) Scalene Triangle
   (B) Isosceles Triangle
   (C) Equilateral Triangle
   (D) None of the above

8. To construct a bisector of a given angle, we need:
   (A) A ruler
   (B) A compass
   (C) A protractor
   (D) Both ruler and compass

9. To construct an angle of 60 degrees, we need to draw first:
   (A) A ray (B) An arc
   (C) Two rays (D) A straight line

10. If we want to construct a triangle, given its perimeter, then we need to know:
    (A) Sum of two sides of triangle
    (B) Difference between two sides of triangle
    (C) One base angles
    (D) Two base angles

11. With the help of a ruler and a compass, it is possible to construct an angle of
    (A) 35° (B) 37.5°
    (C) 40° (D) 47.5°

12. With the help of a ruler and a compass it is not possible to construct an angle of
    (A) 22.5° (B) 37.5°
    (C) 40° (D) 67.5°

13. Which of the following angles can be constructed using ruler and compasses?
    (A) 35° (B) 45°
    (C) 95° (D) 55°

14. In $\triangle$ ABC if $\angle$B = $\angle$C = 300, which of the following is the longest side?
   (A) BC
   (B) AC
   (C) AB
   (D) none
15. An external bisector of an angle measuring 70° will divide the angle into two angles measuring
   (A) 35°
   (B) 55°
   (C) 70°
   (D) 110°
16. The side length of 2 cm, 3 cm, and 4 cm can be the sides of
   (A) Scalene triangle
   (B) Isosceles triangle
   (C) Equilateral triangle
   (D) None of the above
17. The side length of 5 cm, 3 cm, and 5 cm can be the sides of
   (A) Scalene triangle
   (B) Isosceles triangle
   (C) Equilateral triangle
   (D) None of the above
18. The internal and external bisectors of an angle forms
   (A) Acute angle
   (B) Right angle
   (C) Obtuse angle
   (D) Straight angle
19. The bisector of an angle lies in its
   (A) Interior
   (B) Exterior
   (C) Anywhere in the plane
   (D) On the arms of the angle
20. The point of occurrence of three angle bisectors of a triangle is called
   (A) Incentre
   (B) Circumcentre
   (C) Orthocentre
   (D) Centroid

HOTS (ACHIEVERS SECTION)

21. On a ray AB with initial point A, Taking A as centre and some radius, draw an arc of a circle, which intersects AB, say at a point D. Taking D as centre and with the same radius as before, draw an arc intersecting the previously drawn arc, say at a point E. Draw the ray AC passing through E. Then, the measure of $\angle$CAB is
   (A) 30°
   (B) 60°
   (C) 45°
   (D) 15°
22. To construct a $\triangle$ABC in which BC = 10 cm and $\angle$B= 60 degrees and AB + AC = 14 cm, then the length of BD used for construction.
   (A) 7 cm
   (B) 14 cm
   (C) 20 cm
   (D) 10 cm
23. The construction of a triangle ABC in which AB = 4 cm, $\angle$A = 60° is not possible when the difference of BC and AC is equal to
   (A) 2.5 cm
   (B) 3 cm
   (C) 3.5 cm
   (D) 4.5 cm
24. A triangle ABC with AB = 4 cm and $\angle$A= 60° and $\angle$B= 40° is constructed. Then what is the measurement of $\angle$C?
   (A) 40°
   (B) 60°
   (C) 80°
   (D) 100°
25. The construction of a triangle ABC, given that BC = 6 cm, $\angle$B = 45° is not possible when the difference of AB and AC is equal to:
   (A) 4 cm
   (B) 5 cm
   (C) 5.2 cm
   (D) 6.9 cm

—Darken Your Choice with HB Pencil—

1.	Ⓐ Ⓑ Ⓒ Ⓓ	6.	Ⓐ Ⓑ Ⓒ Ⓓ	11.	Ⓐ Ⓑ Ⓒ Ⓓ	16	Ⓐ Ⓑ Ⓒ Ⓓ	21.	Ⓐ Ⓑ Ⓒ Ⓓ
2.	Ⓐ Ⓑ Ⓒ Ⓓ	7.	Ⓐ Ⓑ Ⓒ Ⓓ	12.	Ⓐ Ⓑ Ⓒ Ⓓ	17.	Ⓐ Ⓑ Ⓒ Ⓓ	22.	Ⓐ Ⓑ Ⓒ Ⓓ
3.	Ⓐ Ⓑ Ⓒ Ⓓ	8.	Ⓐ Ⓑ Ⓒ Ⓓ	13.	Ⓐ Ⓑ Ⓒ Ⓓ	18.	Ⓐ Ⓑ Ⓒ Ⓓ	23.	Ⓐ Ⓑ Ⓒ Ⓓ
4.	Ⓐ Ⓑ Ⓒ Ⓓ	9.	Ⓐ Ⓑ Ⓒ Ⓓ	14.	Ⓐ Ⓑ Ⓒ Ⓓ	19.	Ⓐ Ⓑ Ⓒ Ⓓ	24.	Ⓐ Ⓑ Ⓒ Ⓓ
5.	Ⓐ Ⓑ Ⓒ Ⓓ	10.	Ⓐ Ⓑ Ⓒ Ⓓ	15.	Ⓐ Ⓑ Ⓒ Ⓓ	20.	Ⓐ Ⓑ Ⓒ Ⓓ	25.	Ⓐ Ⓑ Ⓒ Ⓓ

HERON'S FORMULA 

➤ Area
➤ Heron's Formula

MULTIPLE CHOICE QUESTIONS

1. The length of median of an equilateral triangle is $2\sqrt{3}$ cm. The length of its side are :

   (A) 3 cm

   (B) 6 cm

   (C) 4cm

   (D) $4\sqrt{3}$ cm

2. The length of median of an equilateral triangle is $\sqrt{3}$ cm. The area of triangle is

   (A) $2\sqrt{3}$ cm²

   (B) $4\sqrt{3}$ cm²

   (C) $\sqrt{3}$ cm²

   (D) $3\sqrt{3}$ cm²

3. The base and hypotenuse of a right triangle are 5cm, 13cm long. The length of altitude from the vertex containing right angle to the hypotenuse will be:

   (A) $\dfrac{30}{13}$ cm

   (B) $\dfrac{90}{13}$ cm

   (C) $\dfrac{60}{13}$ cm

   (D) $\dfrac{120}{13}$ cm

4. In the figure, $PQ : QR = 3 : 2$. If the area of $\triangle PRT = 40$ cm², then area of $\triangle TQR$ is:

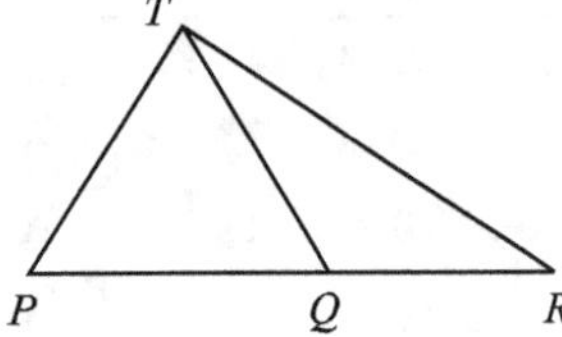

5. Find the area of the rhombus ABCD.

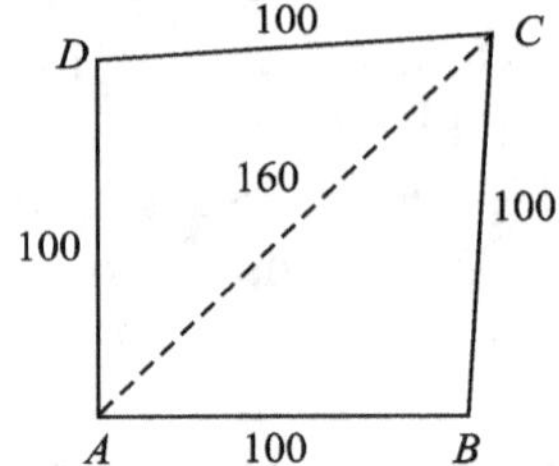

   (A) 15cm²

   (B) 16cm²

   (C) 35cm²

   (D) 30cm²

   (A) 4800 cm²

   (B) 5600 cm²

   (C) 9600 cm²

   (D) 8800 cm²

6. Find the length of BD, in the previous question:

   (A) 120 cm

   (B) 60 cm

   (C) 80 cm

   (D) 160 cm

7. If a square and rhombus have same perimeter, and area of square is S and area of rhombus is R, then

   (A) $S > R$

   (B) $R > S$

   (C) $R = S$

   (D) data insufficient

8. If a square and equilateral triangle have same perimeter and square has area A_1 and equilateral triangle has area A_2, then

   (A) $A_1 = A_2$

   (B) $A_1 > A_2$

   (C) $A_2 > A_1$

   (D) $A_2 = \dfrac{2}{3}A_1$

9. Find the area of kite in the adjoining figure if $AC = BD = 32$ cm, DE = DF 6cm and EF = 8cm.

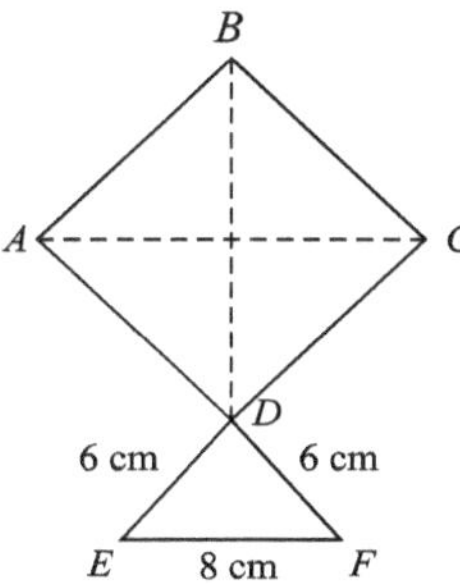

(A) 512 cm² (B) 529.84 cm²
(C) 512.84 cm² (D) 517.84 cm²

10. Two parallel sides of a trapezium are 60cm and 77cm and other sides are 25cm and 26cm. The area of the trapezium is
(A) 622 cm² (B) 822 cm²
(C) 1244 cm² (D) 1644 cm²

11. Area of parallelogram, in the adjoining figure will be :

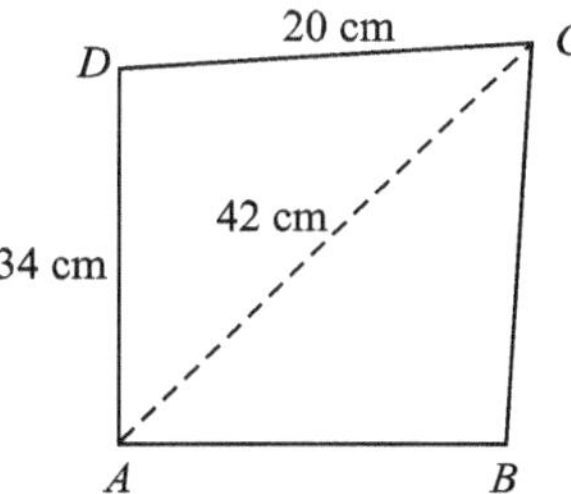

(A) 336 cm² (B) 672 cm²
(C) 1008 cm² (D) 1080 cm²

12. The area of rhombus whose perimeter is 80m and one of the diagonal is 24m will be
(A) 284m² (B) 384m²
(C) 192m² (D) 374m²

13. Find the area of the shaded region.

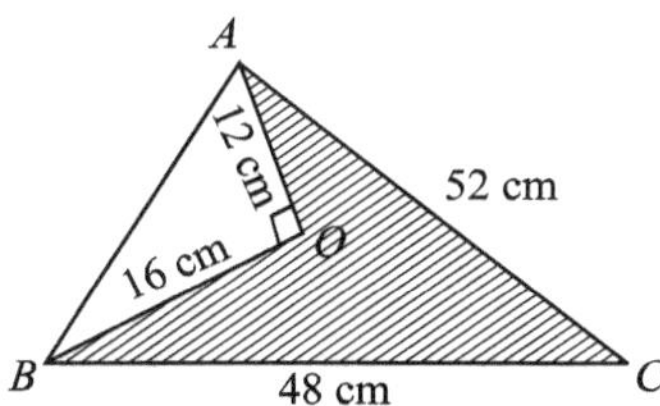

(A) 278 cm² (B) 384 cm²
(C) 364 cm² (D) 284 cm²

14. Area of the figure is :

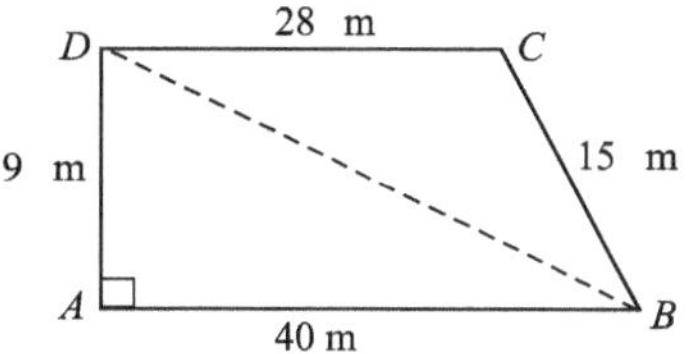

(A) 216 m² (B) 316 m²
(C) 306 m² (D) 206 m²

15. A square and an equilateral triangle have equal perimeters. If the diagonal of the square is $12\sqrt{2}$ cm, the area of the triangle is :

(A) $24\sqrt{2}$ cm² (B) $48\sqrt{3}$ cm²

(C) $24\sqrt{3}$ cm² (D) $64\sqrt{3}$ cm²

16. Find the cost of fencing a triangular park having area = $20\sqrt{2}$ m² and two of its sides as 11m and 6 m. (Cost of fencing = ₹ 10/m).
(A) ₹ 280 (B) ₹ 400
(C) ₹ 320 (D) ₹ 270

17. The third side of triangle whose two sides are 26cm and 28 cm and area is 336 cm², is
(A) 29 cm (B) 27 cm
(C) 30 cm (D) 32 cm

18. The area of a trapezium whose parallel sides are 25 cm and 13 cm and other sides are 15 cm each is :
(A) $56\sqrt{20}$ cm² (B) $56\sqrt{21}$ cm²

(C) $57\sqrt{21}$ cm² (D) $61\sqrt{21}$ cm²

19. The length of sides of a triangle are in the ratio 3 : 4 : 5 and its perimeter is 144 cm, then, the height corresponding to the longest side is:
(A) 27.8 cm (B) 26.8 cm
(C) 28.8 cm (D) 30.8 cm

20. The diagonal of a parallelogram divides it in 2 parts, the area of the two parts:
(A) will be equal
(B) will be unequal
(C) cannot be compared
(D) $\dfrac{2}{3}$ of the area of parallelogram

21. A rhombus shaped field has green grass for 18 cows to graze. If each side of the rhombus is 30 m and its longer diagonal is 48 m, then in how much area of grass field will each cow be grazing?

 (A) 24 m²
 (B) 36 m²
 (C) 48 m²
 (D) 96 m²

22. A cone and a hemisphere have equal bases and equal volumes. What is the ratio of their heights?

 (A) 1 : 2
 (B) 2 : 1
 (C) 1 : 3
 (D) 3 : 1

23. The area of a triangle with given two sides 18 cm and 10 cm, respectively and a perimeter equal to 42 cm is:

 (A) 20√11 cm²
 (B) 19√11 cm²
 (C) 22√11 cm²
 (D) 21√11 cm²

24. A quadrilateral whose sides are 3 cm, 4 cm, 4 cm, 5 cm and one of the diagonal is equal to 5 cm as per the below figure. The area of the quadrilateral is:

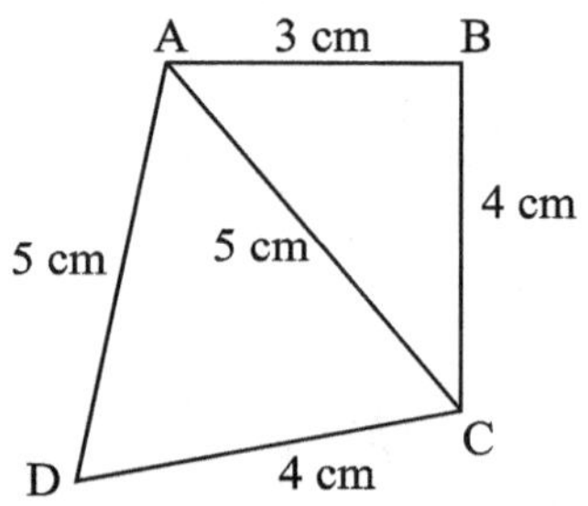

 (A) 19.17 sq.cm
 (B) 15.17 sq.cm
 (C) 20.17 sq.cm
 (D) 22.17 sq.cm.

25. The sides of a parallelogram are 100 m each and the length of the longest diagonal is 160 m. The area of a parallelogram is:

 (A) 9600 sq.m
 (B) 9000 sq.m
 (C) 9200 sq.m
 (D) 8800 sq.m

1.	Ⓐ Ⓑ Ⓒ Ⓓ	6.	Ⓐ Ⓑ Ⓒ Ⓓ	11.	Ⓐ Ⓑ Ⓒ Ⓓ	16	Ⓐ Ⓑ Ⓒ Ⓓ	21.	Ⓐ Ⓑ Ⓒ Ⓓ
2.	Ⓐ Ⓑ Ⓒ Ⓓ	7.	Ⓐ Ⓑ Ⓒ Ⓓ	12.	Ⓐ Ⓑ Ⓒ Ⓓ	17.	Ⓐ Ⓑ Ⓒ Ⓓ	22.	Ⓐ Ⓑ Ⓒ Ⓓ
3.	Ⓐ Ⓑ Ⓒ Ⓓ	8.	Ⓐ Ⓑ Ⓒ Ⓓ	13.	Ⓐ Ⓑ Ⓒ Ⓓ	18.	Ⓐ Ⓑ Ⓒ Ⓓ	23.	Ⓐ Ⓑ Ⓒ Ⓓ
4.	Ⓐ Ⓑ Ⓒ Ⓓ	9.	Ⓐ Ⓑ Ⓒ Ⓓ	14.	Ⓐ Ⓑ Ⓒ Ⓓ	19.	Ⓐ Ⓑ Ⓒ Ⓓ	24.	Ⓐ Ⓑ Ⓒ Ⓓ
5.	Ⓐ Ⓑ Ⓒ Ⓓ	10.	Ⓐ Ⓑ Ⓒ Ⓓ	15.	Ⓐ Ⓑ Ⓒ Ⓓ	20.	Ⓐ Ⓑ Ⓒ Ⓓ	25.	Ⓐ Ⓑ Ⓒ Ⓓ

SURFACE AREA AND VOLUME 

➤ Area

➤ Heron's Formula

MULTIPLE CHOICE QUESTIONS

1. A rectangular reservoir is 120 m long and 75 m wide. At what speed per hour must water flow into it through a square pipe 20 cm wide so that the water rises by 2.4 m in 18 hours?
   - (A) 40 km/hour
   - (B) 30 km/hour
   - (C) 45 km/hour
   - (D) 60 km/hour

2. The diameter of roller 1.5 m long is 84 cm. If it takes 100 revolutions to level a playground, what is the cost of leveling the playground at the rate of 50 paise per square meter?
   - (A) ₹ 198
   - (B) ₹ 168
   - (C) ₹ 192
   - (D) ₹ 208

3. The thickness of a hollow wooden cylinder is 2 cm. It is 35 cm long and its inner radius is 12 cm. What is the volume of wood required to make the cylinder if it is open at either end?
   - (A) 5120 cm³
   - (B) 5720 cm³
   - (C) 5820 cm³
   - (D) 5620 cm³

4. The volume of a cylinder is 448 π cm³ and height 7 cm. What is the lateral surface area of the cylinder?
   - (A) 352 cm²
   - (B) 356 cm²
   - (C) 342 cm²
   - (D) 362 cm²

5. A solid cylinder has total surface area of 462 m². Its curved surface area is one-third of total surface area. What is the volume of the cylinder?
   - (A) 569 cm³
   - (B) 539 cm³
   - (C) 529 cm³
   - (D) 549 cm³

6. At a mela, a stall keeper in one of the food stalls has a large cylindrical vessel of base radius 15 cm filled upto a height of 32 cm with fruit juice. The juice is filled in small cylindrical glasses of radius 3 cm upto height of 8cm. How many glasses will be filled by selling the juice completely?
   - (A) 100
   - (B) 125
   - (C) 150
   - (D) 200

7. The height of a right circular cylinder is 10.5 m. Three times the sum of the areas of its two circular faces is twice the area of the curved surface. What is the volume of the cylinder?
   - (A) 1617 m³
   - (B) 1651 m³
   - (C) 1631 m³
   - (D) 1637 m³

8. How many metres of cloth 5 m in width will be required to make a conical tent, the radius of whose base is 7 m and height is 24 m ?
   - (A) 120 m
   - (B) 110 m
   - (C) 125 m
   - (D) 130 m

9. The diameter of a sphere is 6 cm. If it is melted and drawn into a wire of diameter 0.2 cm, then what is the length of the wire?
   - (A) 18 m
   - (B) 26 m
   - (C) 36 m
   - (D) 30 m

10. The diameter of moon is approximately $\frac{1}{4}$th the diameter of earth. What fraction of the volume of earth is the volume of moon?

(A) $\frac{1}{16}$ (B) $\frac{1}{32}$

(C) $\frac{1}{64}$ (D) None of these

11. How many planks each of which is 2 m long, 2.5 cm broad and 4 cm thick can be cut from a wooden block 6m long, 15 cm broad and 40cm thick?

(A) 100   (B) 180

(C) 140   (D) 200

12. Water flows into a tank 150 m × 100 m at the base through a pipe whose cross-section is 2 dm by 1.5 dm at the speed of 15 km per hour. In how many hours will the water be 3 meters deep?

(A) 100 hours   (B) 120 hours

(C) 80 hours   (D) 150 hours

13. What is the length of diagonal of a cube each of whose edge measures 20cm?

(A) 32.64 cm   (B) 17.32 cm

(C) 28.28 cm   (D) None of these

14. If a place receives 5 cm of rain, then what is the volume of water received in 2 hectares?

(A) 2000 m³   (B) 1200 m³

(C) 1000 m³   (D) None of these

15. Total surface area of a cube is 486 cm². What is its lateral surface area?

(A) 324 cm²   (B) 364 cm²

(C) 332 cm²   (D) 348 cm²

16. The curved surface area and the volume of a pillar are 264 m² and 396 m³. What is the height of the pillar?

(A) 12 m

(B) 14 m

(C) 6 m

(D) 8 m

17. Find the number of coins 1.5 cm in diameter and 0.2 cm thick to be melted to form a right circular cylinder of height 5cm and diameter 4.5 cm.

(A) 225

(B) 175

(C) 215

(D) 275

18. The volume of a cone is 1232 cm³ and diameter of its base is 14 cm. What is its slant height?

(A) 24 cm

(B) 25 cm

(C) 26 cm

(D) 27 cm

19. What is the length of longest rod that can placed in a room of dimension 10 m × 10 m × 5 m?

(A) 16 m

(B) 15 m

(C) 12 m

(D) $10\sqrt{5}$ m

20. The radius of a wire is decreased by one third and if volume remains the same, then by how many times will the length increase?

(A) 2 times

(B) 3 times

(C) 6 times

(D) 9 times

21. In the given figure, D is a point between BC in ΔABC such that BD : DC = 3 : 2. If the area of ΔABC is 40 cm², what is the area of shaded region?

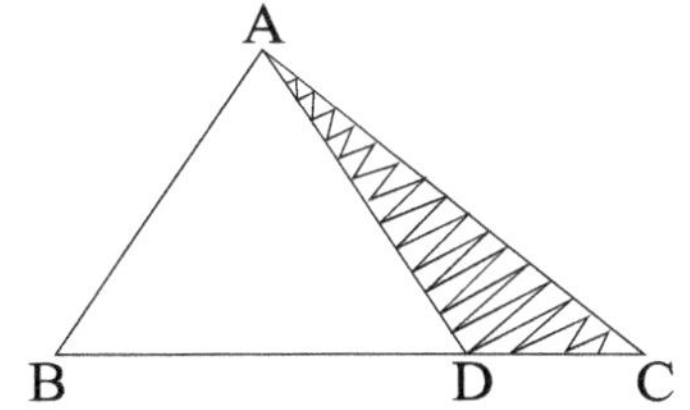

 (A) 12 cm²   (B) 16 cm²
 (C) 18 cm²   (D) 20 cm²

22. What is the area of the shaded region?

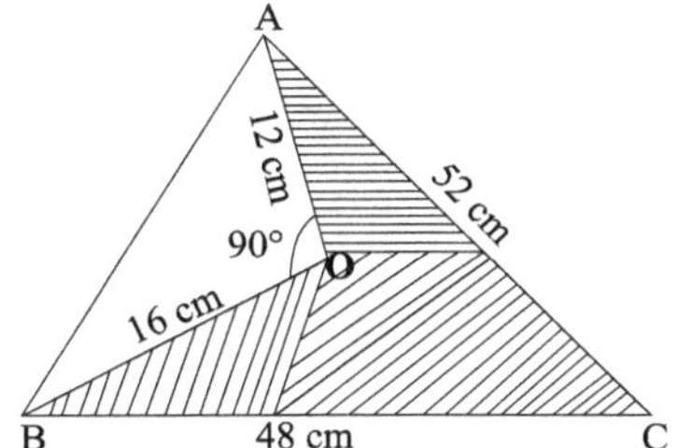

 (A) 404 cm²   (B) 392 cm²
 (C) 388 cm²   (D) 384 cm²

23. A solid cylinder has total surface area of 462 square cm. Its curved surface area is one-third its total surface area. What is the volume of cylinder?

 (A) 529 cm²
 (B) 539 cm³
 (C) 549 cm³
 (D) 559 cm³

24. The surface area of a sphere is 5544 cm². What is the volume of the sphere?

 (A) 38808 cm³
 (B) 38208 cm³
 (C) 38608 cm³
 (D) 38818 cm³

25. Five cubes each of side 5 cm are joined end to end. What is the surface area of the resulting cuboid?

 (A) 475 cm²
 (B) 450 cm²
 (C) 550 cm²
 (D) 575 cm²

Darken Your Choice with HB Pencil

1.	Ⓐ Ⓑ Ⓒ Ⓓ	6.	Ⓐ Ⓑ Ⓒ Ⓓ	11.	Ⓐ Ⓑ Ⓒ Ⓓ	16	Ⓐ Ⓑ Ⓒ Ⓓ	21.	Ⓐ Ⓑ Ⓒ Ⓓ
2.	Ⓐ Ⓑ Ⓒ Ⓓ	7.	Ⓐ Ⓑ Ⓒ Ⓓ	12.	Ⓐ Ⓑ Ⓒ Ⓓ	17.	Ⓐ Ⓑ Ⓒ Ⓓ	22.	Ⓐ Ⓑ Ⓒ Ⓓ
3.	Ⓐ Ⓑ Ⓒ Ⓓ	8.	Ⓐ Ⓑ Ⓒ Ⓓ	13.	Ⓐ Ⓑ Ⓒ Ⓓ	18.	Ⓐ Ⓑ Ⓒ Ⓓ	23.	Ⓐ Ⓑ Ⓒ Ⓓ
4.	Ⓐ Ⓑ Ⓒ Ⓓ	9.	Ⓐ Ⓑ Ⓒ Ⓓ	14.	Ⓐ Ⓑ Ⓒ Ⓓ	19.	Ⓐ Ⓑ Ⓒ Ⓓ	24.	Ⓐ Ⓑ Ⓒ Ⓓ
5.	Ⓐ Ⓑ Ⓒ Ⓓ	10.	Ⓐ Ⓑ Ⓒ Ⓓ	15.	Ⓐ Ⓑ Ⓒ Ⓓ	20.	Ⓐ Ⓑ Ⓒ Ⓓ	25.	Ⓐ Ⓑ Ⓒ Ⓓ

STATISTICS

LEARNING OBJECTIVES

- ➤ Data
- ➤ Exclusive Method
- ➤ Graphical Representation of Data
- ➤ Important Formulae
- ➤ Frequency Distribution
- ➤ Cumulative Frequency Distribution
- ➤ Measures of Central Tendency

MULTIPLE CHOICE QUESTIONS

1. Tallys are usually marked in a bunch of :
   (A) 3   (B) 5
   (C) 4   (D) 6

2. Let 'l' be the lower limit of a class interval in a frequency distribution and 'm' be the midpoint of the class. Then the upper limit of the class is:
   (A) $m - 2l$ (B) $2m - l$
   (C) $\dfrac{3l + m}{2}$ (D) $\dfrac{2l + m}{2}$

3. The mid-value and upper limit of a class interval are 41 and 47 respectively. The class size will be :
   (A) 6   (B) 12
   (C) 10   (D) 18

4. The mid value of a class interval is 14 and the class size is 2. The lower limit of the class is :
   (A) 15   (B) 13
   (C) 17   (D) 18

5. The x-and y-axes in the histogram represent :
   (A) Class interval and frequency
   (B) Class interval and cumulative frequency
   (C) Frequency and class interval
   (D) Cumulative frequency and class interval

6. A frequency polygon is constructed by plotting frequency of the class interval and the
   (A) Upper limit of the class
   (B) Lower limit of the class
   (C) Mid value of the class
   (D) Any values of the class

7. In the 'more-than' type of ogive the cumulative frequency is plotted against :
   (A) The lower limit of the concerned class interval
   (B) The mid value of the concerned class interval
   (C) The upper limit of the concerned class interval
   (D) Any value of the concerned class interval

8. Ogives are the graphical representation of
   (A) Cumulative frequency
   (B) Frequency
   (C) Raw data
   (D) Relative frequency

9.

OLYMPIAD WORKBOOK (IMO) CLASS— 9

The frequency of students is highest in the class interval :

(A) $0-10$ (B) $20-30$
(C) $30-40$ (D) $40-50$

10. Total number of students (Q 14) are :

(A) 66   (B) 76
(C) 56   (D) 54

11. The mean of $x_1, x_2, \ldots, x_n$ is $\overline{X}$, then the value of:

$$\left(x_1 - \overline{X}\right) + \left(x_2 - \overline{X}\right) + \left(x_3 - \overline{X}\right) + \left(x_4 - \overline{X}\right)$$
$$\ldots + \left(x_n - \overline{X}\right) =$$

(A) n (B) $n-1$
(C) zero   (D) 1

12. If the mean of $x_1, x_2, x_3 \ldots, x_n$ is $\overline{X}$ and 5 is added to each number, the new mean will be :

(A) $\overline{X} + 5n$ (B) $\overline{X} - 5n$
(C) $\overline{X} + 5$ (D) $\overline{X} - 5$

13. If each number in (Prob - 17) is multiplied by k, the new mean will be :

(A) $k\overline{X}$ (B) $k^2\overline{X}$
(C) $k^n\,\overline{X}$ (D) $\dfrac{\overline{X}}{k}$

14. The mean of 10 numbers is 16. If two consecutive numbers are excluded, the new mean is 18. The sum of the excluded numbers is:

(A) 15   (B) 16
(C) 18   (D) 21

15. If $x_1, x_2, \ldots, x_n$ are n values of variable x, such that,

$$\sum_{i=1}^{n}(x_i - 2) = 110 \text{ and } \sum_{i=1}^{n}(x_i - 5) = 20 \text{ then}$$

value of the mean is :

(A) $\dfrac{16}{3}$ (B) 5
(C) $\dfrac{17}{3}$ (D) $\dfrac{20}{3}$

16. The sum of deviations of a set of n values $x_1, x_2, \ldots x_n$ measured from 50 is -10 and the sum of deviations of the values from 46 is 70. The value of n is :

(A) 21   (B) 20
(C) 23   (D) 25

17. The mean of marks scored by 10 students was found to be 43. Later it was discovered that a score of 30 was misread as 40. The new mean will be (correct):

(A) 41   (B) 44
(C) 43   (D) 42

18. The mean of the following distribution is:

x	10	30	50	70	89
f	7	8	10	15	10

(A) 54   (B) 50
(C) 55   (D) 57

19. The value of p, if the mean of the following distribution is 20.

x	15	17	19	$20+p$	23
f	2	3	4	$5p$	6

(A) 1   (B) 2
(C) 3   (D) 4

20.

x	10	30	70	50	90
f	17	f_1	f_2	32	19

If sum of frequency is 120 and mean $= 50$, then the value of f_1 and f_2 will be

$f_1, f_2 =$

(A) 24, 28   (B) 28, 24
(C) 26, 28   (D) 26, 24

21. The mean of 16 numbers is 8. If 2 is added to every number, then what will be the new mean?

    (A) 9   (B) 10

    (C) 12   (D) 14

22. A student gets the following percentages in an examination English = 50%, Biology = 40%, Mathematics = 60%, Physics = 70%, Chemistry = 80% It was suggested that he has been given double weight age on his marks in Physics and Chemistry than in other subjects. What is the arithmetic weight age mean of marks?

    (A) 57.4   (B) 59.4

    (C) 58.4   (D) 64.28

23. Five students were tested in English and Hindi and the marks obtained by them were as under:

	A	B	C	D	E
English	55	60	82	65	75
Hindi	21	25	86	90	99

    Which subject has a better median value:

    (A) Hindi

    (B) English

    (C) Both

    (D) None of these

24. In a school 90 boys and 30 girls appeared for a public examination. The mean marks of boys was found to be 45% whereas the mean marks of girls was 70%. What is the average marks % of the school?

    (A) 61.50%   (B) 51.25%

    (C) 40.50%   (D) 51.52%

25. The data in the table below shows the number of people at each table at a restaurant. What is the median of this data?

Number of people	5	6	7	8	9	10	11	12
Frequency	1	0	3	9	12	7	4	2

    (A) 7   (B) 9

    (C) 9.5   (D) 9.25

—Darken Your Choice with HB Pencil—

1.	Ⓐ Ⓑ Ⓒ Ⓓ	6.	Ⓐ Ⓑ Ⓒ Ⓓ	11.	Ⓐ Ⓑ Ⓒ Ⓓ	16	Ⓐ Ⓑ Ⓒ Ⓓ	21.	Ⓐ Ⓑ Ⓒ Ⓓ
2.	Ⓐ Ⓑ Ⓒ Ⓓ	7.	Ⓐ Ⓑ Ⓒ Ⓓ	12.	Ⓐ Ⓑ Ⓒ Ⓓ	17.	Ⓐ Ⓑ Ⓒ Ⓓ	22.	Ⓐ Ⓑ Ⓒ Ⓓ
3.	Ⓐ Ⓑ Ⓒ Ⓓ	8.	Ⓐ Ⓑ Ⓒ Ⓓ	13.	Ⓐ Ⓑ Ⓒ Ⓓ	18.	Ⓐ Ⓑ Ⓒ Ⓓ	23.	Ⓐ Ⓑ Ⓒ Ⓓ
4.	Ⓐ Ⓑ Ⓒ Ⓓ	9.	Ⓐ Ⓑ Ⓒ Ⓓ	14.	Ⓐ Ⓑ Ⓒ Ⓓ	19.	Ⓐ Ⓑ Ⓒ Ⓓ	24.	Ⓐ Ⓑ Ⓒ Ⓓ
5.	Ⓐ Ⓑ Ⓒ Ⓓ	10.	Ⓐ Ⓑ Ⓒ Ⓓ	15.	Ⓐ Ⓑ Ⓒ Ⓓ	20.	Ⓐ Ⓑ Ⓒ Ⓓ	25.	Ⓐ Ⓑ Ⓒ Ⓓ

PROBABILITY

LEARNING OBJECTIVES

➤ Experiment
➤ Compound Event

➤ Empirical Probability

MULTIPLE CHOICE QUESTIONS

1. A dice is rolled 600 times and the occurrence of the outcomes are given below :

Outcomes	1	2	3	4	5	6
Frequency	200	30	120	100	50	100

The probability of getting a composite number is :

(A) $\dfrac{2}{3}$ (B) $\dfrac{1}{3}$

(C) $\dfrac{11}{60}$ (D) $\dfrac{71}{125}$

2. A dice is rolled twice and the outcomes are noted down. The probability of getting even no. as a sum is :

(A) $\dfrac{19}{36}$

(B) $\dfrac{17}{36}$

(C) $\dfrac{1}{2}$

(D) $\dfrac{5}{9}$

3. The unit place digit of 200 people's mobile number is observed and the following table is plotted :

Unit place digit	0	1	2	3	4	5	6	7	8	9
Frequency	23	26	23	20	19	11	14	30	14	20

A number is chosen at random. The probability that its unit place has prime number is:
(A) 0.42   (B) 0.43   (C) 0.84   (D) 0.48

4. With reference to Qn 8 the probability of getting odd number as a unit place digit is:

(A) $\dfrac{103}{200}$ (B) $\dfrac{97}{200}$

(C) $\dfrac{107}{200}$ (D) $\dfrac{121}{200}$

5. A dice is rolled twice. Find the probability of getting prime number as a sum.

(A) $\dfrac{5}{12}$ (B) $\dfrac{1}{2}$

(C) $\dfrac{7}{36}$ (D) $\dfrac{17}{36}$

6. A coin is tossed 1000 times. If the probability of getting a tail is $\dfrac{3}{8}$ then how many times is

(A) 325 (B) 525
(C) 625 (D) 725

7. A coin is tossed 1000 times and the following frequencies are observed:

Head: 455, tail : 545.

The probability of getting tail is:

(A) $\dfrac{109}{200}$ (B) $\dfrac{91}{200}$

(C) $\dfrac{9}{20}$ (D) $\dfrac{108}{200}$

8. The distribution of marks of 90 students are as follows :

Marks	0-20	20-30	30-40	40-50	50-60
Numbers of students	27	10	10	23	20

The probability that a student obtained 40 or more marks is :

(A) $\dfrac{27}{90}$ (B) $\dfrac{47}{90}$ (C) $\dfrac{43}{90}$ (D) $\dfrac{53}{90}$

9. Two coins are tossed simultaneously. The probability of getting at least one tail is:

(A) $\dfrac{3}{4}$ (B) $\dfrac{1}{4}$

(C) $\dfrac{1}{2}$ (D) 1

10. One card is drawn from a well shuffled deck of 52 cards. What is the probability of drawing a red card?

(A) $\dfrac{6}{13}$ (B) $\dfrac{1}{2}$

(C) $\dfrac{2}{13}$ (D) $\dfrac{4}{13}$

11. One card is drawn from a well-shuffled deck of 52 cards. What is the probability of getting a king?

(A) $\dfrac{3}{26}$ (B) $\dfrac{1}{13}$

(C) $\dfrac{2}{13}$ (D) $\dfrac{5}{26}$

12. There are 36 students in a class of which 20 are boys and remaining are girls. What is the probability that a student chosen is a girl?

(A) $\dfrac{5}{9}$ (B) $\dfrac{4}{9}$

(C) $\dfrac{2}{3}$ (D) $\dfrac{1}{3}$

13. Three coins are tossed simultaneously. The probability of getting exactly 2 heads is:

(A) $\dfrac{2}{8}$ (B) $\dfrac{3}{8}$

(C) $\dfrac{4}{8}$ (D) $\dfrac{5}{8}$

14. Two dice are thrown simultaneously. What is the probability of getting a double?

(A) $\dfrac{5}{36}$ (B) $\dfrac{1}{9}$

(C) $\dfrac{1}{6}$ (D) $\dfrac{7}{36}$

15. A bag contains numbers 1, 2, 3, 4 …., 35. What is the probability of getting a multiple of 8?

(A) $\dfrac{2}{35}$ (B) $\dfrac{3}{35}$

(C) $\dfrac{4}{35}$ (D) $\dfrac{1}{7}$

16. A bag contains 6 red balls, 8 white balls, 5 green balls and 3 black balls. One ball is drawn at random from the bag. The probability that the ball is neither white nor black is:

(A) $\dfrac{1}{3}$

(B) $\dfrac{17}{22}$

(C) $\dfrac{1}{2}$

(D) $\dfrac{9}{22}$

17. From a pack of 52 playing cards jacks, queens, kings and aces of red colour are removed. A card is drawn at random. The probability of drawing a black king is:

(A) $\dfrac{1}{24}$

(B) $\dfrac{1}{22}$

(C) $\dfrac{1}{26}$

(D) $\dfrac{1}{44}$

18. A bag contains 5 red and some black balls. If the probability of drawing a black ball is thrice that of a red ball, the number of black balls in the bag is:

(A) 5

(B) 10

(C) 15

(D) 20

19. Two men were born in the same year, i.e., 1987. What is the probability that their birthday will fall on different days?

(A) $\dfrac{364}{366}$

(B) $\dfrac{364}{365}$

(C) $\dfrac{1}{365}$

(D) $\left(1+\dfrac{364}{365}\right)$

20. A box contains 200 bulbs out of which 20 are defective. A bulb is drawn at random. What is the probability of drawing a non–defective bulb?

(A) $\dfrac{1}{10}$

(B) $\dfrac{9}{10}$

(C) $\dfrac{7}{10}$

(D) $\dfrac{4}{5}$

21. The probability of getting 53 Fridays in a leap year is:

(A) $\dfrac{1}{7}$

(B) $\dfrac{3}{7}$

(C) $\dfrac{2}{7}$

(D) $\dfrac{3}{14}$

22. The sum of probabilities of all the outcomes of an experiment is:

(A) Zero

(B) Less than zero

(C) 1

(D) Less than 1

23. A bag contains cards marked with numbers 51, 52, …., 100. A number is selected at random. What is the probability of getting a number which is not a multiple of 5?

(A) $\dfrac{1}{5}$

(B) $\dfrac{2}{5}$

(C) $\dfrac{3}{5}$

(D) $\dfrac{4}{5}$

24. One card is drawn from a well–shuffled deck of 52 cards. The probability of drawing a red face card is:

(A) $\dfrac{3}{26}$

(B) $\dfrac{3}{13}$

(C) $\dfrac{3}{52}$

(D) $\dfrac{1}{13}$

25. Two dice are rolled simultaneously. Find the probability of getting their product as a odd number.

(A) $\dfrac{1}{2}$

(B) $\dfrac{1}{3}$

(C) $\dfrac{5}{36}$

(D) $\dfrac{1}{4}$

26. A bag contains 12 balls out of which x are red. If three more red balls are put in the bag the probability of drawing the red balls is twice then the value of x is:

(A) 2   (B) 4

(C) 6   (D) 5

27. A number "a" is selected from numbers 1, 2, 3 and then the second number "b" is randomly selected from the numbers 1, 4 and 9. The probability that the product ab of the two numbers will be less than 8 is...... .

(A) $\dfrac{4}{9}$ (B) $\dfrac{1}{3}$

(C) $\dfrac{5}{9}$ (D) $\dfrac{2}{9}$

28. A card is drawn from a well-shuffled deck of 52 cards. What is the probability of getting a king of the red suits?

(A) $\dfrac{3}{36}$ (B) $\dfrac{1}{26}$

(C) $\dfrac{3}{26}$ (D) $\dfrac{1}{16}$

29. What is the probability of getting an odd number less than 4, if a die is thrown?

(A) $\dfrac{1}{6}$ (B) $\dfrac{1}{2}$

(C) $\dfrac{1}{3}$ (D) 0

30. Three coins were tossed 200 times. The number of times 2 heads came up is 72. Then the probability of 2 heads coming up is:

(A) $\dfrac{1}{25}$ (B) $\dfrac{2}{25}$

(C) $\dfrac{7}{25}$ (D) $\dfrac{9}{25}$

1. Ⓐ Ⓑ Ⓒ Ⓓ	7. Ⓐ Ⓑ Ⓒ Ⓓ	13. Ⓐ Ⓑ Ⓒ Ⓓ	19 Ⓐ Ⓑ Ⓒ Ⓓ	25. Ⓐ Ⓑ Ⓒ Ⓓ
2. Ⓐ Ⓑ Ⓒ Ⓓ	8. Ⓐ Ⓑ Ⓒ Ⓓ	14. Ⓐ Ⓑ Ⓒ Ⓓ	20. Ⓐ Ⓑ Ⓒ Ⓓ	26. Ⓐ Ⓑ Ⓒ Ⓓ
3. Ⓐ Ⓑ Ⓒ Ⓓ	9. Ⓐ Ⓑ Ⓒ Ⓓ	15. Ⓐ Ⓑ Ⓒ Ⓓ	21. Ⓐ Ⓑ Ⓒ Ⓓ	27. Ⓐ Ⓑ Ⓒ Ⓓ
4. Ⓐ Ⓑ Ⓒ Ⓓ	10. Ⓐ Ⓑ Ⓒ Ⓓ	16. Ⓐ Ⓑ Ⓒ Ⓓ	22. Ⓐ Ⓑ Ⓒ Ⓓ	28. Ⓐ Ⓑ Ⓒ Ⓓ
5. Ⓐ Ⓑ Ⓒ Ⓓ	11. Ⓐ Ⓑ Ⓒ Ⓓ	17. Ⓐ Ⓑ Ⓒ Ⓓ	23. Ⓐ Ⓑ Ⓒ Ⓓ	29. Ⓐ Ⓑ Ⓒ Ⓓ
6. Ⓐ Ⓑ Ⓒ Ⓓ	12. Ⓐ Ⓑ Ⓒ Ⓓ	18. Ⓐ Ⓑ Ⓒ Ⓓ	24. Ⓐ Ⓑ Ⓒ Ⓓ	30. Ⓐ Ⓑ Ⓒ Ⓓ

LOGICAL REASONING

LEARNING OBJECTIVES

➤ Analogy
➤ Simple Analogy

➤ Detecting Analogy

MULTIPLE CHOICE QUESTIONS

1. Misogamy : Marriage : : Misogyny : ?
   (A) Husband   (B) Women
   (C) Relations   (D) Children

2. Coherent : Consistent : : Irate : ?
   (A) Unhappy   (B) Irritated
   (C) Angry   (D) Unreasonable

3. Skirmish : War : : Disease : ?
   (A) Patient   (B) Medicine
   (C) Infection   (D) Epidemic

Direction (1 to 3): In each of the following questions four words have been given. Out of which three are alike while the fourth one is different. Choose the odd one.

4. (A) Pallete   (B) Trigger
   (C) Muzzle   (D) Barrel

5. (A) Avalancle   (B) Hurricane
   (C) Explosion   (D) Earthquake

6. (A) Pepper   (B) Cinnamon
   (C) Groundnut   (D) Clove

7. 3, 4, 5, 5, 12 , 13, 7, 24, 25, 9, ?, 41

   (A) 40   (B) 35
   (C) 24   (D) 16

8. 1, 3, 6, 10, 15, 21,?

   (A) 26   (B) 25
   (C) 28   (D) 30

9. 10, 17, 26, 37, 50,?

   (A) 76   (B) 65
   (C) 95   (D) 84

10. In a certain code ZIP = 198, VIP = 222 then ZAP will be equal to
    (A) 256   (B) 296
    (C) 246   (D) 276

11. In a certain system of coding, the word STATEMENT is written as TNEMETATS. In the same system of coding what would be the code for the word POLITICAL?
    (A) LATILIOP   (B) LCATILIOP
    (C) LACITILOP   (D) LCAITIOLP

12. In a certain code 134 means 'good and tasty', 478 means 'see good pictures', 428 means 'pictures are faint. Which of the following digit stands for pictures?
    (A) 4   (B) 7
    (C) 8   (D) 2

13. Raju is 5th from the left and Pankaj is 12th from the right end in a row of students. If Pankaj shifts three places towards Raju, his position is 10th from the left. How many students are there in the row?
    (A) 24   (B) 28
    (C) 26   (D) 27

14. If the day after tomorrow is Saturday, what day was three days before yesterday?
(A) Monday
(B) Sunday
(C) Friday
(D) Tuesday

15. In a particular year 1st November is Wednesday, what day was 1st October in that year?
(A) Tuesday
(B) Sunday
(C) Friday
(D) Monday

16. If the English alphabets are written in reverse order then what will be the 4th letter to the right of 13th letter from the left?
(A) G
(B) J
(C) L
(D) K

17. If in the English alphabet, starting from 5th letter from the left, if 12 letters are written in reverse order then which letter will be 7th to the left of 14th letter from the right?
(A) L
(B) O
(C) M
(D) N

18. If 1st and 26th, 2nd and 25th, 3rd and 24th and so on, letters of English alphabet are paired then when of the following pair is correct?
(A) CW
(B) IP
(C) GR
(D) EV

19. Pointing towards Meena, Rajan said, " I am the only son of her mother's son. How is Meena related to Rajan?
(A) Mother
(B) Aunt
(C) Niece
(D) Cousin

20. Introducing Rekha, "Sarita said, she is the only daughter of my father's only daughter. How is Sarita related to Rekha?
(A) Mother
(B) Niece
(C) Cousin
(D) Aunt

21. Pointing at Kanchan, Sulekha said, "He is the son of my father's only son." How is Kanchan mother related to Sulekha?
(A) Sister
(B) Aunt
(C) Daughter
(D) Sister-in-law

22. If P means addition, Q means multiplication, R means division, S means subtraction, then what is the value of 4P10Q6R3S8?
(A) 34
(B) 24
(C) 16
(D) 8

23. If A denotes multiplication, B denotes addition, C denotes division and D denotes subtraction, then what is the value of 14A6B8C2D12?
(A) 76
(B) 86
(C) 82
(D) 72

24. If J stands for subtraction, K stands for multiplication, L stands for division and M stands for addition, then find the value of 27J15K2M18L3.
(A) 30
(B) 3
(C) 13
(D) 18

25. A certain number of horses and an equal number of men are going somewhere. Half of the men are on their horse's back while the remaining ones are walking along leading their horses. If the number of legs walking on the ground is 70, find the number of horses.
(A) 16
(B) 10
(C) 14
(D) 12

26. Ram is three times as old as Mohan. Lokesh was twice as old as Ram four years ago. In four year's time Ram will be 31. What is the difference between present ages of Mohan and Lokesh?
(A) 41 years
(B) 36 years
(C) 37 years
(D) 40 years

27. Today is Mukesh's birthday. One year from today he will be twice as old of what he was 12 years ago. What was the age of Mukesh 5 years ago?
(A) 20 years
(B) 25 years
(C) 30 years
(D) 15 years

28.

9		25		4	
1 (324) 81		16 (?) 1		64 (289) 16	
25		81		9	

(A) 361
(B) 381
(C) 369
(D) 389

29.

2		3		8	
4 (384) 6		3 (216) 6		6 (?) 4	
8		4		7	

(A) 1344
(B) 1244
(C) 1342
(D) 1542

30.

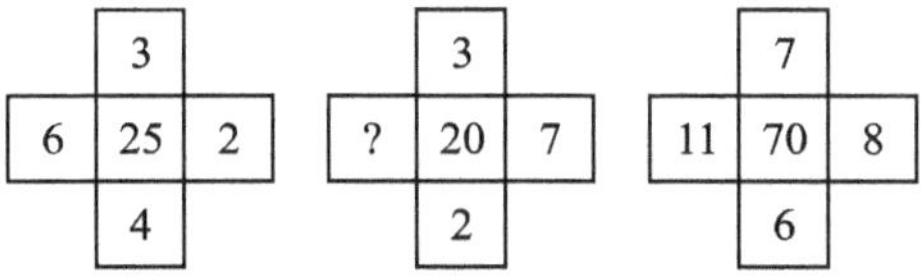

	3	
6	25	2
	4	

	3	
?	20	7
	2	

	7	
11	70	8
	6	

(A) 4
(B) 6
(C) 8
(D) 5

PROBLEM FIGURES   ANSWER FIGURES

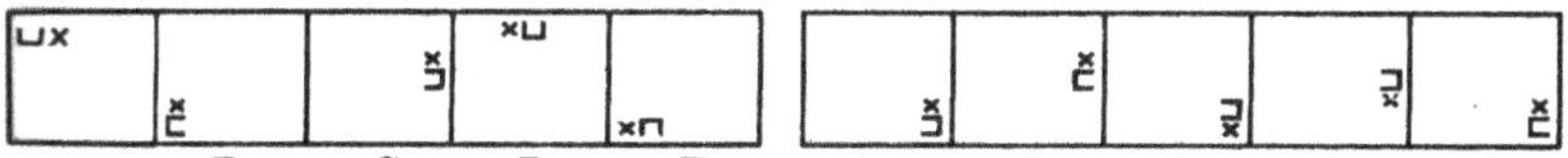

31.

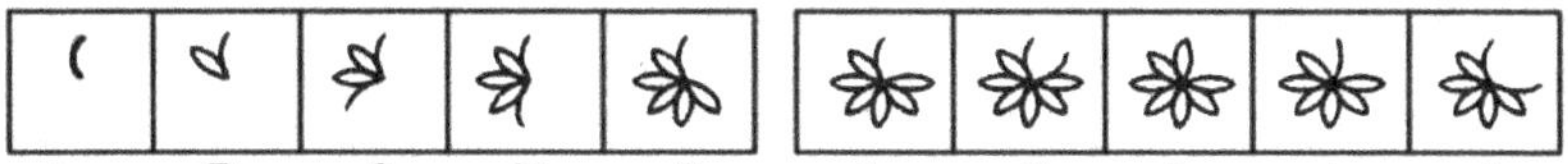

34.

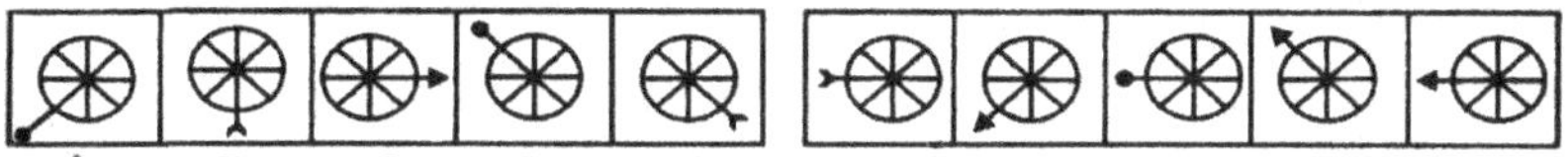

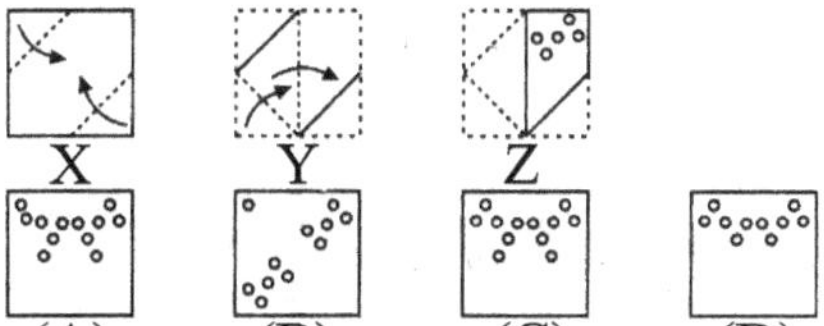

X   Y   Z

(A)   (B)   (C)   (D)

35.

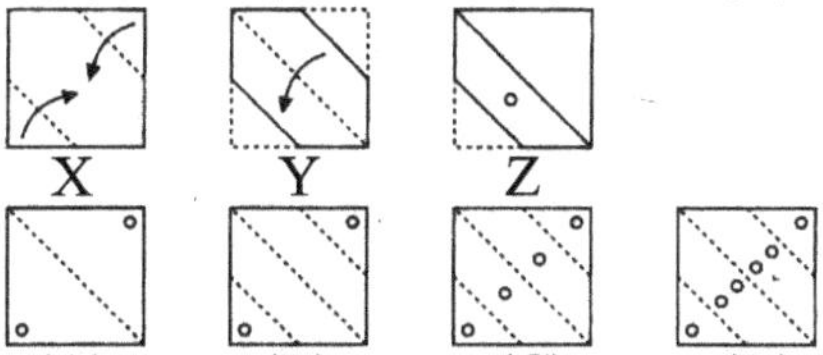

X   Y   Z

(A)   (B)   (C)   (D)

36.

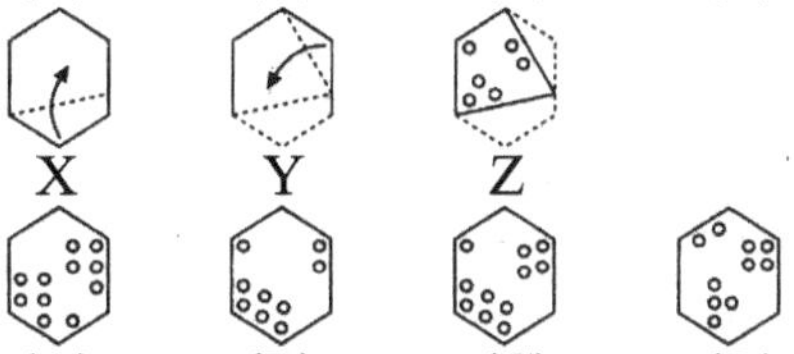

X   Y   Z

(A)   (B)   (C)   (D)

37. NIRMALA

(A) ALAMRIN   (B) AJAMЯIИ

(C) NRILAMA   (D) INRMALA

38. VINAYAKA

(A) INVAYAKA   (B) AKAYANIV

(C) AЯAYAИIV   (D) NIVYAAKA

39. OBSTINATE

(A) ƎTAИITSBO   (B) BOSTINATE

(C) ETANITSBO   (D) SOBTNIATE

40. CORDIAL

(A) LAIDROC   (B) ⅃ΛIDЯOC

(C) COЯDIΛ⅃   (D) ⅃ΛIDЯOƆ

41. PRECARIOUS

(A) ꟼЯECΛЯIOUƧ   (B) ꟼЯECΛЯIOUƧ

(C) SUORECARIP   (D) ꟼЯECΛЯIOUS

42. SUPERFLOUS

(A) ƧUꟼEЯꟻ⅃OUƧ   (B) ƧUꟼEЯꟻ⅃OUƧ

(C) ƧUꟼEЯꟻ⅃OUƧ   (D) ƧUꟼEЯꟻ⅃OUƧ

43.

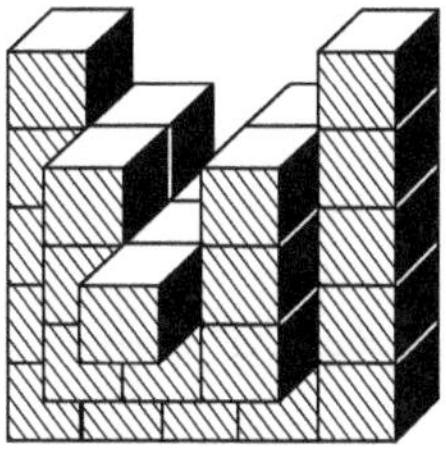

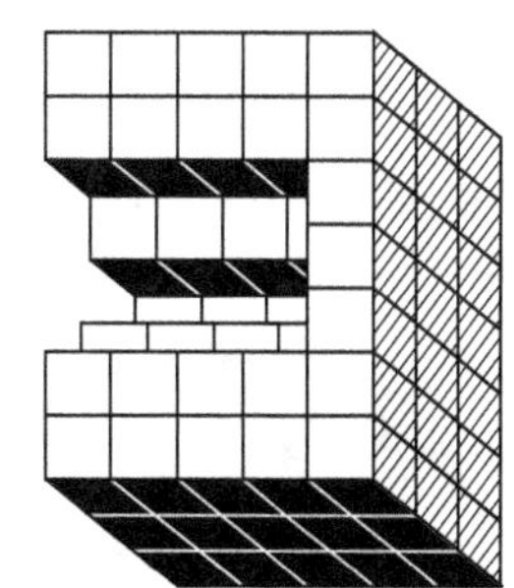

(A) 34   (B) 32
(C) 30   (D) 25

44.

(A) 89   (B) 88

(C) 87   (D) 81

(A) 150

(B) 168

(C) 158

(D) 144

45. 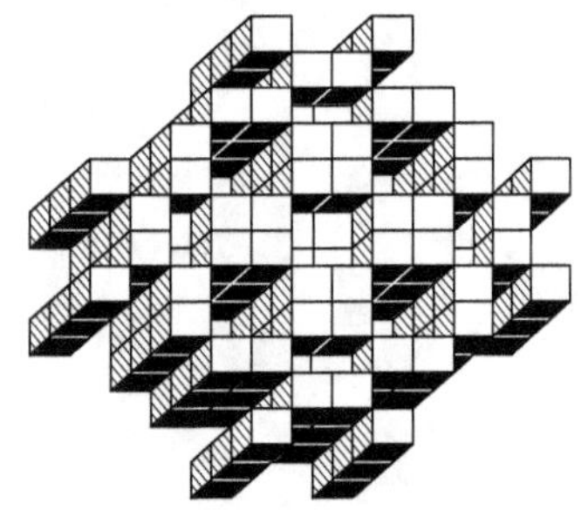

---Darken Your Choice with HB Pencil---

1.	Ⓐ Ⓑ Ⓒ Ⓓ	10.	Ⓐ Ⓑ Ⓒ Ⓓ	19.	Ⓐ Ⓑ Ⓒ Ⓓ	28.	Ⓐ Ⓑ Ⓒ Ⓓ	37.	Ⓐ Ⓑ Ⓒ Ⓓ
2.	Ⓐ Ⓑ Ⓒ Ⓓ	11.	Ⓐ Ⓑ Ⓒ Ⓓ	20.	Ⓐ Ⓑ Ⓒ Ⓓ	29.	Ⓐ Ⓑ Ⓒ Ⓓ	38.	Ⓐ Ⓑ Ⓒ Ⓓ
3.	Ⓐ Ⓑ Ⓒ Ⓓ	12.	Ⓐ Ⓑ Ⓒ Ⓓ	21.	Ⓐ Ⓑ Ⓒ Ⓓ	30.	Ⓐ Ⓑ Ⓒ Ⓓ	39.	Ⓐ Ⓑ Ⓒ Ⓓ
4.	Ⓐ Ⓑ Ⓒ Ⓓ	13.	Ⓐ Ⓑ Ⓒ Ⓓ	22.	Ⓐ Ⓑ Ⓒ Ⓓ	31.	Ⓐ Ⓑ Ⓒ Ⓓ	40.	Ⓐ Ⓑ Ⓒ Ⓓ
5.	Ⓐ Ⓑ Ⓒ Ⓓ	14.	Ⓐ Ⓑ Ⓒ Ⓓ	23.	Ⓐ Ⓑ Ⓒ Ⓓ	32.	Ⓐ Ⓑ Ⓒ Ⓓ	41.	Ⓐ Ⓑ Ⓒ Ⓓ
6.	Ⓐ Ⓑ Ⓒ Ⓓ	15.	Ⓐ Ⓑ Ⓒ Ⓓ	24.	Ⓐ Ⓑ Ⓒ Ⓓ	33.	Ⓐ Ⓑ Ⓒ Ⓓ	42.	Ⓐ Ⓑ Ⓒ Ⓓ
7.	Ⓐ Ⓑ Ⓒ Ⓓ	16.	Ⓐ Ⓑ Ⓒ Ⓓ	25.	Ⓐ Ⓑ Ⓒ Ⓓ	34.	Ⓐ Ⓑ Ⓒ Ⓓ	43.	Ⓐ Ⓑ Ⓒ Ⓓ
8.	Ⓐ Ⓑ Ⓒ Ⓓ	17.	Ⓐ Ⓑ Ⓒ Ⓓ	26.	Ⓐ Ⓑ Ⓒ Ⓓ	35.	Ⓐ Ⓑ Ⓒ Ⓓ	44.	Ⓐ Ⓑ Ⓒ Ⓓ
9.	Ⓐ Ⓑ Ⓒ Ⓓ	18.	Ⓐ Ⓑ Ⓒ Ⓓ	27.	Ⓐ Ⓑ Ⓒ Ⓓ	36.	Ⓐ Ⓑ Ⓒ Ⓓ	45.	Ⓐ Ⓑ Ⓒ Ⓓ

MODEL TEST PAPER

1. If sky is called star, star is cloud, cloud is earth, earth is tree, tree is pencil then where do the birds fly?
   (A) Sky
   (B) Cloud
   (C) Star
   (D) Tree

2. In the given question, which number will replace the question mark?

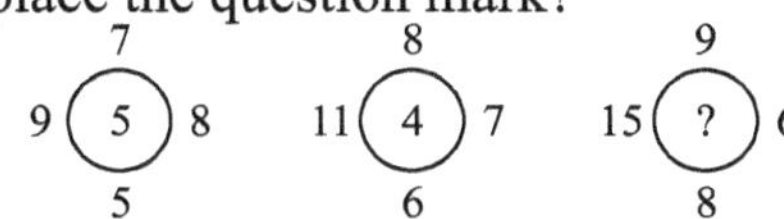

   (A) 3
   (B) 4
   (C) 5
   (D) 6

3. Sohan is brother of Mohan. Mona is daughter of Mohan. Sheela is sister of Sohan. Kunal is brother of Mona. Who is the uncle of Kunal?
   (A) Sohan
   (B) Mohan
   (C) Mona
   (D) Sheela.

4. If $66 \times 345 = 144$, $251 \times 42 = 48$ and $523 \times 345 = 120$ then $732 \times 236 =?$
   (A) 132
   (B) 122
   (C) 142
   (D) 112

5. In the given matrix the value of A, B, C respectively are

9	A	12
B	10	7
8	C	11

   (A) $A = 13, B = 14, C = 6$
   (B) $A = 15, B = 4, C = 14$
   (C) $A = 16, B = 13, C = 15$
   (D) $A = 14, B = 16, C = 18$

6. In the given figure, square represents teacher, triangle represents ladies, circle represents singers. Which letter represent the ladies who are both teachers and singers?

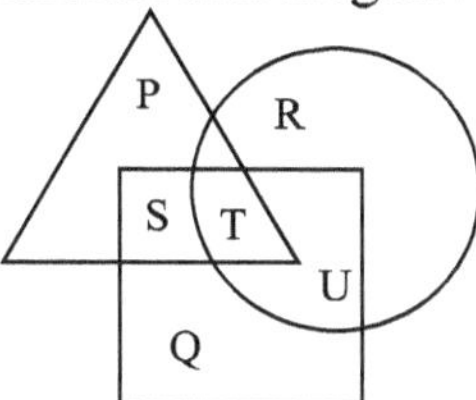

   (A) T
   (B) U
   (C) S
   (D) R

7. The last four letters of the word 'CONCENTRATION' are written in reverse order followed by next two in the reverse order and next three in reverse order and then followed by first four in reverse order. Starting from the end which letter will be eighth in the new arrangement?
   (A) T
   (B) N
   (C) R
   (D) E

8. Which number will replace the question mark?

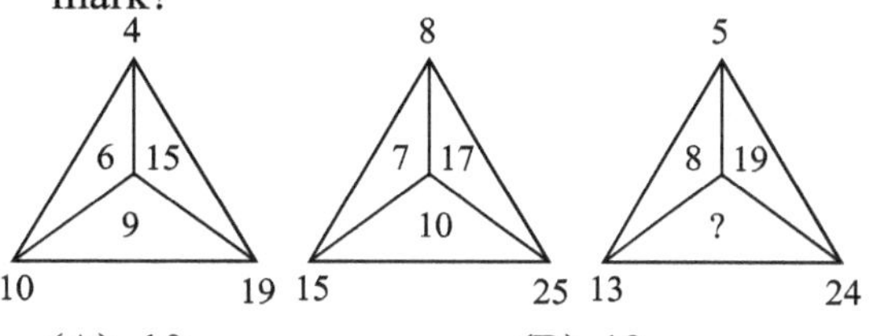

   (A) 10
   (B) 12
   (C) 11
   (D) 13

9. If $2 \times 1 = 81$, $1 \times 3 = 19$, then $2 \times 5 =?$
   (A) 425
   (B) 825
   (C) 825
   (D) 8025

10. Pointing to Akash, Rekha said, "His mother's brother is the father of my son Ankush. How is Akash related to Rekha?
    (A) Nephew
    (B) Aunt
    (C) Niece
    (D) Sister-in-law

11. Aflatoxin is related to food poisoning in the same way as histamine is related to _____ ?
(A) Head ache   (B) Inhabited
(C) Anthrax   (D) Allergy

12. In the given number series find out the wrong term?

841, 529, 361, 289, 160, 121
(A) 160   (B) 121
(C) 289   (D) 361

13. In the given words, three of them are alike in a certain way and so form a group. Find the one that does not belong to that group.
(A) Artist   (B) Musician
(C) Actor   (D) Poet

14. Ravi's house is to the East of a University. He intendes to travel to the University and starts heading North. He comes to a crossing from where a road runs West to a theatre and the road he is an further heads North to a hospital. To which direction is the University now, with respect to Ravi's position?
(A) North   (B) South
(C) East   (D) West

15. Find the figure which contains the figure (X) as its embedded part.

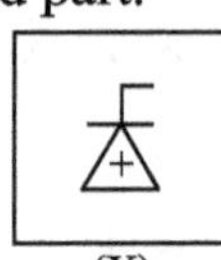
(X)

(a) 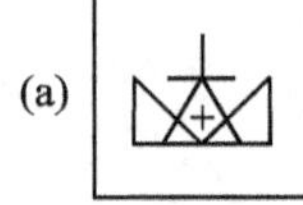   (b) 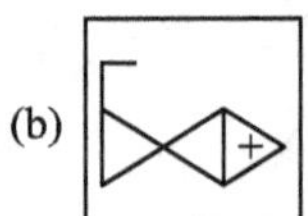

(c) 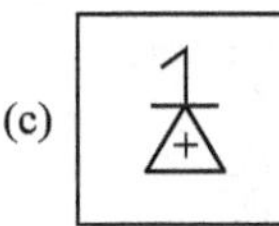   (d) 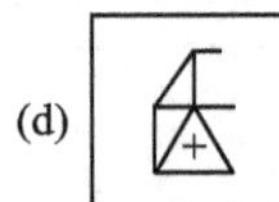

16. 5, 6, 10, 19, 35, ?
(A) 60   (B) 55
(C) 50   (D) 71

17. Select that lettered pair which has the same relationship as the original pair of words

Sprain : Fracture
(A) Devotion : Blessing
(B) Excitement : Frenzy

(C) Sleep : Dream
(D) Fever : Malaria

18. Choose the one which is different from the other three.
(A) 2936   (B) 9627
(C) 5814   (D) 4836

19. If ZEBRA can be written as 2652181. How can CAMEL be written?
(A) 3113512   (B) 3112511
(C) 3112412   (D) 3211513

20. If train is called bus; bus is called tractor, tractor is called car, car is called scooter, scooter is called bicycle, then which is used to plough a field?
(A) Tractor   (B) Car
(C) Scooter   (D) Bus

21. If $8^{x+1} = 64$ then what is the value of 3^{2x+1}?
(A) 1   (B) 3
(C) 9   (D) 27

22. If $\dfrac{a}{b} + \dfrac{b}{a} = -1$ then what is the value of $a^3 - b^3$?

(A) 0   (B) $\dfrac{1}{2}$

(C) −1   (D) 1

23. In the given figure if $\dfrac{y}{x} = 5$ and $\dfrac{z}{x} = 4$ then what is the value of x?

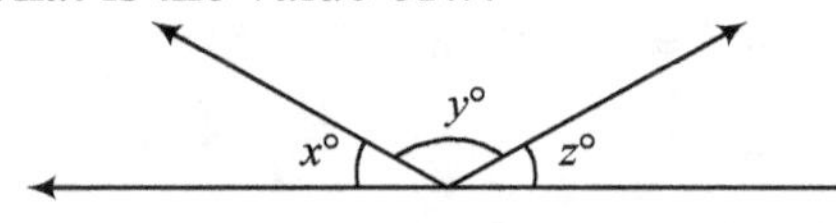

(A) 12°   (B) 15°
(C) 8°   (D) 18°

24. The abscissa of a point is positive in the
(A) First & fourth quadrant
(B) First & second quadrant
(C) Second & third quadrant
(D) Third & fourth quadrant

25. The graph of the equation 4x + 3y = 12 cuts the co−ordinate axes at point A and B, then what is the length of hypotenuse of right triangle AOB?
(A) 3 units   (B) 4 units
(C) $4\sqrt{2}$ units   (D) 5 units

26. Diagonals of a quadrilateral $ABCD$ bisect each other. If $\angle A = 45°$ what is the value of $\angle B$?
(A) 135°   (B) 120°
(c) 115°   (D) 125°

27. $ABCD$ is rectangle with O as any point in its interior. If area(ΔAOD) = 3 cm², area (ΔBOC) = 6 cm², then what is the area of rectangle $ABCD$?
(A) 12 cm²   (B) 20 cm²
(C) 18 cm²   (D) 24 cm²

28. In the given figure what is the measure of $\angle POR$?

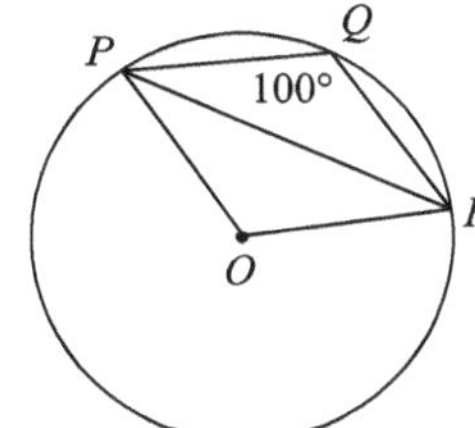

(A) 10°   (B) 20°
(C) 30°   (D) 80°

29. If the heights of two cones are in the ratio 1:4 and radii of their bases are in the ratio of 4 : 1 then what is the ratio of their volumes?
(A) 4:1   (B) 4:3
(C) 3:4   (D) 3:2

30. If the mean of a, b, c, d, e is 28, the mean of b and d is 34, then what is the mean of a, c and e?
(A) 22   (B) 24
(C) 32   (D) 28

31. In a football match, a player makes 4 goals from 10 penalty kicks. The probability of converting a penalty kick into a goal by player is
(A) $\dfrac{1}{5}$ (B) $\dfrac{2}{5}$
(C) $\dfrac{3}{5}$ (D) $\dfrac{4}{5}$

32. The chord of a circle is equal to its radius. The angle subtended by this chord at the minor arc of the circle is
(A) 120°   (B) 150°
(C) 180°   (D) 90°

33. The ratio of the volume of a right circular cylinder and a right circular cone of the same height and base is
(A) 1 : 3   (B) 3 : 4
(C) 1 : 2   (D) 3 : 1

34. If $a + b + c = 0$ then what is the value of $\dfrac{a^2}{bc} + \dfrac{b^2}{ca} + \dfrac{c^2}{ab}$?
(A) 2   (B) 3
(C) 4   (D) 5

35. What is the value of k if $x + 3$ is a factor of $3x^2 + kx + 6$?
(A) 5   (B) 7
(C) 9   (D) 11

36. An angle is 14° more than its complementing angle, then what is its measure?
(A) 48°   (B) 52°
(C) 58°   (D) 28°

37. The surface area of sphere of radius 5 cm is five times the area of the curved surface of a cone of radius 4 cm. What is the height of the cone?
(A) 3 cm   (B) 4 cm
(C) 2cm   (D) 5cm

38. The sides of a triangle are 11 cm, 60 cm and 61 cm. What is the length of altitude to the smallest side?
(A) 66 cm   (B) 60 cm
(C) 11cm   (D) 50 cm

39. If $x^{140} + 2x^{151} + k$ is divisible by $x + 1$, then what is the value of k?
(A) 2   (B) 3
(C) 1   (D) 4

40. If $(a^2 + b^2 + ab - a + b + 1)$ is the one factor of $a^3 - b^3 + 1 + 3ab$, then what is the other factor?
(A) $a - b + 1$ (B) $a + b - 1$
(C) $b - a - 1$ (D) None of these

41. If $x^2 + \dfrac{1}{x^2} = 23$ then what is the value of $x + \dfrac{1}{x}$?
(A) 4   (B) 5
(C) 6   (D) 3

42. In $\triangle ABC$, $AB = AC$ and $\angle ACD = 120°$ what is the value of $\angle A$?

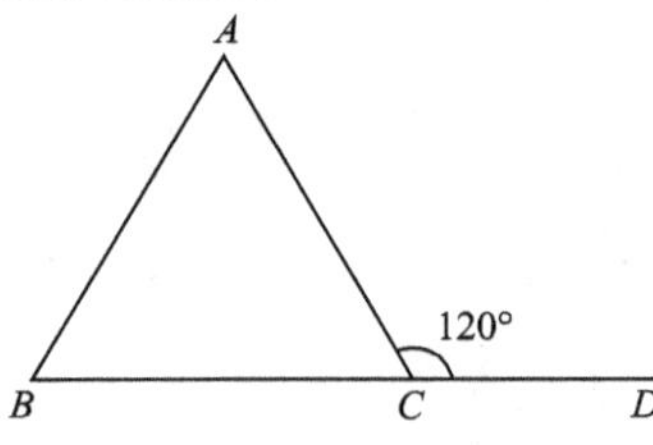

(A) 90°   (B) 60°
(C) 70°   (D) 50°

43. Amar and Raju are friends. Each has some money. If Amar gives ₹ 30 to Raju then Raju will have twice the money left with Amar. But if Raju gives ₹10 to Amar then Amar will have thrice as much as is left with Raju. How much money does Amar and Raju have ?

(A) ₹ 62, ₹ 34   (B) ₹ 60, ₹ 34
(C) ₹ 60, ₹ 30   (D) ₹ 62, ₹ 30

44. Probability of an event can be

(A) $\dfrac{11}{9}$ (B) -0.7

(C) 1.001   (D) 0.6

45. The perimeter of a circle is equal to the perimeter of a square. Then what is the ratio of their areas?

(A) 4 : 1   (B) 22 : 7
(C) 11 : 7   (D) 14 : 11

46. A hollow garden roller of height 63 cm with a girth of 440 cm is made of iron 4 cm thick. What is the volume of iron used?

(A) 54982 cm³   (B) 57636 cm³
(C) 56372 cm³   (D) 107712 cm²

47. A group of students decided to collect as many paisa from each member of the group as the number of members. If the total collection amounts to ₹59.29 what is the number of members in the group?

(A) 77   (B) 87
(C) 67   (D) 57

48. In how many years will a sum of ₹ 800 at 10% per annum compounded half yearly becomes ₹ 926.10?

(A) $1\dfrac{1}{3}$ (B) $1\dfrac{1}{2}$

(C) $2\dfrac{1}{3}$ (D) $2\dfrac{1}{2}$

49. What is the remainder when $9x^3 - 3x^2 + x - 5$ is divided by $x - \dfrac{2}{3}$?

(A) 3   (B) 2
(C) -3 (D) -2

50. If $4^{44} + 4^{44} + 4^{44} + 4^{44} = 4^x$, then what is the value of x ?

(A) 45   (B) 44
(C) 172   (D) 11

—Darken Your Choice with HB Pencil—

1. Ⓐ Ⓑ Ⓒ Ⓓ	11. Ⓐ Ⓑ Ⓒ Ⓓ	21. Ⓐ Ⓑ Ⓒ Ⓓ	31. Ⓐ Ⓑ Ⓒ Ⓓ	41. Ⓐ Ⓑ Ⓒ Ⓓ
2. Ⓐ Ⓑ Ⓒ Ⓓ	12. Ⓐ Ⓑ Ⓒ Ⓓ	22. Ⓐ Ⓑ Ⓒ Ⓓ	32. Ⓐ Ⓑ Ⓒ Ⓓ	42. Ⓐ Ⓑ Ⓒ Ⓓ
3. Ⓐ Ⓑ Ⓒ Ⓓ	13. Ⓐ Ⓑ Ⓒ Ⓓ	23. Ⓐ Ⓑ Ⓒ Ⓓ	33. Ⓐ Ⓑ Ⓒ Ⓓ	43. Ⓐ Ⓑ Ⓒ Ⓓ
4. Ⓐ Ⓑ Ⓒ Ⓓ	14. Ⓐ Ⓑ Ⓒ Ⓓ	24. Ⓐ Ⓑ Ⓒ Ⓓ	34. Ⓐ Ⓑ Ⓒ Ⓓ	44. Ⓐ Ⓑ Ⓒ Ⓓ
5. Ⓐ Ⓑ Ⓒ Ⓓ	15. Ⓐ Ⓑ Ⓒ Ⓓ	25. Ⓐ Ⓑ Ⓒ Ⓓ	35. Ⓐ Ⓑ Ⓒ Ⓓ	45. Ⓐ Ⓑ Ⓒ Ⓓ
6. Ⓐ Ⓑ Ⓒ Ⓓ	16. Ⓐ Ⓑ Ⓒ Ⓓ	26. Ⓐ Ⓑ Ⓒ Ⓓ	36. Ⓐ Ⓑ Ⓒ Ⓓ	46. Ⓐ Ⓑ Ⓒ Ⓓ
7. Ⓐ Ⓑ Ⓒ Ⓓ	17. Ⓐ Ⓑ Ⓒ Ⓓ	27. Ⓐ Ⓑ Ⓒ Ⓓ	37. Ⓐ Ⓑ Ⓒ Ⓓ	47. Ⓐ Ⓑ Ⓒ Ⓓ
8. Ⓐ Ⓑ Ⓒ Ⓓ	18. Ⓐ Ⓑ Ⓒ Ⓓ	28. Ⓐ Ⓑ Ⓒ Ⓓ	38. Ⓐ Ⓑ Ⓒ Ⓓ	48. Ⓐ Ⓑ Ⓒ Ⓓ
9. Ⓐ Ⓑ Ⓒ Ⓓ	19. Ⓐ Ⓑ Ⓒ Ⓓ	29. Ⓐ Ⓑ Ⓒ Ⓓ	39. Ⓐ Ⓑ Ⓒ Ⓓ	49. Ⓐ Ⓑ Ⓒ Ⓓ
10. Ⓐ Ⓑ Ⓒ Ⓓ	20. Ⓐ Ⓑ Ⓒ Ⓓ	30. Ⓐ Ⓑ Ⓒ Ⓓ	40. Ⓐ Ⓑ Ⓒ Ⓓ	50. Ⓐ Ⓑ Ⓒ Ⓓ

HINTS AND SOLUTIONS

1. NUMBER SYSTEM

Answer Key

1. (B)	2. (B)	3. (C)	4. (B)	5. (C)	6. (D)	7. (B)	8. (C)	9. (D)	10. (A)
11. (D)	12. (C)	13. (A)	14. (A)	15. (D)	16. (B)	17. (B)	18. (B)	19. (D)	20. (B)

1.(B)

$\pi = 3.14157......$

(Non-repeating non-terminating decimal)

$\dfrac{22}{7} = 3.142871$

$\therefore \dfrac{22}{7}$ is a rational number.

2.(B)

Rationalising the denominator we have

$$\dfrac{\sqrt{3}+1}{2-\sqrt{3}} \times \dfrac{2+\sqrt{3}}{2+\sqrt{3}} = \dfrac{\left(\sqrt{3}+1\right)\left(\sqrt{3}+2\right)}{(2)^2 - \left(\sqrt{3}\right)^2}$$

$$= \dfrac{3+2\sqrt{3}+\sqrt{3}+2}{4-3}$$

$$= 5 + 3\sqrt{3} = x + y\sqrt{3}$$

$$\therefore \ x = 5, y = 3$$

3.(C)

Here

$$x = \dfrac{\sqrt{3}+\sqrt{2}}{\sqrt{3}-\sqrt{2}} + \dfrac{\sqrt{3}-\sqrt{2}}{\sqrt{3}+\sqrt{2}}$$

$$= \dfrac{3+2+2\sqrt{6}}{\left(\sqrt{3}\right)^2 - \left(\sqrt{2}\right)^2} + \dfrac{3+2-2\sqrt{6}}{(\sqrt{3})^2 - (\sqrt{2})^2}$$

$$= 5 + 2\sqrt{6} + 5 - 2\sqrt{6} = 10$$

$\therefore$ Required value $= 10 \times 50 = 500$

4.(B)

Given $x = 2 + \sqrt{3}$ then

$$\dfrac{1}{x} = \dfrac{1}{2+\sqrt{3}} = \dfrac{1}{2+\sqrt{3}} \times \dfrac{2-\sqrt{3}}{2-\sqrt{3}}$$

$$= \dfrac{2-\sqrt{3}}{(2)^2 - \left(\sqrt{3}\right)^2} = \dfrac{2-\sqrt{3}}{4-3} = 2 - \sqrt{3}$$

$$\therefore \ x + \dfrac{1}{x} = \left(2+\sqrt{3}\right) + \left(2-\sqrt{3}\right) = 4$$

5.(C)

We have $\dfrac{16 \times 2^{n+1} - 4 \times 2^n}{16 \times 2^{n+2} - 2 \times 2^{n+2}}$

$$= \dfrac{(2)^4 \times 2^{n+1} - (2)^2 \times 2^n}{(2)^4 \times (2)^{n+2} - 2 \times 2^{n+2}}$$

$$= \dfrac{2^{n+2}\left\{(2)^3 - 1\right\}}{2^{n+3}\left\{(2)^3 - 1\right\}} = \dfrac{1}{2}$$

6.(D)

We have $x =$

$$\dfrac{1}{2-\sqrt{3}} = \dfrac{1}{2-\sqrt{3}} \times \dfrac{2+\sqrt{3}}{2+\sqrt{3}} = 2 + \sqrt{3}$$

$$\Rightarrow \qquad x - 2 = \sqrt{3}$$

Squaring both sides
$$(x-2)^2 = 3$$
$$\Rightarrow \qquad x^2 + 4 - 4x = 3$$
$$\Rightarrow \qquad x^2 - 4x + 1 = 0 \qquad \text{...(i)}$$
$$x^3 - 2x^2 - 7x + 5$$
$$= x(x^2 - 4x + 1) + 2(x^2 - 4x + 1) + 3$$
$$= x \times 0 + 2 \times 0 + 3 = 0 + 3 = 3 \text{ (using eq (i))}$$

7.(B)

Here $y = \dfrac{(x^{a+b})^2 (x^{b+c})^2 (x^{c+a})^2}{(x^a x^b x^c)^4}$

$$= \dfrac{(x^{a+b+b+c+c+a})^2}{(x^{a+b+c})^4}$$

$$= \dfrac{x^{4(a+b+c)}}{x^{4(a+b+c)}} = 1$$

8.(C)

Given $5^{x-3} \cdot 3^{2x-8} = 225 = 5^2 \cdot 3^2$

$$\therefore \qquad x - 3 = 2x - 8 = 2$$
$$\Rightarrow \qquad x = 5$$

9.(D)

Here $\sqrt{13 - m\sqrt{10}} = \sqrt{8} + \sqrt{5}$

Squaring both sides, we have
$$13 - m\sqrt{10} = \left(\sqrt{8} + \sqrt{5}\right)^2$$
$$\Rightarrow \quad 13 - m\sqrt{10} = 8 + 5 + 2\sqrt{40}$$
$$\Rightarrow \quad -m\sqrt{10} = 2 \times \sqrt{4 \times 10}$$
$$\Rightarrow \quad -m\sqrt{10} = 2 \times 2\sqrt{10}$$
$$\Rightarrow \qquad m = -4$$

10.(A)

Here $\left[2 - 3(2-3)^3\right]^3 = \left[2 - 3(-1)^3\right]^3$

$$= [2+3]^3 = (5)^3 = 125 = x$$

11.(D)

$$\because \ 10^x = 64 \Rightarrow \left(10^x\right)^{\frac{1}{2}} = (64)^{\frac{1}{2}} = 8$$

$$\therefore \ 10^{\frac{x}{2}} = 8 \Rightarrow 10^{\frac{x}{2}+1} = 10^{\frac{x}{2}} \cdot 10 = 8 \cdot 10 = 80$$

12.(C)

We have $4^x - 4^{x-1} = 24$

$$\Rightarrow \qquad 4^{x-1}(4 - 1) = 24$$
$$\Rightarrow \qquad 4^{x-1} = 8$$
$$\Rightarrow \qquad \dfrac{4^x}{4} = 8$$
$$\Rightarrow \qquad 4^x = 32$$
$$\Rightarrow \qquad (2)^{2x} = (2)^5$$
$$\Rightarrow \qquad x = \dfrac{5}{2}$$

$$\therefore \quad (2x)^x = \left(2 \times \dfrac{5}{2}\right)^{\frac{5}{2}} = (5)^{\frac{5}{2}}$$

$$= (5)^{\frac{4}{2}} \cdot (5)^{\frac{1}{2}} = 25\sqrt{5}$$

13.(A)

$$x^2 + \dfrac{1}{x^2} = 83$$

$$\Rightarrow \left(x - \dfrac{1}{x}\right)^2 = x^2 + \dfrac{1}{x} - 2 = (83 - 2) = 81$$

$$\Rightarrow \qquad \left(x - \dfrac{1}{x}\right) = 9$$

$$\therefore \qquad \left(x - \dfrac{1}{x}\right)^3 = (9)^3$$

$$\Rightarrow \quad x^3 - \dfrac{1}{x^3} - 3 \cdot x \cdot \dfrac{1}{x}\left(x - \dfrac{1}{x}\right) = 729$$

$$\Rightarrow \qquad x^3 - \dfrac{1}{x^3} - 3(9) = 729$$

$$\Rightarrow \qquad x^3 - \dfrac{1}{x^3} = 729 + 27 = 756$$

14.(A)

$$\text{Here}\left(x+\frac{1}{x}\right)^2 = x^2+\frac{1}{x^2}+2$$

$$= (98+2)=100$$

$$\Rightarrow \quad x+\frac{1}{x}=\sqrt{100}=10$$

15.(D)

We have $\dfrac{x}{y}+\dfrac{y}{x}=-1$

$$\Rightarrow \quad x^2+y^2=-xy$$

$$\Rightarrow \quad x^2+y^2+xy=0 \qquad \text{...(i)}$$

We know that,

$$x^3-y^3=(x-y)\left(x^2+y^2+xy\right)=(x-y)(0)$$

$$\text{[Using (i)]}$$

$$= 0$$

16.(B)

Here $xy=1$

$$y=\frac{1}{x}=\frac{1}{7+4\sqrt{3}}=\frac{1}{7+4\sqrt{3}}\times\frac{7-4\sqrt{3}}{7-4\sqrt{3}}$$

$$=\frac{7-4\sqrt{3}}{(7)^2-\left(4\sqrt{3}\right)^2}=\frac{7-4\sqrt{3}}{1}=7-4\sqrt{3}$$

$$\therefore \quad \frac{1}{x^2}+\frac{1}{y^2}=\frac{1}{x^2}+x^2$$

$$=\left(x+\frac{1}{x}\right)^2-2=(7+4\sqrt{3}+7-4\sqrt{3})^2-2$$

$$=(14)^2-2=196-2=194$$

17.(B)

$$\because \ x^{-2}=64$$

$$\Rightarrow \qquad x^{-1}=8$$

$$\Rightarrow \qquad x=\frac{1}{8}$$

$$\Rightarrow \qquad x^{\frac{1}{3}}=\left(\frac{1}{8}\right)^{\frac{1}{3}}=\frac{1}{2}$$

$$x^0+x^{\frac{1}{3}}=1+\frac{1}{2}=\frac{3}{2}$$

18.(B)

The given equation can be written as

$$\left\{(23+4)^{\frac{2}{3}}+(121)^{\frac{1}{2}}\right\}^2$$

$$=\left\{(27)^{\frac{2}{3}}+(121)^{\frac{1}{2}}\right\}^2$$

$$=\left\{(3)^2+11\right\}^2=\{9+11\}^2$$

$$=[20]^2=400$$

19.(D)

Let $7+4\sqrt{3}=\left(a+b\sqrt{3}\right)^2$

$$\Rightarrow \quad 7+4\sqrt{3}=a^2+3b^2+2ab\left(\sqrt{3}\right)$$

$$\Rightarrow \quad \left(a^2+3b^2\right)=7 ,\ ab=2$$

$$\therefore \ a=2, b=1.$$

$$\Rightarrow \quad \sqrt{7+4\sqrt{3}}=2+\sqrt{3}$$

20.(B)

Here $\dfrac{\sqrt{2}-1}{\sqrt{2}+1}=\dfrac{\sqrt{2}-1}{\sqrt{2}+1}\times\dfrac{\sqrt{2}-1}{\sqrt{2}-1}$

$$=\frac{\left(\sqrt{2}-1\right)^2}{\left(\sqrt{2}\right)^2-(1)^2}$$

$$=\frac{2+1-2\sqrt{2}}{2-1}=3-2\sqrt{2}$$

Let, $\sqrt{3-2\sqrt{2}}=a+b\sqrt{2}$

$$\Rightarrow 3-2\sqrt{2}=a^2+b^2\cdot 2+2ab\sqrt{2}$$

$$\Rightarrow a^2+2b^2=3,\ ab=-1$$

Solving these two equations, we have

$$a=-1, b=+1$$

$$\therefore \text{ The required value} = \sqrt{2}-1=1.4142-1$$

$$= 0.4142$$

21. (B)	22. (B)	23. (A)	24. (C)	25. (B)

21. (B)

$$x + \frac{1}{x+1} = 1$$

$$\Rightarrow x = 1 - \frac{1}{x+1}$$

$$\Rightarrow x = \frac{x+1-1}{x+1}$$

$$\Rightarrow x+1 = 1$$

$$\Rightarrow (x+1)^5 + \frac{1}{(x+1)^5}$$

$$\Rightarrow \quad (1)^5 + \frac{1}{(1)^5}$$

$$\Rightarrow \quad 1+1$$

$$\Rightarrow \quad 2$$

22. (B)

$$\frac{1}{x-5} = x$$

$$(x-5) = \frac{1}{x}$$

$$x - \frac{1}{x} = 5$$

$$\Rightarrow \left(x - \frac{1}{x}\right)^2 = (5)^2$$

$$\Rightarrow x^2 + \frac{1}{x^2} - 2 = 25$$

$$\Rightarrow x^2 + \frac{1}{x^2} = 23 = 27$$

$$\left(x + \frac{1}{x}\right)^2 = x^2 + \frac{1}{x^2} + 2$$

$$\left(x + \frac{1}{x}\right)^2 = 23 + 2 = 27 + 2 = 29$$

$$x + \frac{1}{x} = \sqrt{25} = 5 \quad 5\sqrt{29}$$

$$\left(x - \frac{1}{x}\right)\left(x + \frac{1}{x}\right)^2 = x^2 - \frac{1}{x^2}$$

$$\Rightarrow \quad 5 \times 5 = x^2 - \frac{1}{x^2} = 5\sqrt{29}$$

23. (A)

$f(1) = 0$

$4(1)^3 + 3(1)^2 - 4(1) + K = 0$

$4 + 3 - 4 + K = 0 \Rightarrow K = -3$

24. (C)

$$\left(a + \frac{1}{a}\right)^2 = b$$

$$a + \frac{1}{a} = \sqrt{b}$$

$$\left(a + \frac{1}{a}\right)^3 = \left(\sqrt{b}\right)^3$$

$$a^3 + \frac{1}{a^3} + 3\left(a + \frac{1}{a}\right) = b^{3/2}$$

$$a^3 + \frac{1}{a^3} = b^{3/2} - 3\sqrt{b} = b^{3/2} - 3b^{1/2}$$

25. (B)

$$\frac{\sqrt{5} + \sqrt{3}}{\sqrt{5} - \sqrt{3}} = \frac{(\sqrt{5} + \sqrt{3})}{(\sqrt{5} - \sqrt{3})} \times \frac{\sqrt{5} + \sqrt{3}}{\sqrt{5} + \sqrt{3}}$$

$$= \frac{5 + 3 + 2\sqrt{15}}{5 - 3} = \frac{8 + 2\sqrt{15}}{2}$$

$$= 4 + \sqrt{15} = a + \sqrt{15}\,b$$

So, $a = 4$, $b = 1$

Answer Key

1. (A)	2. (A)	3. (D)	4. (C)	5. (A)	6. (D)	7. (A)	8. (A)	9. (B)	10. (C)
11. (D)	12. (C)	13. (D)	14. (A)	15. (D)	16. (B)	17. (B)	18. (C)	19. (B)	20. (A)

1. (A)

$(x-y-z)^2$ will contain 6 terms in its simplied form.

2. (A)

Given $a^2 + 4b^2 + 9c^2 + 6ac + 4ab + 12bc$

$$= (A)^2 + (2b)^2 + (3c)^2 + 2(3c)(A)$$
$$+ 2(A)(2b) + 2(3c)(2b)$$
$$= (a + 2b + 3c)^2$$

$\therefore$ Square root of the above expression will be $(a + 2b + 3c)$.

3. (D)

Here $(a + b + c)^2 = (a^2 + b^2 + c^2)$
$$+ 2(ab + bc + ca)$$
$\Rightarrow (a + b + c)^2 = (16) + 2(10) = 16 + 20 = 36$

$\Rightarrow (a + b + c) = \sqrt{36} = \pm 6$

4. (C)

$9a^2 + 4b^2 + 16c^2 + 12ab - 24ac - 16bc$
$$= (3a)^2 + (2b)^2 + (-4c)^2 + 2(3a)(2b)$$
$$+ 2(3a)(-4c) + 2(2b)(-4c)$$
$$= (3a + 2b - 4c)^2$$

Putting $a = 2$, $b = 1$, $c = -2$, we have required expression as

$$[3(2) + 2(1) - 4(-2)]^2$$
$$= [6 + 2 + 8]^2 = (16)^2 = 256$$

5. (A)

$$x^4 + \frac{1}{x^4} = 47$$

$$\Rightarrow \left(x^2 + \frac{1}{x^2}\right)^2 = \left(x^4 + \frac{1}{x^4}\right) + 2$$

$$= (47 + 2) = 49$$

$$\Rightarrow x^2 + \frac{1}{x^2} = 7$$

$$\therefore \left(x + \frac{1}{x}\right)^2 = \left(x^2 + \frac{1}{x^2}\right) + 2$$

$$\Rightarrow \left(x + \frac{1}{x}\right)^2 = 7 + 2 = 9 \Rightarrow \left(x + \frac{1}{x}\right) = 3,$$

$$\therefore \left(x + \frac{1}{x}\right)^3 = \left(x^3 + \frac{1}{x^3}\right) + 3\left(x + \frac{1}{x}\right)$$

$$\Rightarrow x^3 + \frac{1}{x^3} = \left(x + \frac{1}{x}\right)^3 - 3\left(x + \frac{1}{x}\right)$$

$$\Rightarrow x^3 + \frac{1}{x^3} = (3)^3 - 3(3) = 27 - 9 = 18$$

6. (D)

$$x + \frac{1}{x} = -3$$

$$\therefore \left(x^3 + \frac{1}{x^3}\right) = \left(x + \frac{1}{x}\right)^3 - 3\left(x + \frac{1}{x}\right)$$

$$= (-3)^3 - 3(-3)$$
$$= -27 + 9 = -18$$

7. (A)

We have $\dfrac{27}{x^3} - \dfrac{8}{x^6} - \dfrac{54}{x^4} + \dfrac{36}{x^5}$

$$= \left(\frac{3}{x}\right)^3 + \left(\frac{-2}{x^2}\right)^3 + 3 \times \left(\frac{3}{x}\right)^2 \times \left(\frac{-2}{x^2}\right)$$

$$+ 3 \times \left(\frac{3}{x}\right) \times \left(\frac{-2}{x^2}\right)^2$$

$$= \left(\frac{3}{x} - \frac{2}{x^2}\right)^3$$

$\therefore$ Cube root will be $\left(\dfrac{3}{x} - \dfrac{2}{x^2}\right)$.

8. (A)

$(a + b)^3 + (a - b)^3 = 2a^3 + 6ab^2$

$\Rightarrow (x + k)^3 + (x - k)^3 = 2x^3 + 6 \times x \times k^2$

$\Rightarrow \qquad\qquad k^2 = 9$

$\Rightarrow \qquad\qquad k = 3, -3$

9. (B)

$$\left(x - \frac{1}{x}\right)^3 = x^3 - \frac{1}{x^3} - 3\left(x - \frac{1}{x}\right)$$

Let $\left(x - \dfrac{1}{x}\right) = A$, then,

$\Rightarrow A^3 + 3A = 108 + 76\sqrt{2}$

$\Rightarrow \qquad A = 3 + 2\sqrt{2}$

10. (C)

Given $3x + 2y = 13$, $xy = 6$

$\because \quad 3x + 2y = 13$

$\therefore (3x + 2y)^3 = (13)^3$

$\Rightarrow 27x^3 + 8y^3 + 3 \times 3x \times 2y\,(3x + 2y)$

$\qquad\qquad\qquad\qquad = (169) \times 13$

$\Rightarrow 27x^3 + 8y^3 + 18xy\,(3x + 2y) = (169) \times 13$

$\Rightarrow 27x^3 + 8y^3 + 18 \times 6 \times (13) = (169) \times 13$

$\Rightarrow 27x^3 + 8y^3 = 61 \times 13 = 793$

11. (D)

Given $x + y = 4$, $xy = 4$.

$\Rightarrow \quad (x + y)^2 = (x - y)^2 + 4xy$

$\Rightarrow \quad (4)^2 = (x - y)^2 + 4 \times 4$

$\Rightarrow \quad (x - y)^2 = 16 - 16 = 0$

$\Rightarrow \qquad\qquad x = y$

$\therefore$ if $\quad x + y = 4$

$\Rightarrow \qquad\qquad y = x = 2$

Hence $2x^3 + y^3 = 3x^3 = 3(2)^3 = 24$

12. (C)

Here $\quad a + b = 6$, $ab = 8$

$\therefore \qquad (a + b)^2 = (6)^2$

$\Rightarrow a^2 + b^2 + 2ab = 36$

$\Rightarrow a^2 + b^2 = 36 - 2(ab) = 36 - (16) = 20$

$\therefore (a^2 + b^2 - ab) = 20 - 8 = 12$

13. (D)

We have $(x - 1)(x^2 + x + 1) = (x^3 - 1)$

Now,

Let $x^3 = p$, then $x^6 = p^2$

$\because \qquad (x^3 - 1)(x^6 + x^3 + 1)$

$\qquad = (p - 1)(p^2 + p + 1) = (p^3 - 1)$

$\qquad = (x^3)^3 - 1$

$\qquad = x^9 - 1$

14. (A)

Here $(a + b + c)^2 = (15)^2$

$\Rightarrow (a^2 + b^2 + c^2) = (15)^2 - 2(ab + bc + ca)$

$\Rightarrow \dfrac{(83) - 225}{2} = -(ab + bc + ca)$

$\Rightarrow \qquad -71 = -(ab + bc + ca) \qquad \ldots(i)$

$\Rightarrow \qquad ab + bc + ca = 71 \qquad \ldots(i)$

15. (D)

$a^3 + b^3 + c^3 - 3abc = (a + b + c)$

$\qquad\qquad\qquad (a^2 + b^2 + c^2 - ab - bc - ca)$

$\qquad = (15)(83 - 71)[\text{see sol. 19 from eq (i)}]$

$\qquad = 15\,(12)$

$\qquad = 180$

16. (B)

Given $\dfrac{x^2 + y^2}{xy} = -1$

$\Rightarrow \qquad x^2 + y^2 = -xy$

$\Rightarrow \qquad x^2 + y^2 + xy = 0 \qquad \ldots(i)$

$\therefore x^3 - y^3 = (x - y)(x^2 + y^2 + xy)$

$\qquad\qquad = (x - y)(0) = 0 \qquad [\text{using (i)}]$

17. (B)

Let $a = 30$, $b = 20$ $c = -50$

$\because \qquad a + b + c = 0$

$\therefore \qquad a^3 + b^3 + c^3 = 3abc$

$$= 3\,(30)\,(20)\,(-50)$$
$$= -\,90{,}000$$

18. **(C)**

Given $a + b + c = 6$, and,
$$a^3 + b^3 + c^3 = 18 + 3abc$$
$$\Rightarrow a^3 + b^3 + c^3 - 3abc = 18$$
$$\Rightarrow a^3 + b^3 + c^3 - 3abc = 18$$
$$= (a + b + c)(a^2 + b^2 + c^2 - ab - bc - ca)$$
$$\Rightarrow a^2 + b^2 + c^2 - ab - bc - ca = 3 \qquad \text{...(i)}$$

Now,
$$(a + b + c)^2 = a^2 + b^2 + c^2 + 2(ab + bc + ca)$$
$$\Rightarrow (6)^2 = a^2 + b^2 + c^2 + 2(ab + bc + ca) \ \text{...(ii)}$$

Subtracting eq (i) from eq (ii), we get
$$(36 - 3) = 3(ab + bc + ca)$$
$$\Rightarrow ab + bc + ca = \frac{33}{3} = 11$$

19. **(B)**

Here $3x^2 - 27 = 3(x^2 - 9)$
$$= 3[(x)^2 - (3)^2]$$
$$= 3(x + 3)(x - 3)$$

20. **(A)**

$\because a^3 + b^3 + c^3 - 3abc$
$$= (a + b + c)(a^2 + b^2 + c^2 - ab - bc - ca)$$
If $a \neq b \neq c$, then,

For $a^3 + b^3 + c^3 = 3abc$, $(a + b + c)$ Must posses zero value.

HOTS (ACHIEVERS SECTION)

21. (C)	22. (C)	23. (A)	24. (B)	25. (B)

21. **(C)**

$$a = \frac{2^{x-1}}{2^{x-2}} = 2^{(x-1)-(x-2)} = a = 2^{x-1-x+2} = 2$$

$$b = \frac{2^{-x}}{2^{x+1}} = 2^{(-x)-(x+1)} \ \ b = 2^{-2x-1}$$

$$2 - 2^{-2x-1} = 0$$

$$[\because a - b = 0]$$

$$-2^{-2x-1} = -2$$

$$-2x - 1 = 1$$

$$\Rightarrow -2x = 2$$

$$\Rightarrow x = -1$$

22. **(C)**

$$1 + \frac{x}{y} = 1 + \frac{2}{3}, \ \ 1 - \frac{x}{y} = 1 - \frac{2}{3}$$

$$\frac{y + x}{y} = \frac{5}{3}, \qquad \frac{y - x}{y} = \frac{1}{3}$$

$$\frac{\dfrac{y - x}{y}}{\dfrac{y + x}{y}} = \frac{\dfrac{3}{5}}{\dfrac{5}{3}} = \frac{1}{5}$$

$$\frac{4}{5} + \frac{y - x}{y + x} = \frac{4}{5} + \frac{1}{5}$$

$$\frac{4}{5} + \frac{y - x}{y + x} = 1$$

23. **(A)**

$$\left(x + \frac{1}{x}\right)^3 = x^3 + \frac{1}{x^3} + 3x\,\frac{1}{x}\left(x + \frac{1}{x}\right)$$

$$\left(x + \frac{1}{x}\right)^3 = 110 + 3\left(x + \frac{1}{x}\right)$$

$$\left(x + \frac{1}{x}\right)^3 - 3\left(x + \frac{1}{x}\right) = 110$$

$$\left(x + \frac{1}{x}\right)^3 - 3\left(x + \frac{1}{x}\right) = (5)^3 - 3(5)$$

By comparing, we have

$$x + \frac{1}{x} = 5$$

24. (B)

$f(x) = x^4 - 2x^3 + 3x^2 - ax + b$

$f(1) = (1)^4 - 2(1)^3 + 3(1)^2 - a(1) + b = 5$

$f(1) = 1 - 2 + 3 - a + b = 5$

$2 - a + b = 5$

$-a + b = 3$ ....(1)

$f(-1) = (-1)^4 - 2(-1)^3 + 3(-1)^2 - a(-1) + b = 19$

$1 + 2 + 3 + a + b = 19$

$a + b = 13$ ....(2)

From (1) & (2)

$2b = 16 \Rightarrow b = 8$

$a = 5$

$f(x) = x^4 - 2x^3 + 3x^2 - 5x + 8$

$f(2) = 2^4 - 2(2)^3 + 3(2)^2 - 5(2) + 8$

$= 16 - 16 + 12 - 10 + 8 = 10$

25. (B)

$$\frac{3 + \sqrt{7}}{3 - \sqrt{7}} \times \frac{3 + \sqrt{7}}{3 + \sqrt{7}} = a + b\sqrt{3} \ \sqrt{7}$$

$$\frac{9 + 7 + 2 \times 3 \times \sqrt{7}}{9 - 7} = a + b\sqrt{3} \ \sqrt{7}$$

$$\frac{16 + 6\sqrt{7}}{2} = a + b\sqrt{3} \ \sqrt{7}$$

$$8 + 3\sqrt{7} = a + b\sqrt{3} \ \sqrt{7}$$

$\Rightarrow a = 8 \quad b = 3, \Rightarrow a = 8 \quad b = 3$

Difference of a & $b = 8 - 3 = 5$

---

3. CO-ORDINATE GEOMETRY

Answer Key

1. (B)	2. (B)	3. (A)	4. (A)	5. (D)	6. (C)	7. (B)	8. (A)	9. (B)	10. (A)
11. (C)	12. (A)	13. (B)	14. (B)	15. (A)	16. (A)	17. (C)	18. (C)	19. (A)	20. (B)

1.(B)

Minimum distance of point (a, b) from x-axis = Perpendicular distance between point and x-axis =

|y-coordinate (ordinate) of the point|

$= |6| = 6$

2.(B)

O is the centre of circle and A is the point of tangency.

∵ Point of tangency lies on x-axis

∴ Ordinate of point = 0

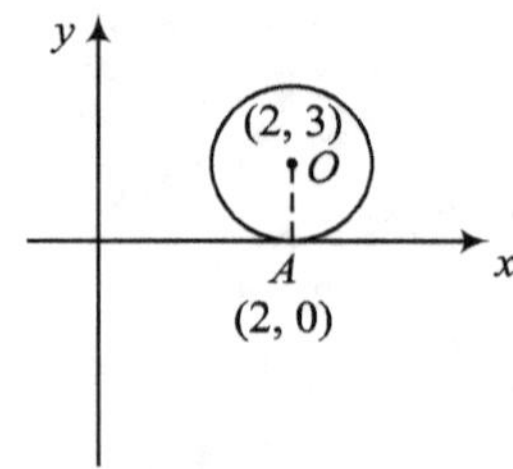

3.(A)

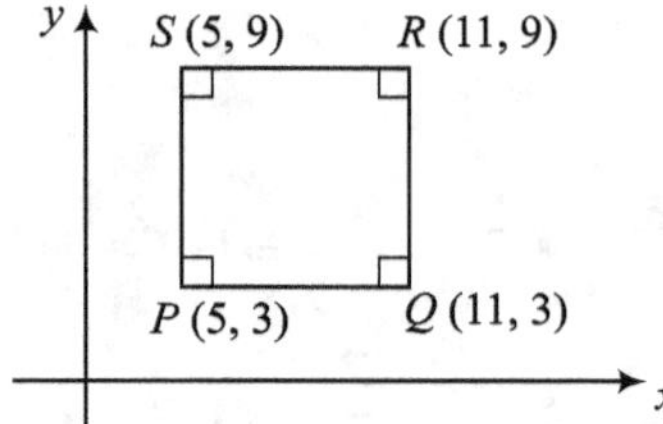

Perimeter of square $= 4a = 24 \Rightarrow a = 6$

∵ (5, 3) can be any of the vertices

∴ We will find the ordinates of other three points assuming (5, 3) to be coordinates of *PQR* and *S* respectively.

If P (5, 3) then Q has ordinate = 3

S has coordinates (5, 3 + 6) = (5, 9)

∴ R and S have ordinates = 9

If Q (5, 3) then P has ordinate = 3

R has coordinates (5, 9)

∴ R and S have ordinates = 9

Similarly,

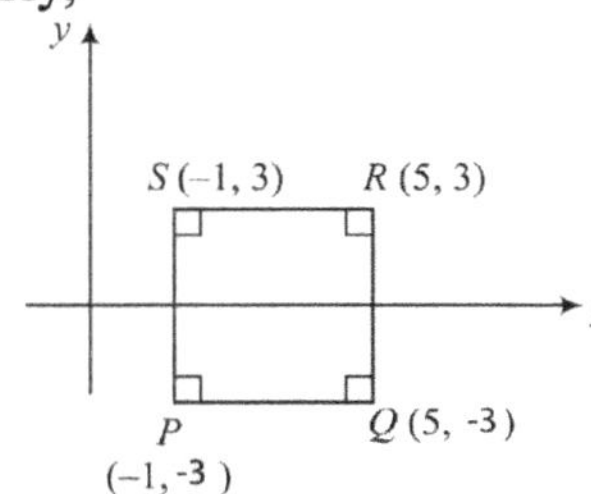

If R or S is conceded as (5,3) then

P and Q have ordinates = 3 − 6 = −3

∴ Possible ordinates are 9, −3 and 3.

4.(A)

Perpendicular distance from y−axis

$$= |\text{ abscissa }| = |-11| = 11$$

5.(D)

Point (4 , −3) have (+, −) sign convention, that belongs to IVth quadrant.

6.(C)

If abscissa = ordinate, i.e, $x = y$ then using this relation in equation of line, we have

$$x = 3x + 2 \implies x = -1$$

∴ Point has coordinates = $(-1, -1)$

Point has sign convection of $(-, -)$

∴ Point will lie in 3rd quadrant

7.(B)

Let the coordinates of point M be $(0, k)$

$$\{\because \text{ M is on } y\text{-axis}\}$$

∴ Coordinates of point $N = (0, -K)$

∴ Distance between point M and N

$$= |K - (-K)| = 2|K|$$

8.(A)

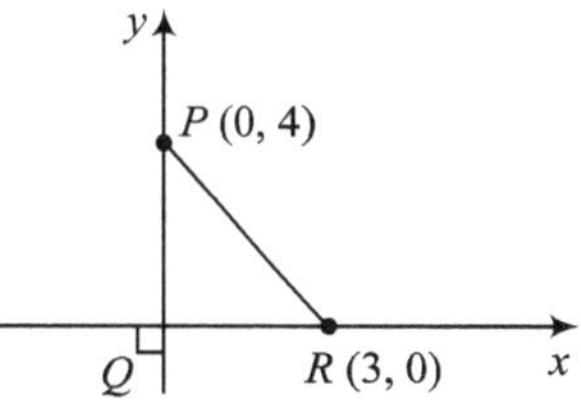

$$QP = 4 \text{ units[From the figure]}$$
$$QR = 3 \text{ units}$$
$$\therefore \quad \angle PQR = 90°$$

∴ In ΔPQR

$$PQ^2 + QR^2 = PR^2 \text{ \{Pythagoras Theorem\}}$$
$$\implies \quad 4^2 + 3^2 = PR^2$$
$$\implies PR = \sqrt{4^2 + 3^2} = \sqrt{25} = 5 \text{ units}$$

∴ Perimeter of $\Delta PQR = PQ + QR + PR$
$$= 4 + 3 + 5$$
$$= 12 \text{ units}$$

9.(B)

$$\text{Area of } PQR = \frac{1}{2} \times PQ \times QR$$

$$= \frac{1}{2} \times 4 \times 3 = 6 \text{ (units)}^2$$

10.(A)

∵ Centroid of any Δ lies within it, and all the coordinates A, B and C are in Ist quadrant (Positive)

∴ centroid will lie in Ist quadrant.

11.(C)

∵ $(-3, -2)$ has $(-, -)$ sign convention.

∴$(-3, -2)$ belongs to 3rd quadrant.

12.(A)

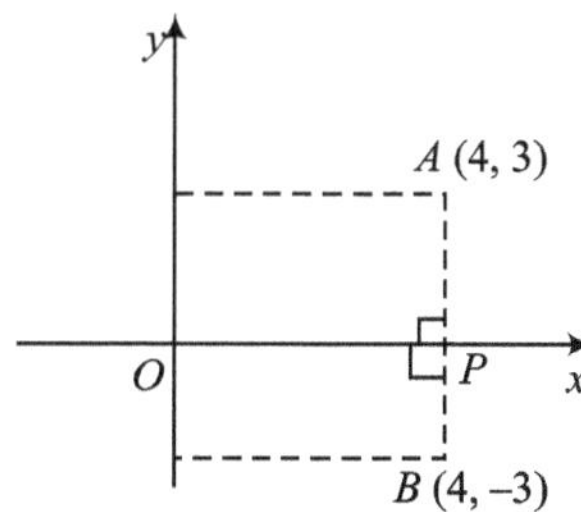

Point A is 3 units above x-axis.

$\therefore$ Its mirror image will be 3 units below x-axis, and the x-coordinate will remain the same.

$\therefore$ Coordinates of point $B \equiv (4, -3)$

13.(B)

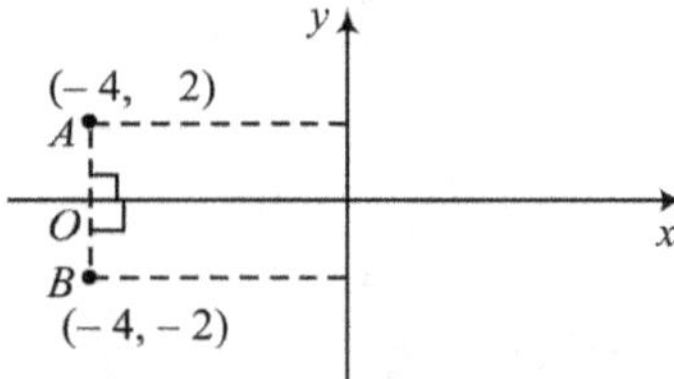

Point A is the reflected point.

Point A will have coordinates where abscissa will not change and ordinate will change sign

$\therefore$ Reflected point will lie in 2nd quadrant.

14.(B)

When ordinate = abscissa, then $y = x$

$\therefore \qquad 2x + 3x = 5$

$\Rightarrow \qquad 5x = 5$

$\Rightarrow \qquad x = 1$

$\therefore$ $x = y = 1$ will be point on line having equal abscissa and ordinate

$\therefore$ Point $P = (1, 1)$

$\therefore$ Its image about y-axis will be $(-1, 1)$.

15.(A)

A has coordinate $\equiv (3, 2)$

Point Q has coordinate $\equiv (3, -2)$

$\qquad\qquad$ {ordinate will change sign}

Now,

After reflection of point Q about y-axis the ordinate will not vary but abscissa will change sign.

$\therefore$ Coordinates of final point $\equiv (-3, -2)$

16.(A)

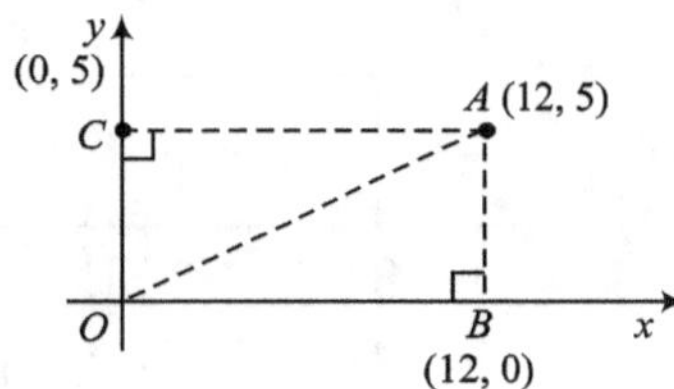

In $\triangle OAB$

$OA^2 = OB^2 + AB^2$

$\qquad = (12)^2 + (OC)^2 = (12)^2 + (5)^2$

$\qquad\qquad = 169$

$\Rightarrow OA = \sqrt{169} = 13$ units

17.(C)

After plotting figure, it can be clearly seen that ABC is an isosceles triangle in which, $AB = (6 - 2) = 4$ units

$CD = (6 - 0) = 6$ units

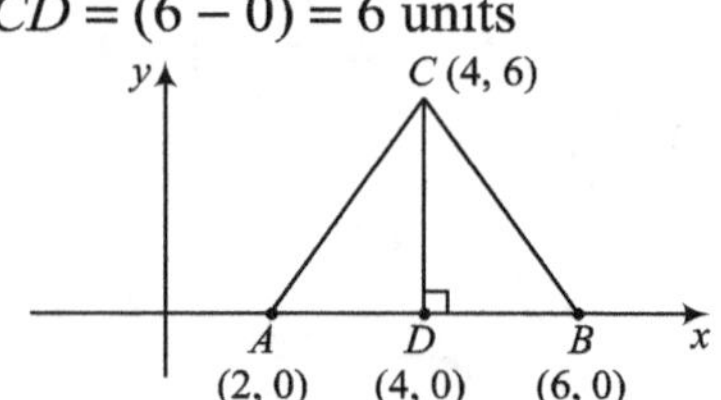

$\therefore$ Ares of $\triangle ABC = \dfrac{1}{2} \times AB \times CD$

$\qquad\qquad = \dfrac{1}{2} \times 4 \times 6 = 12$ sq. units

18.(C)

On every point of y-axis, abscissa $= 0$

$\therefore$ $x = 0$ is the equation of y-axis

19.(A)

Consider a point B on the line

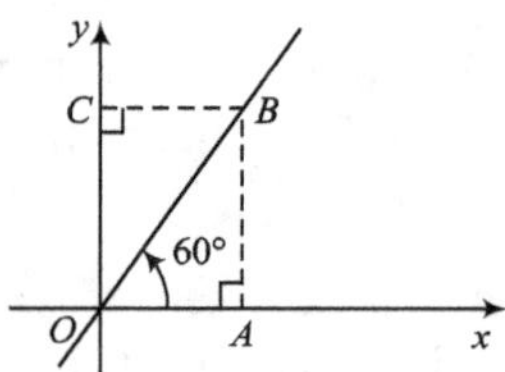

$\therefore$ In $\triangle OAB$,

$\qquad \tan 60° = \dfrac{AB}{OA} = \sqrt{3}$

$\Rightarrow \qquad \dfrac{OC}{OA} = \sqrt{3}$

$\Rightarrow \qquad OC = \sqrt{3}\, OA$

$\Rightarrow \qquad y = \sqrt{3}x$

20.(B)

Consider a point P on line

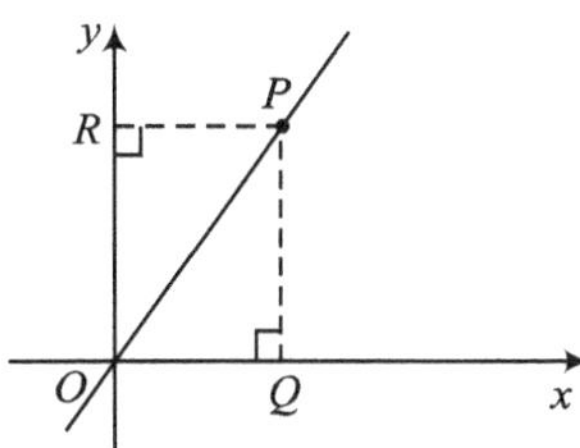

$\therefore$ In $\Delta\ POQ$,

$$\frac{OQ}{PQ} = \tan 45° = 1$$

$$\Rightarrow \qquad OQ = PQ$$
$$\Rightarrow \qquad OQ = OR$$
$$\Rightarrow \qquad x = y$$

HOTS (ACHIEVERS SECTION)

21. (B)	22. (A)	23. (C)	24. (C)	25. (A)

4. LINEAR EQUATIONS IN TWO VARIABLES

Answer Key

1. (A)	2. (A)	3. (B)	4. (B)	5. (B)	6. (C)	7. (A)	8. (B)	9. (C)	10. (A)
11. (B)	12. (B)	13. (C)	14. (C)	15. (B)	16. (D)	17. (B)	18. (D)	19. (C)	20. (C)

1.(A)

(k^2, k) will satisfy $x - 5y + 6 = 0$

$$\Rightarrow \qquad k^2 - 5k + 6 = 0$$
$$\Rightarrow \qquad k^2 - 3k - 2k + 6 = 0$$
$$\Rightarrow \quad k(k-3) - 2(k-3) = 0$$
$$\Rightarrow \qquad (k-3)(k-2) = 0$$
$$\Rightarrow \quad k - 2 = 0 \text{ or, } k - 3 = 0$$
$$\Rightarrow \qquad\qquad k = 2 \text{ or } 3$$

2.(A)

(a^2, a) is a solution of the equation

$$x - y + 1 = 0$$
$$\Rightarrow \qquad a^2 - a + 1 = 0$$

$\Rightarrow$ The above equation has negative discriminant.

$\therefore$ value of a cannot be determined

3.(B)

$(k^3, 0)$ satisfies the equation, $x - y + 8 = 0$

$$\Rightarrow \qquad k^3 - (0) + 8 = 0$$
$$\Rightarrow \qquad\qquad k^3 = -8$$
$$\Rightarrow \qquad\qquad k = (-8)^{\frac{1}{3}} = -2$$

4.(B)

$(2, 3)$ satisfies the equation

$x + 3y + 4k = 6$ then ,

$$2 + 3(3) + 4k = 6$$
$$\Rightarrow \qquad 2 + 9 + 4k = 6$$
$$\Rightarrow \qquad\qquad 4k = -5$$
$$\Rightarrow \qquad\qquad k = \frac{-5}{4}$$

5.(B)

$$x + 3y - 3x - y + x - y = a - b$$
$$\Rightarrow \qquad -x + y = a - b$$
$$\Rightarrow \qquad y - x = a - b$$

$\therefore (x, y)$ is satisfied by (b, a)

6.(C)

$$k(x^3 - y^3) = x^2 + y^2 + xy$$

$$\Rightarrow k = \frac{\left(x^2 + y^2 + xy\right)}{(x-y)(x^2 + xy + y^2)}$$

$$\Rightarrow x - y = \frac{1}{k} \Rightarrow x = \frac{1}{k} + y = \frac{1}{k} + \frac{1}{k} = \frac{2}{k}$$

7.(A)

$$x - y = \left(\sqrt{x}\right)^2 - \left(\sqrt{y}\right)^2$$

$$= \left(\sqrt{x} + \sqrt{y}\right) \times \left(\sqrt{x} - \sqrt{y}\right)$$

$$\Rightarrow x - y + \left(\sqrt{x} + \sqrt{y}\right) = \left(\sqrt{x} + \sqrt{y}\right)$$

$$\left\{\sqrt{x} - \sqrt{y} + 1\right\}$$

$$= \left(\sqrt{x} + \sqrt{y}\right)\left(\sqrt{x} - \sqrt{y} + 1\right)$$

According to the question

$$\left(\sqrt{x} + \sqrt{y}\right)\left(\sqrt{x} - \sqrt{y} + 1\right) = 10$$

$$\Rightarrow \left(\sqrt{9} + \sqrt{y}\right)\left(\sqrt{9} - \sqrt{y} + 1\right) = 10$$

$$\Rightarrow \left(\sqrt{y} + 3\right)\left(3 - \sqrt{y} + 1\right) = 10$$

$$\Rightarrow \left(\sqrt{y} + 3\right)\left(4 - \sqrt{y}\right) = 10$$

Let $\sqrt{y} = p$

$$\Rightarrow (p + 3)(4 - p) = 10$$
$$\Rightarrow p = 2$$
$$\therefore y = p^2 = 4$$

8.(B)

Here $x + y = \left(x^{\frac{1}{3}}\right)^3 + \left(y^{\frac{1}{3}}\right)^3$

$$= \left(x^{\frac{1}{3}} + y^{\frac{1}{3}}\right)\left(x^{\frac{2}{3}} + y^{\frac{2}{3}} - x^{\frac{1}{3}}y^{\frac{1}{3}}\right)$$

$\Rightarrow$ The equation will be reduced to,

$$\left(x^{\frac{1}{3}} + y^{\frac{1}{3}} + 1\right)\left(x^{\frac{2}{3}} + y^{\frac{2}{3}} - x^{\frac{1}{3}}y^{\frac{1}{3}}\right) = 12$$

$$\Rightarrow \left(3 + y^{\frac{1}{3}}\right)\left(4 + y^{\frac{2}{3}} - 2y^{\frac{1}{3}}\right) = 12$$

$$\Rightarrow 12 + y - 2y^{\frac{2}{3}} + 3y^{\frac{2}{3}} + 4y^{\frac{1}{3}}6y^{\frac{1}{3}}$$

$$- 2y^{\frac{2}{3}} + 3y^{\frac{2}{3}} + 4y^{\frac{1}{3}}6y^{\frac{1}{3}} = 12$$

$$\Rightarrow y + y^{\frac{2}{3}} - 2y^{\frac{1}{3}} = 0$$

$$\Rightarrow y^{\frac{2}{3}} - y^{\frac{1}{3}} + y^{\frac{2}{3}} - y^{\frac{1}{3}} - 2 = 0$$

Let,

$$y^{\frac{1}{3}} = k$$

$$\therefore k^2 + k - 2 = 0$$
$$\Rightarrow k = 1 \Rightarrow y = 1$$

9.(C)

Here $(2k - 3, k)$ satisfies the equation

$$6x + 2y = k - 5$$
$$\therefore \quad 6(2k - 3) + 2k = k - 5$$
$$\Rightarrow 12k - 18 + 2k - k + 5 = 0$$
$$\Rightarrow \quad 13k = 13$$
$$\Rightarrow \quad k = 1$$

10(A)

Let the amount donated by Kajol be ₹ x

$\therefore$ Amount donated by Arun = ₹ $(2x - 80)$

According to the question

$$x + 2x - 80 = 100$$
$$\Rightarrow \quad 3x = 180$$
$$\Rightarrow \quad x = 60$$

$\therefore$ Money donated by Arun = ₹ $(2 \times 60 - 80)$

$$= ₹ \ 40$$

11.(B)

Let the unit's place digit be x,

and tens place digit be y,

$\therefore$ Number $= 10y + x$

The new number after reversing the digits

$$= 10x + y$$

$\therefore$ Difference $= (10y + x) - (10x + y)$

$$= 9y - 9x = 9(y - x)$$

According to the question

$$9(y - x) = 27$$
$$\Rightarrow \quad y - x = 3$$

$\Rightarrow \qquad y - 3 = 3$

$\Rightarrow \qquad\qquad y = 6$

$\therefore$ If one of the digit is 3, then other is 6.

12.(B)

Point (4,5) lies on the graph of the equation $3y = ax + 3$

$\therefore \qquad 3 \times 5 = 4a + 3$

$\Rightarrow \qquad 4a = 12 \Rightarrow a = 3$

13.(C)

$A(3, 5)$ and $B(1, 4)$ lie on graph of line

$$ax + by = 7$$

$\therefore \qquad 3a + 5b = 7 \qquad \text{...(i)}$

$\qquad\qquad a + 4b = 7 \qquad \text{...(ii)}$

$\therefore$ From equations (i) and (ii), we get

$$b = 2, a = -1$$

$\therefore (a, b) \equiv (-1, 2)$

14.(C)

Let the numerical value of temperature be x

$\therefore \qquad x = \dfrac{(x - 32) \times 5}{9}$

$\Rightarrow \qquad 9x = 5x - 160$

$\Rightarrow \qquad 4x = -160$

$\Rightarrow \qquad x = -40$

$\therefore$ the temperature is equal in both the scales at $-40°$C.

15.(B)

The given curve intersect the x and y-axes at $A(4, 0)$ and $B(0, 5)$ respectively then

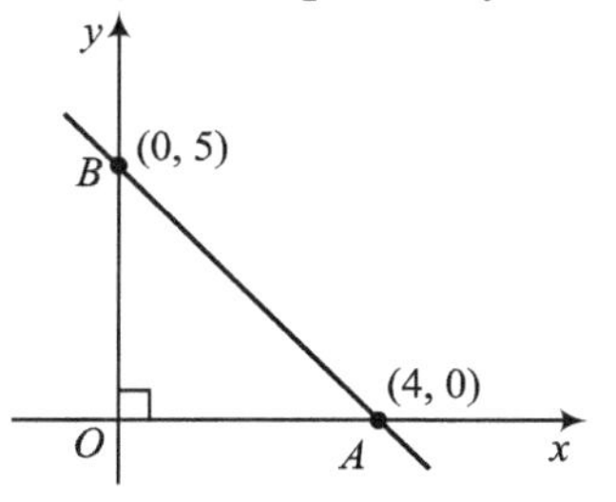

$$\text{Area of } \Delta OAB = \frac{1}{2} \Delta OAB = \frac{1}{2} \times 4 \times 5$$

$$= 10 \text{ sq. units}$$

16.(D)

Let the point of intersection of lines be (a, b).

$\therefore \qquad 3a + 4b = 12, \text{ and}$

$\qquad\qquad 6a + 8b = 48$

The above two equations have no solutions for (a, b)

$\therefore$ The graph will not intersect.

17.(B)

$\therefore$ The ordinate of every point on x-axis $= 0$

$\therefore$ The line $3x + 4y = 15$ and the x-axis will intersect where y value of the line becomes zero

$\therefore \qquad 3x = 15$

$\Rightarrow \qquad x = 5$

$\therefore$ The point of intersection is $(5,0)$

18.(D)

On y – axis, abscissa $= 0$

$\therefore \qquad x = 0$

$\Rightarrow \qquad 36y = 108$

$\Rightarrow \qquad y = 3$

$\therefore$ point of intersection $= (0,3)$

19.(C)

The distance between the graphs

$$= 3 - (-3) = 3 + 3 = 6 \text{ units}$$

20.(C)

The equation can be written as,

$$y = \frac{8 - 3x}{2}$$

$\therefore$ For different values of x, different values of y will exist.

$\therefore$ The above equation has many solutions.

<table>
<tr><td colspan="5" align="center">HOTS (ACHIEVERS SECTION)</td></tr>
<tr><td>21. (D)</td><td>22. (C)</td><td>23. (A)</td><td>24. (D)</td><td>25. (B)</td></tr>
</table>

HINTS AND SOLUTIONS

21. (D)

$$9^{x+2} = 240 + 9^x$$

$$9^x \times 9^2 = 240 + 9x$$

$$81 \times 9^x - 9^x = 240$$

$$9^x(81-1) = 240 \Rightarrow 9^x = \frac{240}{80} = 3$$

$$\left((3)^2 = 3 \Rightarrow 3^{2x} = 3\right)^x = 3 \Rightarrow 3^{2x} = 3$$

$$2x = 1 \Rightarrow x = \frac{1}{2} = 0.5$$

22. (C)

$$a + b + c = 9$$
$$a^2 + b^2 + c^2 = 35$$

$$a^3 + b^3 + c^3 - 3abc = ?$$

$$(a + b + c)^2 = a^2 + b^2 + c^2 + 2(ab + bc + ca)$$

$$9^2 = 35 + 2(ab + bc + ca)$$

$$(ab + bc + ca) = \frac{81-35}{2} = \frac{46}{2} = 23$$

$$a^3 + b^3 + c^3 - 3abc$$
$$= (a + b + c)\,[a^2 + b^2 + c^2 - (ab + bc + ca)]$$
$$= 9 \times [35 - 23] = 9 \times 12 = 108$$

23. (A)

Let $g(x) = x + 1 = 0 \Rightarrow x = -1$

$$f(x) = x^{51} + 51$$

$$f(-1) = (-1)^{51} + 51 = -1 + 51 = 50$$

5. INTRODUCTION TO EUCLID'S GEOMETRY

Answer Key

1. (A)	2. (A)	3. (A)	4. (D)	5. (C)	6. (A)	7. (A)	8. (A)	9. (D)	10. (A)
11. (D)	12. (A)	13. (B)	14. (C)	15. (B)	16. (C)	17. (B)	18. (B)	19. (B)	20. (A)

1.(A)

Line are formed using 3 non–collinear points.

∴ 3 non-collinear points will form 1 plane.

2.(A)

Axiom does not require a proof.

3.(A)

Through 2 given points, 1 and only one line can be drawn.

4.(D)

Only one line can be drawn parallel to a given line and passing through a fixed point.

5.(C)

Concurrent lines.

6.(A)

$\overleftrightarrow{AB}$ is a line.

∴ It has no end point.

7.(A)

Two circles are congruent, iff they have equal radii.

8.(A)

∵ $AB \parallel CD$, and

$CD \parallel PQ$

∴ $AB \parallel QP$

9.(D)

Two straight lines can intersect in one and only one point.

10.(A)

Minimum 2 lines are required for determination of a plane.

11.(D)

Point is dimensionless, ie having no dimension.

12.(A)

A surface has 2-dimensions i.e., a surface is 2D figure.

13.(B)

A surface has curved boundary and curve contains infinite points.

14.(C)

Two planes can intersect each other in minimum 1 point.

15.(B)

Let the measure of angle be $x°$

Then, its complementary angle will be

$$(90° - x°) = 20°$$
$$\Rightarrow \qquad x = 70°$$

16.(C)

Let the measure of angle be $x°$ then, its complementary angle will be $90° - x°$ supplement $= 180° - x°$.

$$\therefore \quad 5(90° - x°) = 2(180° - x°) - 12°$$
$$\Rightarrow \qquad x = 34°$$

17.(B)

Boundary of surface is curved and boundary of solid is surface.

18.(B)

Parallel.

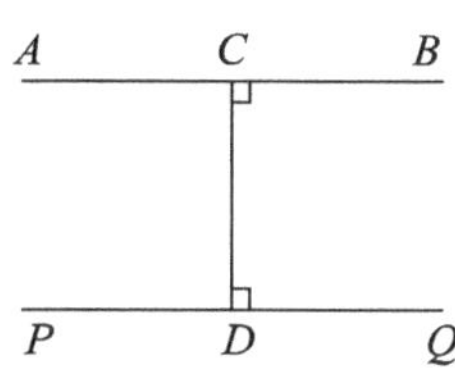

$$\{\because \text{ Sum of interior angles} = 90° + 90° = 180°\}$$

19.(B)

$$\text{No. of lines} = \frac{n(n-1)}{2} = \frac{4 \times 3}{2} = 6$$

20.(A)

$$\text{No. of lines} = \frac{n(n-1)}{2} - \frac{m(m-1)}{2} + 1$$
$$= \frac{4(4-1)}{2} - \frac{3(3-1)}{2} + 1$$
$$= 6 - 3 + 1 = 4$$

HOTS (ACHIEVERS SECTION)

21. (D)	22. (B)	23. (A)	24. (A)	25. (C)

6. LINES AND ANGLES

Answer Key

1. (B)	2. (A)	3. (B)	4. (B)	5. (B)	6. (A)	7. (A)	8. (B)	9. (B)	10. (B)
11. (B)	12. (A)	13. (B)	14. (B)	15. (C)	16. (A)	17. (C)	18. (D)	19. (C)	20. (B)

1.(B)

$$\angle AOB = 180°$$
$$\Rightarrow \angle AOP + \angle POB = 180°$$
$$\Rightarrow \angle AOP + \angle POQ + \angle BOQ = 180°$$
$$\Rightarrow 90° + 3x + x = 180°$$
$$\Rightarrow \qquad 4x = 90°$$
$$\Rightarrow \qquad x = \frac{90°}{4} = 22.5°$$

2.(A)

$$\angle AOC + \angle BOC = 180°$$
$$\Rightarrow \qquad 7x + 3y = 180° \qquad \text{...(i), and}$$
$$y - x = 10°$$
$$\Rightarrow \qquad x = y - 10° \qquad \text{...(ii)}$$

Using (ii) and (i)

$$7(y - 10°) + 3y = 180°$$
$$\Rightarrow \qquad 10y = 250°$$

$$\Rightarrow \quad y = 25°$$

3.(B)

$\because$ Sum of angles around a point = 360°

$$\angle AOB + \angle BOC + \angle AOC = 360°$$
$$\Rightarrow \quad 90° + a + b = 360°$$
$$\Rightarrow \quad a + b = 270° \qquad ...(i) \text{ and}$$
$$b = a + 20° \qquad ...(ii)$$

Using (ii) in (i)

$$a + (a + 20°) = 270°$$
$$\Rightarrow \quad 2a = 250°$$
$$\Rightarrow \quad a = 125°$$

4.(B)

Let the measure of $\angle POS$ be $x°$

$\because \qquad \angle POQ = 180°$
$$\Rightarrow \quad \angle POS + \angle ROS + \angle QOR = 180°$$
$$\Rightarrow \quad \angle POS + \angle ROS + 90° = 180°$$
$$\Rightarrow \quad \angle ROS = (90° - x).$$
$$\angle QOS = 90° + (90° - x) = 180° - x$$
$$\therefore \quad \angle POS = x = \angle QOS - 2\angle ROS.$$

5.(B)

$\angle m = \angle x \qquad$ [Vertically opposite $\angle$s]

$\because \angle AOB = 180°$
$$\Rightarrow \angle BOF + \angle COF + \angle AOC = 180°$$
$$\Rightarrow \angle BOF + \angle DOE + \angle AOC = 180°$$
$$\Rightarrow x° + 2x° + 3x° = 180°$$
$$\Rightarrow \quad 6x° = 180°$$
$$\Rightarrow \quad x = 30°$$
$$\therefore \quad m = 30°$$

6.(A)

$q = 5p$, $r = 3p$ and

$\because \angle POQ = 180°$
$$\Rightarrow p + q + r = 180°$$
$$\Rightarrow p + 5p + 3p = 180°$$
$$\Rightarrow 9p = 180° \Rightarrow p = 20°$$
$$r = 3p = 3 \times 20° = 60°$$
$$\therefore r + p = 60° + 20° = 80°$$

7.(A)

Here $\angle COQ = \angle POD$

[vertically opposite $\angle$s]

$\because \quad \angle AOB = 180°$

(AOB is a straight line)
$$\Rightarrow \angle POA + \angle POD + \angle BOD = 180°$$
$$\Rightarrow 2x° + 3x° + 20° + 3x° = 180°$$
$$\Rightarrow \quad 8x = 160°$$
$$\Rightarrow \quad x = 20°$$

8.(B)

$\because \angle POQ = 180° \quad$ [PQ is a straight line]
$$\Rightarrow \angle AOQ + \angle AOP = 180°$$
$$\Rightarrow \quad 5k + 7k = 180°$$
$$\Rightarrow \quad 12k = 180°$$
$$\Rightarrow \quad k = 15°$$
$$\therefore \angle BOQ = \angle AOP = 7 \times 15° = 105°$$

[vertically opposite $\angle$s]

9.(B)

$$x = 3y , z = \frac{21}{6} y = \frac{7}{2} y.$$

$\therefore \quad x + y + z = 180°$
$$\Rightarrow 3y + y + \frac{7}{2} y = 180°$$
$$\Rightarrow \quad 4y + \frac{7}{2} y = 180°$$
$$\Rightarrow \quad 15y = 180° \times 2$$
$$\Rightarrow \quad y = 24°$$

10.(B)

$\angle BOD = \angle AOC = 40°$

[vertically opposite $\angle$s]

$\because \angle SOB$ is a straight angle
$$\therefore \angle AOB = 180°$$
$$\Rightarrow \angle AOC + \angle COE + \angle BOE = 180°$$
$$\Rightarrow \angle COE = 180° - (\angle AOC + \angle BOE)$$
$$= 180° - 70° = 110°$$
$$\Rightarrow \angle AOC + \angle BOE = 70°$$
$$\angle BOE = 70° - 40° = 30°$$
$$\therefore \text{reflex } (\angle BOE) = 360° - 30 = 330°$$

11.(B)

$\angle AOD = \angle BOC$ [vertically opposite $\angle$s]

$\Rightarrow \quad y = 60° + x \qquad$ ...(i) and ,

$\because \qquad \angle DOC = 180°$

$\Rightarrow 60° + x + 100° = 180°$

$\Rightarrow \qquad x = 20°$

12.(A)

$\because \angle COD = 180°$

$\Rightarrow \angle BOC + \angle BOQ + \angle DOQ = 180°$

$\Rightarrow 55° + 60° + z = 180°$

$\Rightarrow \qquad z = 65°$

Similarly $\angle BOC = \angle AOD$

$\Rightarrow \qquad 2x + 3° = 55°$

$\Rightarrow \qquad x = 26°$

and,

$\qquad \angle AOP = \angle BOQ$ [vertically opposite $\angle$s]

$\Rightarrow \qquad 5y - 10° = 60°$

$\Rightarrow \qquad y = \dfrac{70°}{5} = 14°$

$\therefore x - y + z = 26° - 14° + 65° = 77°$

13.(B)

It is clear from the figure that,

$\qquad 105° + 5x = 180°$

$\Rightarrow \qquad 5x = 75°$

$\Rightarrow \qquad x = 15°$

14.(B)

$\angle ANP + \angle PNO = 180° \qquad$ [Straight angle]

$\Rightarrow \angle PNO = 180° - 120° = 60°$

$\therefore \angle PNO = \angle PCM = 60°$ [corresponding $\angle$S]

15.(C)

Here $\angle RQB + \angle RQP = 180°$

$\qquad\qquad\qquad (\because AB$ is a straight line)

$\Rightarrow \quad \angle RQP = 180° - 115° = 65°$

Now $\angle PRQ = 30°$

$\because \angle PRQ, \angle RQP$ and $\angle RPQ$ are the $\angle$s of Δ

$\therefore \angle PRQ + \angle RQP + \angle RPQ = 180°$

$\Rightarrow \angle RPQ = 180° - 65° - 30° = 85°$

$\qquad \angle APC = \angle RPQ$ [Vertically opposite $\angle$s]

$\therefore \quad \angle APC = 85°$

16. (A)

$\because AB \parallel CD$

$\therefore \angle DRM = \angle BPR = 127°$

$\qquad\qquad\qquad$ (corresponding $\angle$S)

$\qquad \angle BPR = \angle BPR = 127°$

$\qquad\qquad\qquad$ [Vertically opposite $\angle$S]

$\therefore \angle LPQ = \dfrac{\angle APL}{3} = \dfrac{127°}{3} = \left(42\dfrac{1}{3}\right)^0$

17. (C)

$\because x : y = 2 : 3$

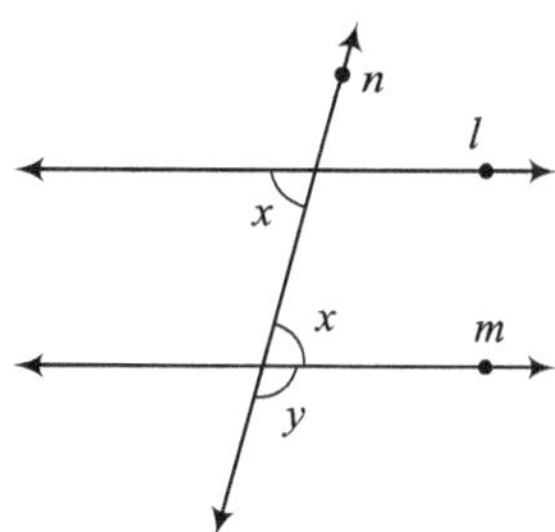

$\therefore$ Let the angles x and y be $2k$ and $3k$ respectively.

$\therefore \qquad 2k + 3k = 180°$

[Sum of $\angle$s in the interior of transversal]

$\Rightarrow \quad 5k = 180° \Rightarrow k = 36°$

$\therefore \qquad y = 3k = 3 \times 36° = 108°$

18. (D)

Extending GH to M, we have ,

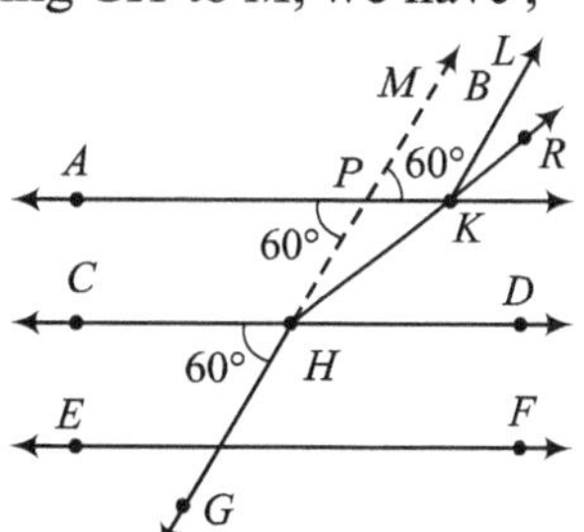

$\angle CHG = \angle APH = 60°$ [Corresponding $\angle$s]

$\angle APH = \angle MPK = 60°$

$\qquad\qquad\qquad$ [Vertically opposite $\angle$s]

$\angle APH = \angle MPD$, then,

$\angle MPK + \angle LKP = 180°$ [Sum of interior$\angle$s]

$\Rightarrow \angle LKP = 180° - 60° = 120°$, also

$\quad \angle KHD = \angle PKH = 25°$ (Alternate $\angle$s)

$\therefore \ \angle HKL = \angle LKP + \angle PKH$

$\qquad = 120° + 25° = 145°$

19.(C)

$\angle PA_1 B_1 + \angle RB_1 A_1 = 180°$

$\qquad\qquad$ [Sum of interior $\angle$s]

Also,

$$\angle MA_1 B_1 = \angle MB_1 A_1 = \frac{180°}{2} = 90°$$

$\quad$ ($\because MA_1$ and MB_1 are angle bisectors)

$\therefore \ \ \angle A_1 MB_1 = 180° - 90° = 90°$

20.(B)

Construct a line $l \parallel AB$,

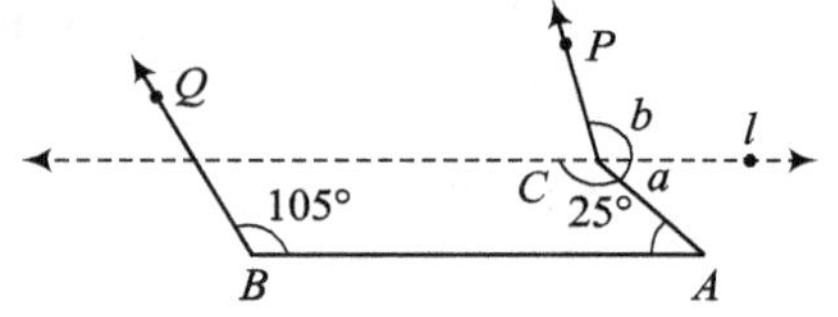

$\qquad \angle a = 25°\qquad$ [Alternate $\angle$s]

$\qquad \angle c = 105°$

$\therefore \ \angle b = 105°\qquad$ [Vertically opposite $\angle$s]

$\therefore \ x = a + b = 25° + 105° = 130°$

HOTS (ACHIEVERS SECTION)

21. (D)	22. (B)	23. (D)	24. (D)	25. (B)

21. (D)

$x = 40° + 30° + 60°$

$x = 130°$

22. (B)

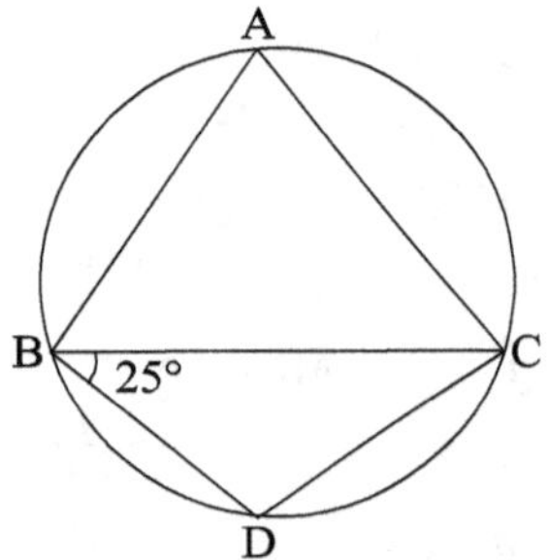

In $\triangle BCD$,

$BD = DC$

$\angle BCD = 25°$

$\angle DCB + \angle DBC + \angle BDC = 180°$

$25° + 25° + \angle BDC = 180°$

$\angle BDC = 130°$

ABDC is a cyclic quadrilateral

$\angle BAC = 180° - 130° = 50°$

23. (D)

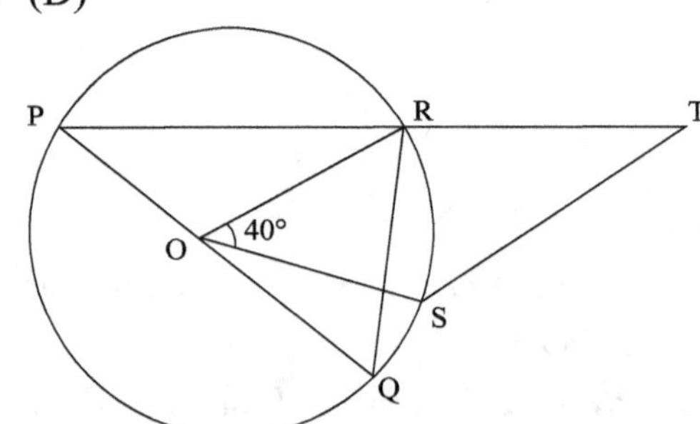

$\angle RQS = \dfrac{1}{2} \angle ROS$

$\qquad = \dfrac{1}{2} \times 40° = 20°$

In $\triangle RQT$,

$\angle QRT + \angle RQS + \angle RTQ = 180°$

$90° + 20° + \angle RTQ = 180°$

$110° + \angle RTQ = 180°$

$$\angle RTQ = 180° - 110°$$
$$\angle RTQ = 70°$$

24. **(D)**

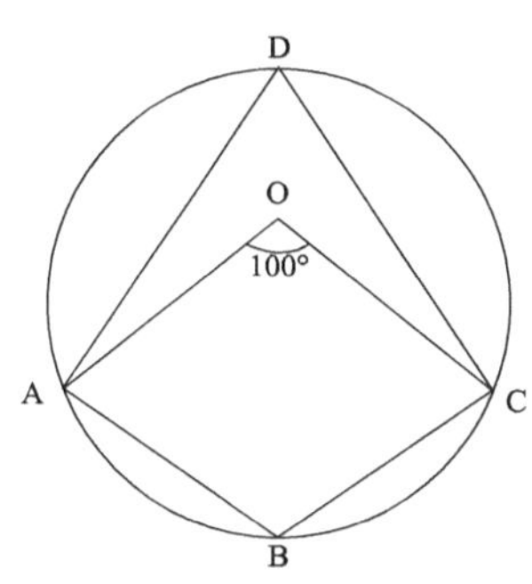

$$\angle ADC = \frac{1}{2} \times \angle AOC$$

$$= \frac{1}{2} \times 100° = 50°$$

$$\angle ABC = \frac{1}{2}(360° - 100°)$$

$$= \frac{1}{2} \times 260° = 130°$$

7. TRIANGLES

Answer Key

1. (B)	2. (D)	3. (D)	4. (B)	5. (A)	6. (A)	7. (A)	8. (C)	9. (B)	10. (C)
11. (C)	12. (C)	13. (A)	14. (C)	15. (A)	16. (B)	17. (B)	18. (C)	19. (B)	20. (B)

1.(B)

In $\triangle ABC$

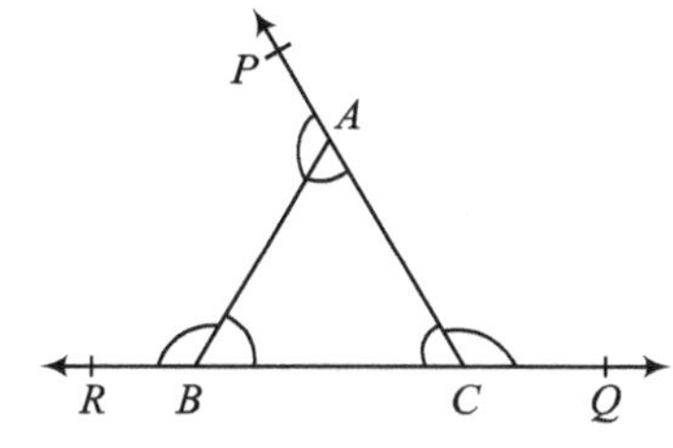

$$\angle ABC + \angle ACB + \angle BAC = 180°$$

Now,

using exterior angle theorem

$$\angle ACB + \angle ABC = \angle BAP \qquad ...(i)$$
$$\angle ABC + \angle BAC = \angle ACQ \qquad ...(ii)$$
$$\angle ACB + \angle BAC = \angle ABR \qquad ...(iii)$$

Adding Eqns (i), (ii) and (iii), we get

$$2(\angle ABC + \angle BAC + \angle ABC)$$
$$= \angle BAP + \angle ACQ + \angle ABR$$

$\Rightarrow$ Sum of all exterior angle $= 2 \times 180° = 360°$

2.(D)

$$x = 90° - \frac{1}{2}\angle A$$

$$= 90° - \frac{1}{2} \times 70°$$

$$= 90° - 35° = 55°$$

3.(D)

$$\because \qquad AB = AC$$
$$\therefore \qquad \angle ABC = \angle ACB \qquad ....(i)$$

$\because \angle CAP$ is an exterior angle for $\triangle ABC$,

$$\because \quad \angle CAP = \angle ABC + \angle ACB \qquad [\text{using (i)}]$$
$$\Rightarrow \quad 108° = 2\angle ABC$$

$$\Rightarrow \angle ABC = \frac{108°}{2} = 54°$$

4.(B)

$$x = 90° + \frac{1}{2}\angle A$$

$$= 90° + \frac{1}{2} \times 72°$$

$$= 90° + 36°$$

$$= 126°$$

5.(A)

$\angle PQX$ and $\angle PRY$ are exterior angles for $\triangle PQR$

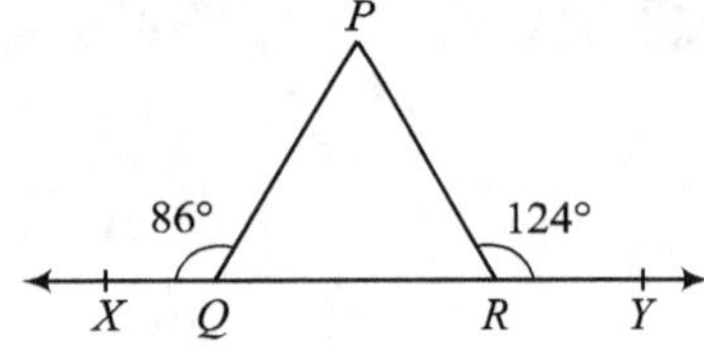

$$\therefore \quad \angle P + \angle PRX = 86° \qquad ...(i)$$
$$\angle P + \angle PQY = 124° \qquad \cdots(ii)$$

Adding (i) and (ii)

$$2\angle P + \angle PRX + \angle PQY = 210°$$
$$\Rightarrow \angle P + (\angle P + \angle PRX + \angle PQX) = 210°$$
$$\Rightarrow \qquad \angle P + 180° = 210°$$
$$\Rightarrow \qquad \angle P = 30°$$

6.(A)

$$\angle APQ = \angle CQF = 65°$$

$$\text{(corresponding } \angle s)$$

$$\angle APR + \angle RPQ = 65°$$
$$\Rightarrow \qquad 25° + q = 65°$$
$$\Rightarrow \qquad q = 40°$$

$\because \angle RQF$ is on exterior angle for $\triangle PQR$

$$\therefore \qquad q + \angle PRQ = 65° + 30°$$
$$\Rightarrow \qquad p + q = 65° + 30$$
$$\Rightarrow \qquad p = 95° - 40° = 55°$$

7. (A)

$\because \angle DBC$ is exterior angle for $\triangle DAB$

$$\therefore \quad \angle ADB + \angle DAB = \angle DBC$$
$$\Rightarrow \quad \angle DBC = 25° + 55° = 80°$$

$\because \angle x$ is an exterior angle for $\triangle EBC$

$$\therefore \qquad \angle EBC + \angle ECB = x$$
$$\Rightarrow \qquad 80° + 40° = x$$
$$\Rightarrow \qquad x = 120°$$

8.(C)

$$\angle ABC + \angle A = \angle ACD$$
$$\Rightarrow \qquad \angle ACD = \angle ABC + 84°$$
$$\Rightarrow \qquad \frac{\angle ACD}{2} = \frac{\angle ABC}{2} + 42°$$
$$\Rightarrow \qquad \angle ECD = \angle EBC + 42° \qquad ...(i)$$

$\because \angle ECD$ is an exterior angle for $\triangle EBC$

$$\therefore \qquad \angle ECD = \angle EBC + x \qquad ...(ii)$$

Comparing (i) and (ii), we get

$$x = 42°$$

9.(B)

In $\triangle s$ ABD and ACD,

$$AB = AC \qquad \text{(Given)}$$
$$AD = AD \qquad \text{(Common)}$$
$$BD = CD \quad (\because AC \text{ is median})$$

$$\therefore \qquad \triangle ABD \cong \triangle ACD$$

$$\text{[By S-S-S congruence criterion]}$$

$$\therefore \angle BAD = \frac{180° - \angle B - \angle C}{2}$$

$$= \frac{180° - 40° - 40°}{2} = 50$$

10.(C)

In $\triangle s$ ABE and DCE

$$\angle ABE = \angle DCE = \frac{\angle B}{2}$$

$$AB = CD \qquad \text{(given)}$$

$$BE = CE (\because \angle ABE = \angle DCE = \frac{\angle B}{2})$$

$$\therefore \triangle ABE \cong \triangle DCE \quad [\text{ By S-S-S congruence}]$$

$$\angle BAC = \left(\frac{108°}{3}\right) \times 2 = 36° \times 2 = 72°$$

11.(C)

$$AB + AC > BC \quad ...(i)$$
$$OB + OC > BC \quad ...(ii)$$

Using (i) and (ii)
$$AB + AC > OB + OC$$

12.(C)

In ΔABC
$$AB + BC > AC \qquad ...(i)$$

InΔADC,
$$AD + DC > AC \qquad ...(ii)$$

Using (i) and (ii)
$$CD + AD + AB + BC > 2AC$$

13.(A)

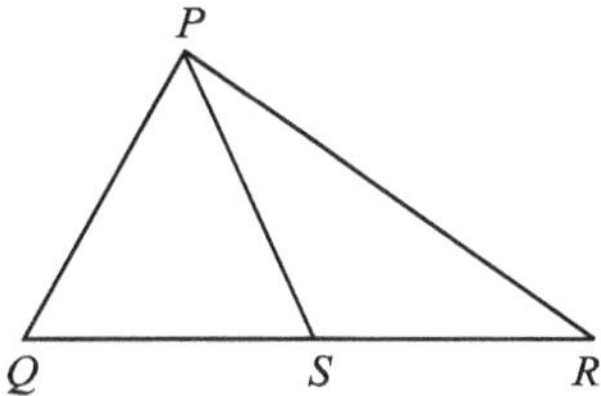

In ΔPQS,
$$PQ + QS > PS \qquad ...(i)$$

In ΔPSR,
$$PR + RS > PS \qquad ...(ii)$$

Using (i) and (ii)
$$PQ + PR + (QS + RS) > 2PS$$
$$\Rightarrow \quad PQ + PR + QR > 2PS$$

14.(C)

In ΔABC,

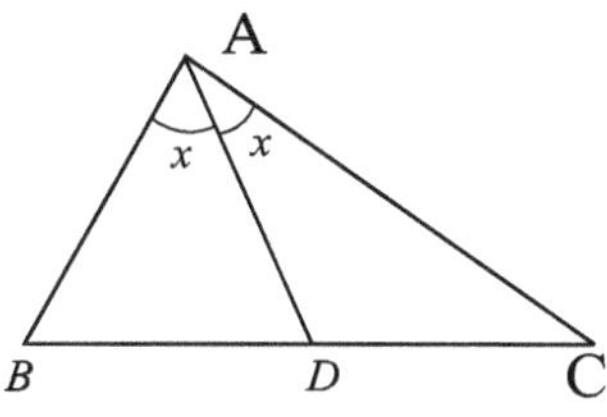

$$\because \qquad AC > AB$$
$$\therefore \qquad \angle ABC > \angle ACB$$
$$\Rightarrow \qquad -\angle ABC < -\angle ACB$$

$$\Rightarrow 180° - \angle ABC < 180° - \angle ACB$$
$$\Rightarrow 180° - \angle ABC - x < 180° - \angle ACB - x$$
$$\Rightarrow \qquad \angle ADB < \angle ADC.$$

15.(A)

$$\angle A = 50°,\ \angle B = 60°$$
$$\angle C = 180° - (\angle A + \angle B)$$
$$= 180° - 110°$$
$$= 70°$$

$\because \angle C$ is the largest angle of ΔABC

$\therefore AB$ is the largest side of ΔABC.

16.(B)

In ΔQTR
$$\angle QTR + \angle Q + \angle R = 180°$$
$$\Rightarrow 90° + 40° + x = 180°$$
$$\Rightarrow \qquad x = 50°$$

$\because \angle PSQ$ is an exterior angle for ΔPRS

$$\therefore \qquad \angle PRS + \angle SPR = y$$
$$\Rightarrow \qquad y = 50° + 30° = 80°$$
$$\therefore \quad x + y = 50° + 80° = 130°$$

17.(B)

$\because \angle BAC$ is the smallest angle

$\therefore BC$ will be the smallest side

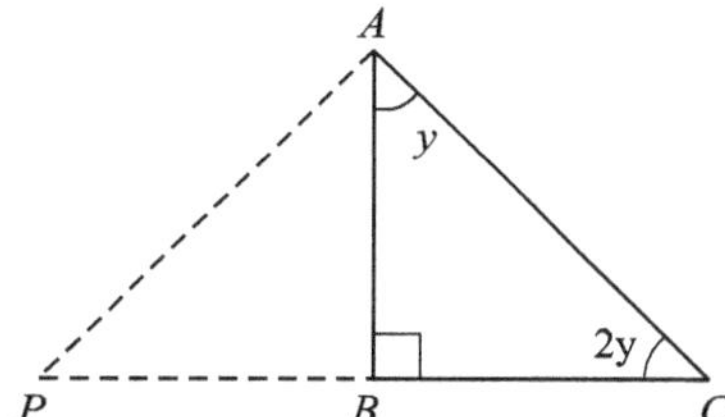

Now,

Connecting ΔAPB in such a way that
$$PB = BC$$

In Δs APB and ACB
$$\angle ABC = \angle ABP = 90°$$
$$PB = BC \ \text{ and } AB \text{ is common}$$
$$\therefore \qquad \Delta ABC \cong \Delta ABP$$
(by S-A-S congruence criterion)
$$\therefore \qquad PA = AC \qquad \text{(CPCT)}$$
$$\therefore \qquad \angle PAB = \angle BAC = y \qquad \text{(say)}$$

Now

In $\triangle APC$

$\because \qquad \angle A = \angle C$

$\therefore \qquad AC = PA$

$\Rightarrow \qquad 2BC = AC$

$\Rightarrow \qquad BC = \dfrac{AC}{2} = \dfrac{x}{2}$

18.(C)

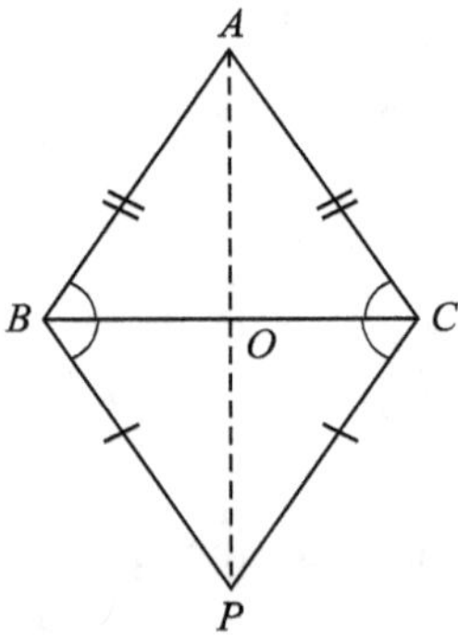

Given : $\triangle ABC$ and $\triangle BCP$ are isosceles Δs with common base BC.

In Δs ABP and ACP

$\qquad AB = AC \qquad$ (given)

$\qquad BP = PC \qquad$ (given)

$\qquad AP = AP \qquad$ (common)

$\therefore \qquad \triangle ABP \cong \triangle ACP$(S-S-S criterion)

$\therefore \qquad BO = OC \qquad$ and

$\qquad \angle AOB + \angle AOC = 180°$

$\Rightarrow \qquad 2\angle AOC = 180°$

$\Rightarrow \qquad \angle AOB = 90°$

19.(B)

In Δs BEC and CFB

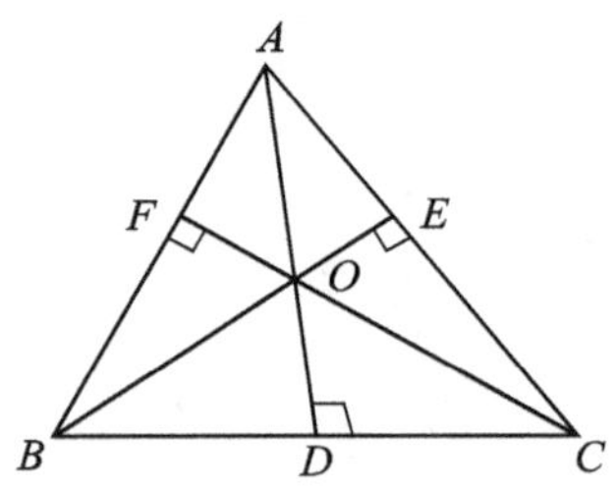

$\qquad BC = BC \qquad$ (Common)

$\qquad BE = CF \qquad$ (Given)

$\qquad \angle BEC = \angle CFB = 90°$

$\therefore \qquad \triangle BEC \cong \triangle CFB$

(By R-H-S congruence criterion)

$\qquad \angle B = \angle C \qquad$ (C-P-C-T)

$\therefore \qquad AB = AC \qquad$ ...(i)

Similarly in Δs ADC and CFA

$\Rightarrow \qquad \angle A = \angle C$

$\therefore \qquad AB = BC \qquad$ ...(ii)

Using (i) and (ii)

$\qquad AB = BC = AC$ (Δ should be equilateral)

20.(B)

In Δs ABC and PQR

$\qquad AB = PQ = 3\text{cm}$

$\qquad BC = QR = 5\text{cm}$

$\qquad \angle ABC = \angle PQR = 50°$

$\therefore \qquad \triangle ABC \cong \triangle PQR$(By S-A-S criterion)

$\qquad \angle BAC = \angle QPR \qquad$ (C.P.C.T)

$\Rightarrow \qquad 2x + 10° = x + 50°$

$\Rightarrow \qquad x = 40°$

HOTS (ACHIEVERS SECTION)

21. (C)	22. (A)	23. (C)	24. (B)	25. (C)

21. (C)

$S - a = 8 \text{ cm} \qquad$ ....(1)

$S - b = 7 \text{ cm} \qquad$ ....(2)

$S - c = 5 \text{ cm} \qquad$ ....(3)

$(1) + (2) + (3)$

$3S - (a + b + c) = 20 \text{ cm}$

$3S - 2S = 20 \text{ cm}$

$S = 20 \text{ cm}$

$\text{Area} = \sqrt{S(S-a)(S-b)(S-c)}$

$\qquad = \sqrt{20 \times 8 \times 7 \times 5}$

$\qquad = \sqrt{10 \times 2 \times 4 \times 2 \times 5 \times 7}$

$$= \sqrt{5 \times 2 \times 2 \times 4 \times 2 \times 7 \times 5}$$

$$= 5 \times 2 \times 2\sqrt{14}$$

$$= 20\sqrt{14} \ cm^2$$

22. (A)

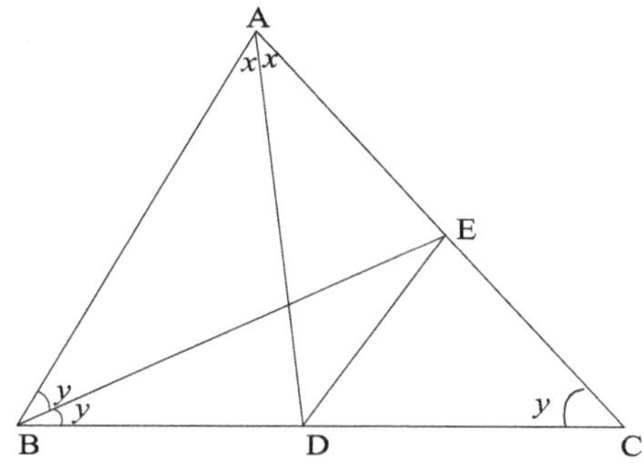

In $\angle ABC$

$\angle B = 2\angle C$

$\angle B = 2y$

Let $\angle BAD = \angle CAD = x$

$\Delta ABE \cong \Delta DCE$

$\angle ABE = \angle DCE = y$

$AB = CD$

$\angle CDE = 2x =$ and $\angle ADE = \angle DAE = x$

$x + 2x = 2y + x$

$x = y$

In ABC;

$\angle A + \angle B + \angle C = 180°$

$2x + 2y + y = 180°$

$2x + 2x + x = 180°$

$x = 36°$

$\angle BAC = 2x = 2 \times 36° = 72°$

23. (C)

$$\Delta = \sqrt{S(S-a)\,(S-b)\,(S-c)}$$

$$S' = \frac{2(a+b+c)}{2} = a+b+c = 2S$$

$$\Delta' = \sqrt{2S\,(2S-2a)\,(2S-2b)\,(2S-2c)}$$

$$= \sqrt{2 \times 2 \times 2 \times 2 \ S(S-a)(S-b)\,(S-c)} = 4\Delta$$

Percentage increase in area =

$$\frac{4\Delta - \Delta}{\Delta} = \times 100 = 300\%$$

8. QUADRILATERALS

Answer Key

1. (B)	2. (A)	3. (C)	4. (B)	5. (C)	6. (B)	7. (A)	8. (B)	9. (B)	10. (D)
11. (B)	12. (C)	13. (C)	14. (A)	15. (B)	16. (B)	17. (C)	18. (C)	19. (B)	20. (C)

1.(B)

∵ Diagonals of a rectangle bisect each other and are also equal in length.

∴ In ΔPOS,

$$OP = OS$$

$\Rightarrow \quad \angle OPS = \angle OSP$

(angles opposite to equal sides are equal)

Also,

$$\angle POS + \angle OSP + \angle OPS = 180°$$

$\Rightarrow \quad 2\angle OPS = 180° - \angle POS$

$$= 180° - 64° \ (\because \angle POS + \angle QOR)$$

$= 116°$ {vertically opposite $\angle$s}

$\Rightarrow \quad \angle OPS = \dfrac{116°}{2} = 58°$

2.(A)

The figure formed by joining the mid-points of consecutive side of a quadrilateral is a parallelogram.

3.(C)

Let the measure of 4th angle be $x°$

∴ $98° + 92° + 70° + x° = 360°$

$$\Rightarrow \qquad x° = 100°$$

4.(B)

Let the angles be $2x, 4x, 5x$ and $7x$ respectively.

$\therefore$ Difference between largest and smallest angle $= 7x - 2x = 5x$

$\because$ Sum of all angles of a quadrilateral $= 360°$

$\Rightarrow 2x + 4x + 5x + 7x = 360°$

$\Rightarrow \qquad 18x = 360°$

$\Rightarrow \qquad x = 20°$

$\therefore$ Required difference

$$= 7x - 2x = 5x$$
$$= 5 \times 20° = 100°$$

5.(C)

$\because$ Diagonals of a rhombus bisect each other at $90°$

In $\triangle AOD$

$$AD = 15 \text{ cm}, AO = 12 \text{ cm},$$

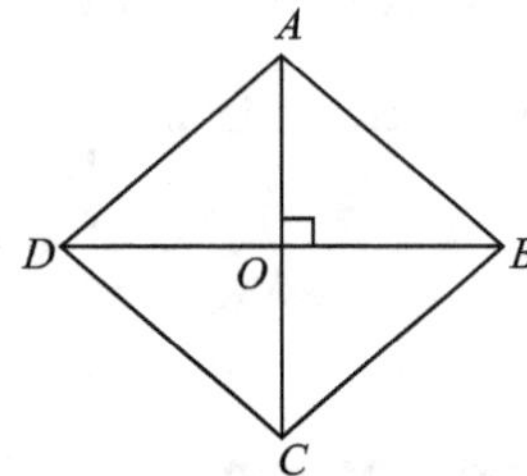

$$\therefore OD = \sqrt{AD^2 - OA^2}$$

$$= \sqrt{(15)^2 - (12)^2} = 9 \text{ cm}$$

$$\therefore BD = 2OD$$

$$= 2 \times 9 = 18 \text{ cm}$$

6.(B)

Let the angle be $x°$

$\therefore$ Its adjacent angle $= (180 - x)°$

A/Q,

$$x° = \frac{2}{3}(180° - x)°$$

$$\Rightarrow \qquad 3x° = 360° - 2x°$$

$$\Rightarrow \qquad 5x = 360°$$

$$\Rightarrow \qquad x = 72°$$

7.(A)

Rectangle has diagonals of equal length

8.(B)

$$\angle P + \angle Q + \angle R + \angle S = 360°$$

$$\Rightarrow \quad 3x + 7x + 6x + 4x = 360°$$

$$\Rightarrow \qquad 20x = 360°$$

$$\Rightarrow \qquad x = 18°$$

$\therefore$ Angles are $54°$ $126, 108°$ $72°$

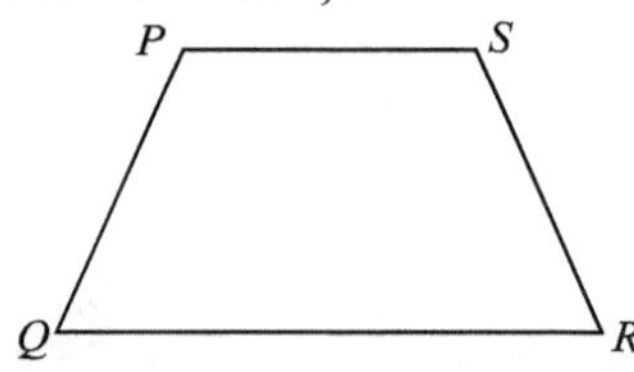

$\because \angle P + \angle Q = \angle R + \angle S = 180°$

$\therefore PQRS$ is a trapezium, because

$$\angle R + \angle Q \neq 180°$$

(only one pair of sides are equal)

9.(B)

Let the angles be $3x, 5x, 9x$ and $13x$

$\therefore$ Sum of largest and smallest angle

$$= 3x + 13x = 16x$$

A/Q,

$$3x + 5x + 9x + 13x = 360°$$

$$\Rightarrow \quad 30x = 360° \Rightarrow x = 12$$

$$\therefore \quad 16x = 16 \times 12° = 192°$$

10.(D)

P, Q, R and S are the mid-points of AB, BC, CD and DA respectively.

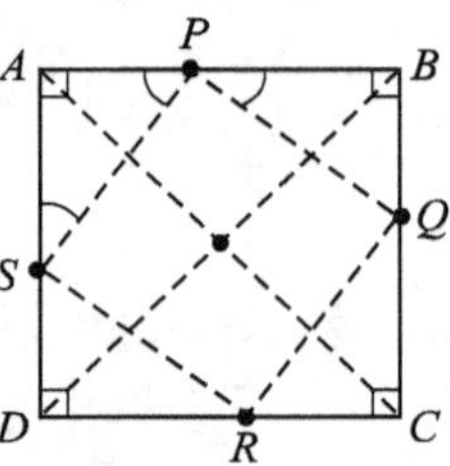

$$\therefore AP = AS = PB = BQ = QC$$

$$= CR = DR = DS = \frac{AB}{2}$$

$\therefore$ In $\triangle APS$

$$AP = AS$$

$$\Rightarrow \angle ASP = \angle APS = \frac{(180° - 90°)}{2} = 45°$$

Similarly

$$\angle ASP = \angle APS = \angle BPQ = \angle BQP = \angle CQR$$
$$= \angle CRQ = \angle DSR = \angle DRS = 45°$$

Now $\angle SPQ + \angle BPQ + \angle APS = 180°$

$\Rightarrow \qquad \angle SPQ = 90°$

Similarly, in PQRS

$$\angle P = \angle Q = \angle R = \angle S = 90°$$

$\therefore$ $PQRS$ is a parallelogram having each of its angles $= 90°$

Now

using midpoint theorem in $\triangle ABC$ and $\triangle ACD$

$$SR = PQ = \frac{1}{2} AC, \text{ and in } \Delta s\ ABD \text{ and } BDC$$

$$SP = RQ = \frac{1}{2} BD = \frac{1}{2} AC\ [\because BD = AC]$$

$\therefore$ $SP = PQ = QR = RS$

$\therefore$ $PQRS$ is a square

11.(B)

In $\triangle ACD$

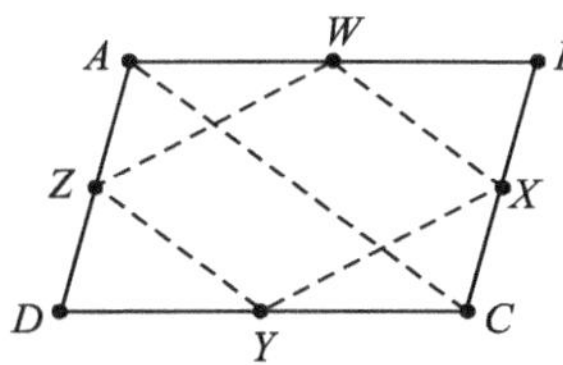

$$ZY \parallel AC \text{ and } YZ = \frac{1}{2} AC$$

[Using mid-point theorem]

12.(C)

In $\triangle ABR$

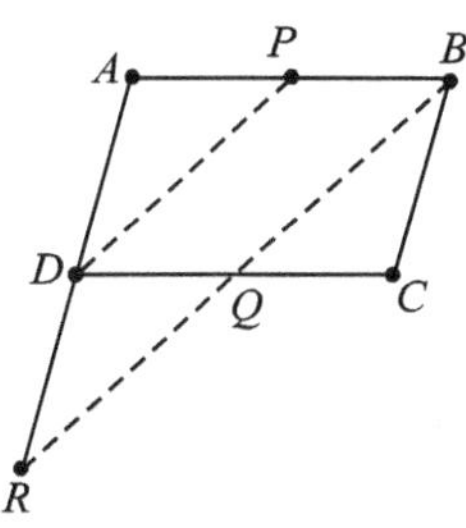

$DP \parallel BR$, and P is the mid-point of side AB

$\therefore$ Using mid-point theorem (converse)

Point P is the mid − point of AB and is parallel to BR.

$\therefore \qquad DP = \frac{1}{2} BR, \text{ and}$

D will be the mid −point of side AR

$\therefore \quad AD = DR = BC = \frac{1}{2} AR$

$\Rightarrow \quad AR = 2BC$

13.(C)

Rhombus is a parallelogram having consecutive sides equal and none of the angles equal to right angle.

14.(A)

$$\angle DAC = \angle DCA = \frac{90°}{2} = 45°$$

15.(B)

$$\angle OPS = \frac{180° - 44°}{2} = \frac{136°}{2} = 68°$$

16.(B)

$$\angle ABC = 56°$$

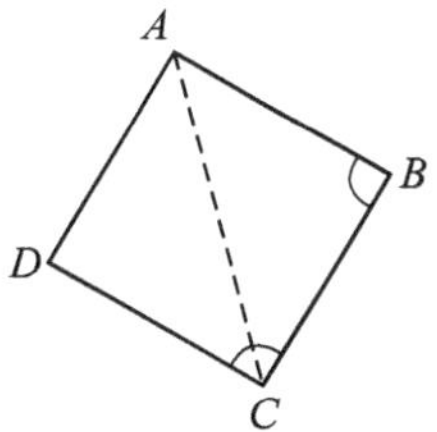

$$\therefore \angle ACD = \frac{180° - 56°}{2} = 90° - 28° = 62°$$

[$\because$ Adjacent angles sum $= 180°$ and diagonal bisect the angle$\angle A$]

17.(C)

$\because$ AD is the median of $\triangle ABC$

$\therefore \qquad BD = DC$

Through D, draw $DR \parallel BF$

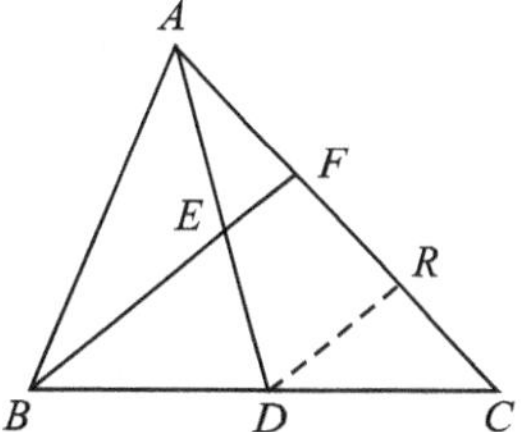

Now, in ΔBFC,

$DR \parallel BF$ and D is the mid-point of BC

$\therefore$ R should be the mid-point of FC (according to converse of mid-point theorem)

$\therefore \qquad FR = RC \qquad \qquad$ ...(i)

Similarly, in ΔADR

E is the mid-point of AD and $EF \parallel DR$

$\therefore$ F should be the mid-point of AR

$\therefore \qquad FR = AF \qquad \qquad$ ...(ii)

Using (i) and (ii)

$$FR = RC = AF$$
$$\Rightarrow \qquad AC = 3AF$$
$$\Rightarrow \qquad AF = \frac{1}{3}AC$$

18.(C)

P, Q, R and S are the midpoints of AB, BC, CD and DA respectively.

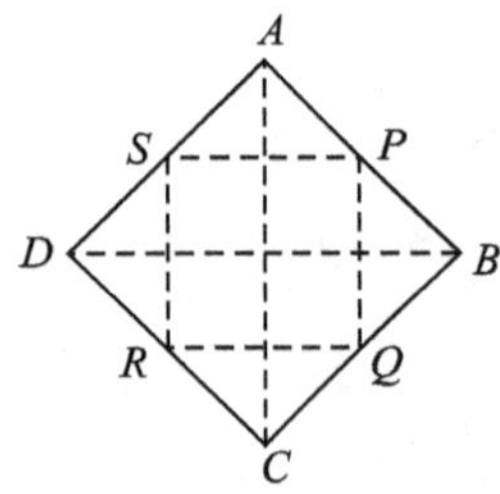

Using midpoint theorem in ΔADB and ΔDBC

$$SP = RQ = \frac{1}{2} DB \text{ and } SP \parallel RQ \parallel BD$$

Similarly in Δs ADC and ΔABC,

$$PQ = SR = \frac{AC}{2} \text{ and } PQ \parallel SR \parallel AC$$

$\therefore$ $AC \perp BD$ and $SP \parallel BD$

$\therefore \qquad \qquad \qquad \angle S = 90°$,

Also,

$$AC \neq BD, \text{ or }, PQ \neq PS$$

$\therefore$ $PQRS$ is a parallelogram having one angle equal to 90° and unequal adjacent sides

$\therefore$ $PQRS$ is a rectangle.

19.(B)

The resulting figure will be a square

20.(C)

Every rhombus is a $\parallel^{gm}$ because its opposite sides are equal and parallel.

<table>
<tr><td colspan="5" align="center">HOTS (ACHIEVERS SECTION)</td></tr>
<tr><td>21. (C)</td><td>22. (A)</td><td>23. (C)</td><td>24. (A)</td><td>25. (B)</td></tr>
</table>

21. (C)

Number of rectangular planks

$$= \frac{Volume\ of\ Cuboid}{Volume\ of\ one\ Plank}$$

$$= \frac{1.104}{2.3 \times 0.75 \times 0.040} = 16$$

9. AREA OF PARALLELOGRAMS AMD TRIANGLES

Answer Key

1. (A)	2. (B)	3. (D)	4. (B)	5. (B)	6. (A)	7. (B)	8. (A)	9. (B)	10. (A)
11. (A)	12. (C)	13. (A)	14. (C)	15. (B)	16. (A)	17. (B)	18. (D)	19. (C)	20. (B)

1.(A)

Joining QS, it can be clearly seen that,
$QS \parallel DC \parallel AB$,

$\therefore$ ar $(PQS) = \dfrac{1}{2}$ ar$(DCQS)$

[Area between QS and DC]

ar $(SRQ) = \dfrac{1}{2}$ ar $(ASQB)$

[Area between QS and AB]

Adding both,

ar $(PQS) +$ ar $(SRQ) = \dfrac{1}{2}$ [ar $(DCQS)$

$+$ ar $(ASQB)$]

ar $(PQRS) = \dfrac{1}{2}$ ar $(ABCD)$

2.(B)

$\because ABCD$ and ΔPDC lie on same base, i.e., CD and between the same parallels, i.e., AB and CD.

$\therefore$ ar $(\Delta PDC) = \dfrac{1}{2}$ ar$(ABCD)$

Similarly,

ar $(\Delta AQD) = \dfrac{1}{2}$ ar$(ABCD)$

$\Rightarrow$ ar $(\Delta PDC) =$ ar (ΔAQD)

$= \dfrac{1}{2}$ ar (quad. $ABCD$)

3.(D)

In ΔABC, AD is the median.

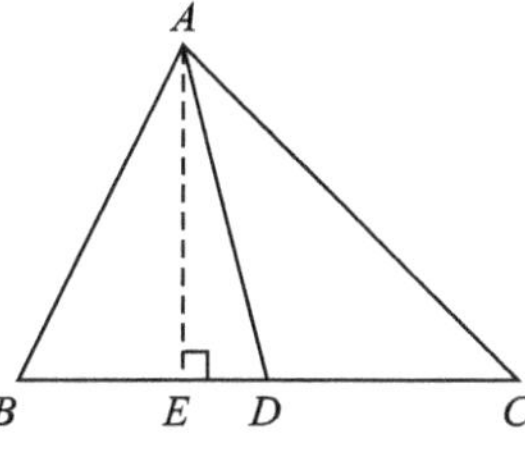

$\therefore \qquad BD = CD$,

Let $AE \perp BC$, then,

ar$(\Delta ABD) = \dfrac{1}{2} \times AE \times BD$,

ar$(\Delta ADC) = \dfrac{1}{2} \times AE \times DC = \dfrac{1}{2} \times AE \times BD$

$\therefore$ ar$(\Delta ABD) =$ ar(ΔADC)

4.(B)

Using midpoint theorem,

$BC = 2\ QR$, $AB = 2\ PQ$, $AC = 2\ PR$.

Let the area of ΔPQR be a, then, ABC is a Δ resulted by doubling the length of every side of ΔPQR.

$\therefore$ ar $(\Delta ABC) = 4$ ar (ΔPQR)

[using Heron's formula]

5.(B)

Area of trapezium $RQBC =$ ar (ΔRBP)

$+$ ar $(\Delta PQR) +$ ar (ΔQPC)

$= 3 \times$ ar (ΔPQR)

$= \dfrac{3}{4}$ ar (ΔABC)

6.(A)

ar (parallelogram $PQRS$)

$= \dfrac{1}{2}$ ar (parallelogram $ABCD$)

$= \dfrac{1}{2} \times 26 = 13\ \text{m}^2$

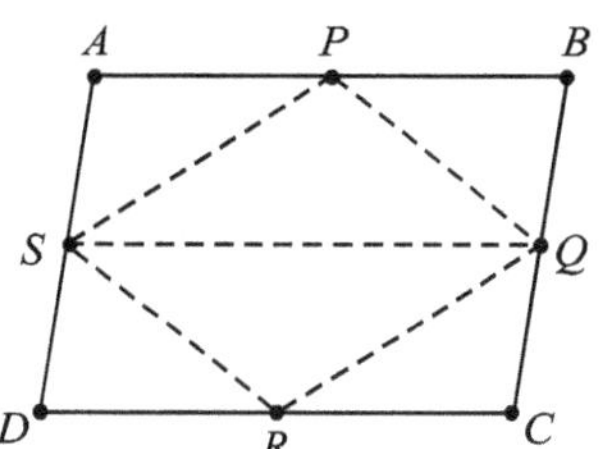

7.(B)

$\because AD$ median of ΔABC

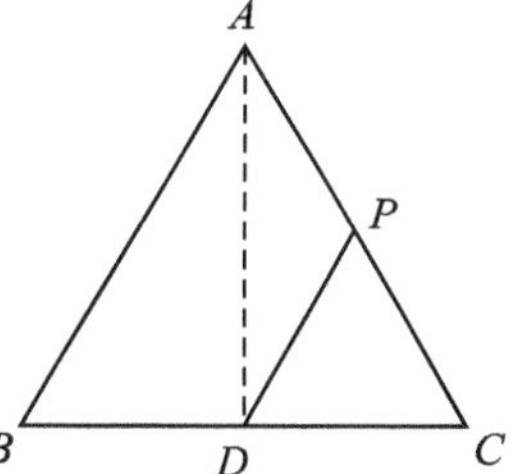

$$\therefore \ \mathrm{ar}\,(ABD) = \mathrm{ar}(ADC) = \frac{1}{2}\,\mathrm{ar}(\Delta ABC)\ldots(i)$$

$$\frac{ar(\Delta ADP)}{ar(\Delta ADC)} = \frac{2}{3}$$

$$\Rightarrow \frac{ar(\Delta PDC)}{ar(\Delta ADC)} = \frac{1}{3} \Rightarrow \frac{2ar(\Delta PDC)}{ar(\Delta ABC)} = \frac{1}{3}$$

$$\therefore \ \text{Required ratio} = \frac{1}{3\times 2} = 1:6$$

8.(A)

Let $AB = x$, $AC = y$, then,

$BC = \sqrt{x^2 + y^2}$ (Pythagoras' theorem)

Area $(ABMN) = x^2$

Area $(ACFG) = y^2$

$$\mathrm{ar}(BCED) = \left(\sqrt{x^2 + y^2}\right)^2 = x^2 + y^2$$

$$\therefore \ \mathrm{ar}(BCED) = \mathrm{ar}(ABMN) + \mathrm{ar}(ACFG)$$

9.(B)

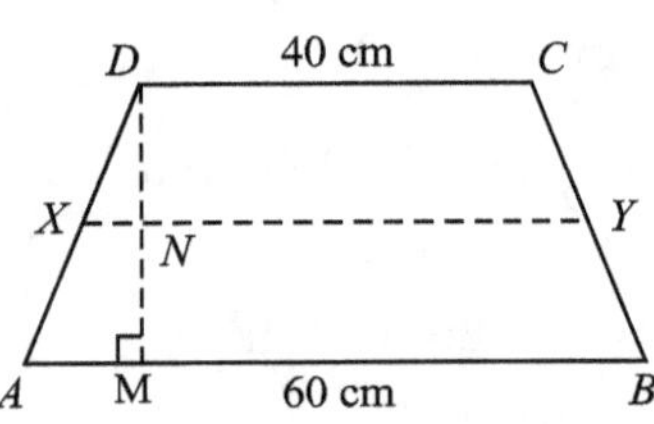

$$\because \qquad XY \parallel AB \parallel DC$$

[Let the length of XY be x cm]

$\because \ \mathrm{ar}\,(DCYX) + \mathrm{ar}\,(XYBA) = \mathrm{ar}\,(ABCD)$

$$\therefore \ \frac{1}{2} \times (40 + x) \times DN + \frac{1}{2} \times (60 + x) \times NM$$

$$= \frac{1}{2} \times (40 + 60) \times DM \qquad \ldots(i)$$

$$\because \ DN = NM = \frac{DM}{2}$$

$\therefore$ The equation (i) reduces to :

$$(40 + x) \times \frac{1}{2} + (60 + x) \times \frac{1}{2} = 100$$

$$\Rightarrow \qquad 100 + 2x = 200$$

$$\Rightarrow \qquad 2x = 100$$

$$\Rightarrow \qquad x = 50 \text{ cm.}$$

10.(A)

According to question

$$\frac{1}{2} \times (40 + x) \times \frac{DM}{2}$$

$$= K\,\frac{1}{2} \times (60 + x) \times \frac{DM}{2}$$

$$\Rightarrow \qquad (40 + 50) = K\,(60 + 50)$$

$$\Rightarrow \qquad K = \frac{9}{11}$$

11.(A)

$$\mathrm{ar}\,(PQRS) = \frac{1}{2} \times (40 + 60) \times 10$$

$$= \frac{1}{2} \times 100 \times 10 = 500 \text{ cm}^2$$

12.(C)

$\because \ \Delta ADC$ and ΔBDC lie on same base DC and between the same parallels, i.e., AB and DC.

$\therefore \quad \mathrm{ar}\,(\Delta ADC) = \mathrm{ar}\,(\Delta BDC)$

$\mathrm{ar}(AOD) + \mathrm{ar}(DOC) = \mathrm{ar}(BOC) + \mathrm{ar}(DOC)$

$\Rightarrow \qquad \mathrm{ar}(AOD) = \mathrm{ar}(BOC).$

13.(A)

In ΔADB,

$$DB = \sqrt{AD^2 + AB^2}$$

$$= \sqrt{9^2 + 12^2} = 15$$

$$\mathrm{ar}(\Delta ADB) = \frac{1}{2} \times 12 \times 9 = 54 \text{ cm}^2$$

$$\mathrm{ar}(\Delta DBC) = \frac{1}{2} \times 15 \times 8 = 60 \text{ cm}^2$$

$\therefore$ Total area $= 54 + 60 = 114 \text{ cm}^2$

14.(C)

Draw $XY \parallel AD \parallel BC$ and $PQ \parallel AB \parallel DC$

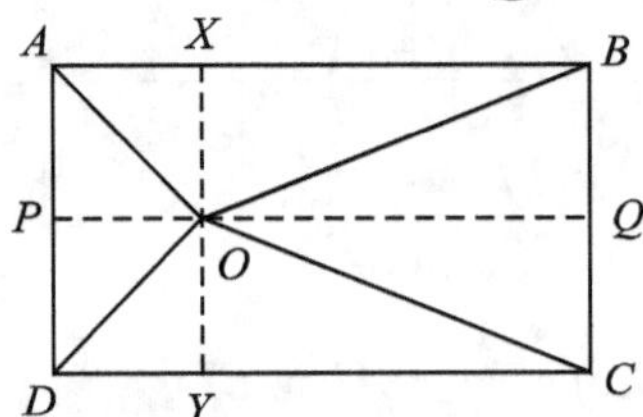

Now ar$(\Delta AOB) = \dfrac{1}{2}$ ar$(ABQP)$

ar$(\Delta DOC) = \dfrac{1}{2}$ ar$(DCQP)$

$\Rightarrow$ ar$(\Delta AOB) +$ ar$(\Delta DOC) = \dfrac{1}{2} \times$ ar$(ABCD)$

$\Rightarrow$ ar$(\Delta AOD) +$ ar$(\Delta BOC) = \dfrac{1}{2} \times$ ar$(ABCD)$

$\Rightarrow$ ar$(ABCD) = 2 \times (3 + 6) = 18$ cm²

15.(B)

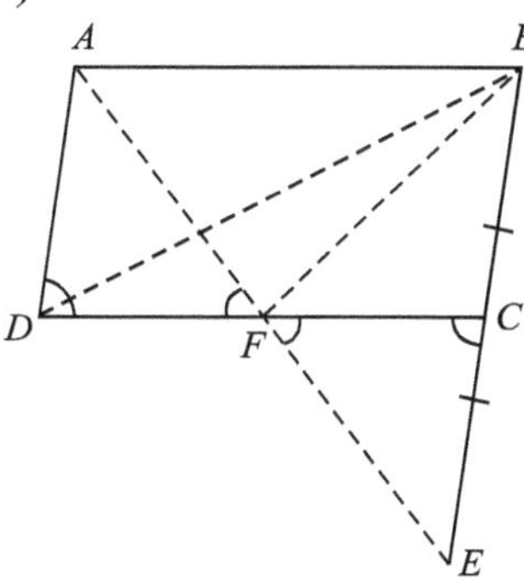

ar$(\Delta AFB) = \dfrac{1}{2}$ ar (parallelogram $ABCD$)

{areas between same parallels and same base}

$\Rightarrow$ ar (parallelogram $ABCD$) $= 2 \times$ ar(ΔAFB)

$= 2 \times$ ar(ΔDCB) …(i)

In Δs ADF and ECF.

$\angle AFD = \angle EFC$

        {vertically opposite angles}

$\angle ECF = \angle ADF$ {alternate angles}

$BC = CE = AD$

$\therefore \ \Delta ADF \cong \Delta ECF$ {by AAS congruency}

$\therefore$ $DF = CF$

ar(parallelogram $ABCD$) $= 2 \times$ ar(ΔDCB)

$= 2 \times 2 \times ($ar$(\Delta DFB))$

$= 2 \times 2 \times 3$

$= 12$ cm²

16.(A)

Here $DE = \sqrt{AD^2 - AE^2}$

$= \sqrt{5^2 - 4^2}$

$= 3$ cm

$\therefore DE = FC = 3$cm, and, $EF = 7$cm.

$\therefore$ ar$(ABCD) = \dfrac{1}{2} \times 4 \times (7 + 7 + 3 + 3)$

$= \dfrac{1}{2} \times 4 \times (20)$

$= 40$ cm²

17.(B)

ar$(\Delta AQE) = \dfrac{1}{2}$ ar (parallelogram $AQED$)

$= \dfrac{1}{2} \times \dfrac{1}{2}$ (ar(parallelogram $ABCD$))

$= \dfrac{1}{4} \times$ (ar(parallelogram $FECG$))

12 cm² $= \dfrac{1}{4} \times$ ar(parallelogram $FECG$)

$\therefore$ ar$(FECG) = 48$ cm²

$\Rightarrow$ ar$(FGQB) = \dfrac{1}{2}$ ar$(FECG) = \dfrac{48}{2} = 24$ cm²

18.(D)

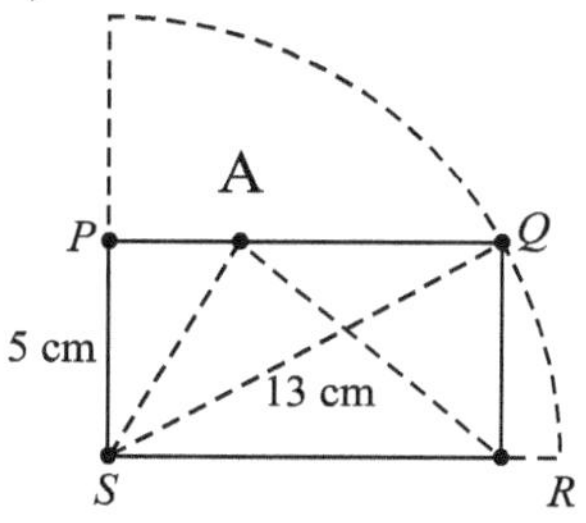

ar$(\Delta ARS) = \dfrac{1}{2}$ ar$(PQRS)$ ….(i)

$\Rightarrow$ $QS^2 = PS^2 + PQ^2$

$\Rightarrow$ $PQ = \sqrt{QS^2 - PS^2}$

$= \sqrt{(13)^2 - (5)^2} = 12$ cm.

$$\therefore\ \mathrm{ar}(\Delta ARS) = \frac{1}{2} \times 12 \times 5 = 30\ \mathrm{cm}^2$$

19. (C)

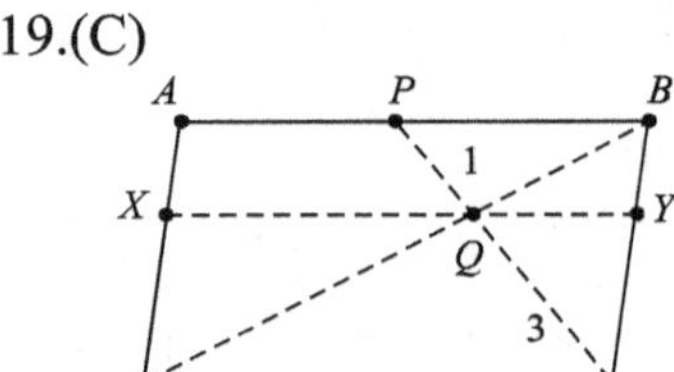

$$\mathrm{ar}(\Delta PQB) + \mathrm{ar}(\Delta DQC)$$
$$= \frac{1}{2}\ \mathrm{ar}(\text{parallelogram } ABCD)$$
$$\Rightarrow\ \mathrm{ar}(\text{parallelogram } ABCD)$$
$$= 2\ [\mathrm{ar}(\Delta PQB) + \mathrm{ar}(\Delta DQC)]$$

$$= 2\ [10\ \mathrm{cm}^2 + \mathrm{ar}(\Delta DQC)]$$
$$\mathrm{ar}(\Delta DQC) = (3 + 3 + 1) \times \mathrm{ar}\ (\Delta PQB)$$
$$= 7 \times 10 = 70\ \mathrm{cm}^2$$
$$\therefore\ \mathrm{ar}(\text{parallelogram } ABCD) = 2 \times 80$$
$$= 160\ \mathrm{cm}^2$$

20. (B)

$$\mathrm{ar}(\text{rhombus}) = \frac{1}{2} \times 8 \times 6 = 24\ \mathrm{cm}^2$$

$$\text{Length of side} = \sqrt{\left(\frac{8}{2}\right)^2 + \left(\frac{6}{2}\right)^2}$$
$$= \sqrt{(4)^2 + (3)^2} = 5$$

$$\therefore\ \text{Ratio} = 24 : 5$$

HOTS (ACHIEVERS SECTION)

21. (B)	22. (C)	23. (C)	24. (C)	25. (B)

21. (B)

$AB \parallel PQ$

$$\angle 1 = 180° - 132°$$
$$\angle 1 = 48°$$
$$\angle 2 = 148° - 48° = 100°$$
$$\angle PCD = 180° - 100° = 80°$$
$$x = 180° - 80 = 100°$$

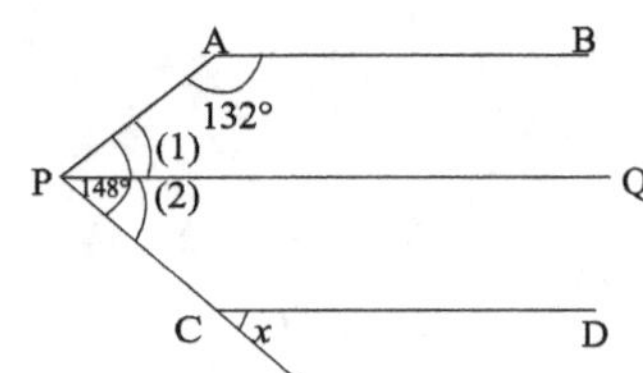

22. (C)

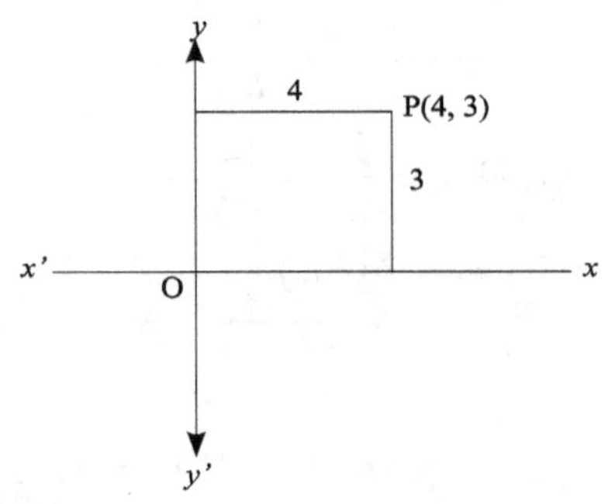

Perpendicular distance from Y- axis of the point $(4, 3) = 4$

23. (C)

Let r be the radius of the cylinder. Volume of spherical shell = volume of the cylinder

$$\frac{4}{3}\pi\ (5^3 - 3^3) = \pi r^2 \times \frac{8}{3}$$
$$125 - 27 = 2r^2$$
$$\frac{98}{2} = r^2 \Rightarrow r = 7\ cm$$
$$Diameter = 2 \times 7 = 14\ cm$$

24. (C)

$$\text{Diagonal of the cuboid} = \sqrt{l^2 + b^2 + h^2}$$
$$\sqrt{251} = \sqrt{l^2 + 9^2 + 7^2}$$
$$251 = l^2 + 81 + 49$$
$$l^2 = 251 - 130 = 121$$
$$l^2 = 11^2 \Rightarrow l = 11$$

OLYMPIAD WORKBOOK (IMO) CLASS— 9

Answer Key

1. (A)	2. (B)	3. (D)	4. (D)	5. (B)	6. (C)	7. (D)	8. (B)	9. (C)	10. (C)
11. (A)	12. (D)	13. (C)	14. (B)	15. (B)	16. (D)	17. (B)	18. (C)	19. (D)	20. (D)

1.(A)

In Δs ABM and ACM

$$AB = AC \qquad \text{(given)}$$
$$AM = AM \qquad \text{(common)}$$
$$OM \perp BC \qquad \text{(given)}$$
$$\text{so } \angle BAM = \angle CAM$$
$$\therefore \quad \Delta ABM \cong \Delta ACM \qquad \text{(by SAS)}$$
$$\therefore \quad BM = CM \qquad \text{(CPCT)}$$

2.(B)

$\because AD$ is the bisector of $\angle BAC$

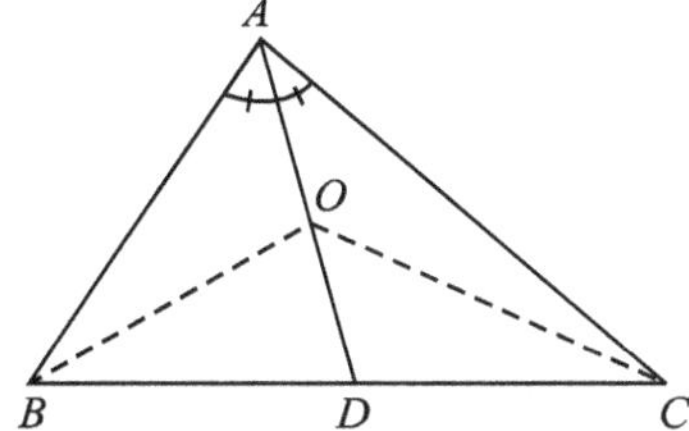

$\therefore AD$ is the $\perp$ bisector of BC.

$\because O$ is the circumcentre of ΔABC.

$$\therefore \quad AB = AC [\because \angle ABD = \angle ACB]$$
$$\text{(By using } \Delta ABD \cong \Delta ACD)$$

3.(D)

In ΔODE,

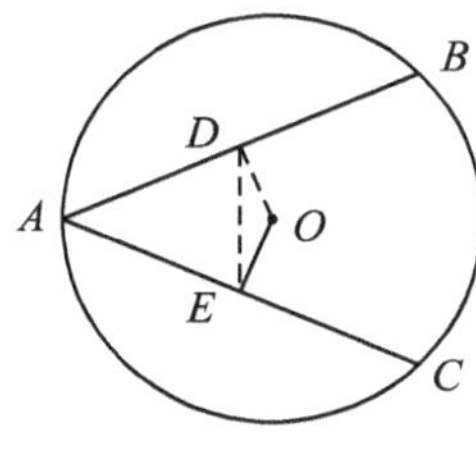

$$OD = OE$$
$$\therefore \quad \angle ODE = \angle OED \qquad \dots\dots\text{(i)}$$

Now,

$$\angle ODA = \angle OEA = 90° \qquad \dots\text{(ii)}$$

Subtracting eq.(i) from (ii), we get

$$\angle ODA - \angle ODE = \angle OEA - \angle OED$$
$$\angle ADE = \angle AED$$
$$\therefore \quad AD = AE \Rightarrow \Delta ADE \text{ is an isosceles triangle.}$$

9.(D)

$$\text{Reflex } \angle AOC = 360° - (110° + 120°)$$
$$= 130°$$
$$\therefore \angle ABC = \frac{\angle AOC}{2} = \frac{130°}{2} = 65°$$

5.(B)

$\because ABCD$ is a parallelogram,

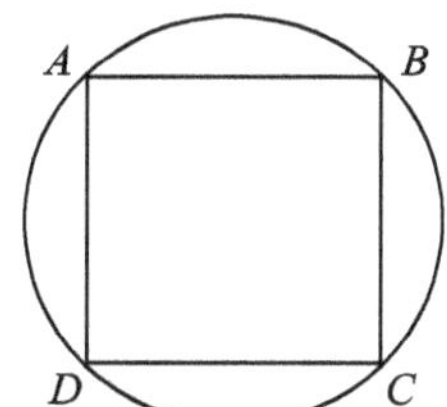

$\therefore \angle A = \angle C$ and $\angle B = \angle D$

Also,

$ABCD$ is a cyclic quadrilateral,

$\angle A + \angle C = 180°$ and $\angle B + \angle D = 180°$

$\Rightarrow \angle A = \angle B = \angle C = \angle D = 90°$

$\therefore ABCD$ is a rectangle.

6.(C)

$\angle BOC = 2 \times \angle BAC$ [Angle subtended at centre is double the angle subtended on the circle]

$$= 2 \times 30° = 60°$$

7.(D)

In ΔABC,

$$AB = AC,$$
$$\Rightarrow \angle ABC = \angle ACB = 40°$$

Also,

$$\angle ABC + \angle BAC + \angle ACB = 180°$$
$$\Rightarrow \angle BAC = 180° - 40° \times 2$$
$$= 100°$$
$$\therefore \ \angle BAC = \angle BDC = 100°$$
(angles in the same segment are equal).

8.(B)

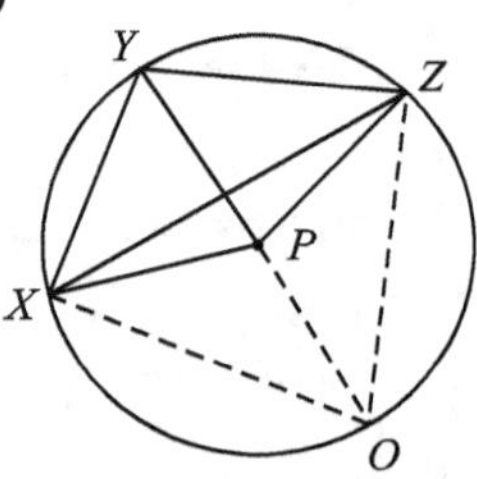

$$\angle XPY = 2\angle XOP.$$
$$\because \qquad \angle XOP = \angle XZY$$
(angles in the same segment)
$$\therefore \qquad \angle XPY = 2\,\angle XZY \qquad …(i)$$
Similarly,
$$\angle YPZ = 2\,\angle YXZ \qquad …(ii)$$
Using (i) and (ii)
$$\angle XPZ = 2\,(\angle XZY + \angle YXZ)$$
$$\Rightarrow \angle YXZ = \frac{\angle XPZ - 2\angle XYZ}{2} = \frac{120° - 2\times 35}{2}$$
$$= \frac{50°}{2} = 25°$$

9.(C)

$\because \angle APC$ is an exterior angle for $\triangle ABP$.
$$\therefore \qquad \angle ABP + \angle PAB = 90°$$
$$\Rightarrow \quad \angle ABP = 90° - 44° = 46°$$
$$\angle ADC = \angle ABP$$
(Angles in the same segment)
$$\therefore \qquad \angle ABP = 46°$$

10.(C)

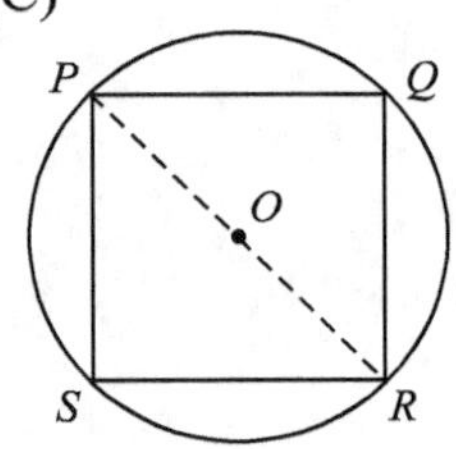

$$\angle P = \angle QPR + \angle SPR$$

$$= 64° + 31°$$
$$= 95°$$
$\because PQRS$ is a cyclic quadrilateral.
$$\therefore \ \angle P + \angle R = 180°$$
$$\Rightarrow \qquad \angle R = 180° - 95° = 85°$$

11.(A)

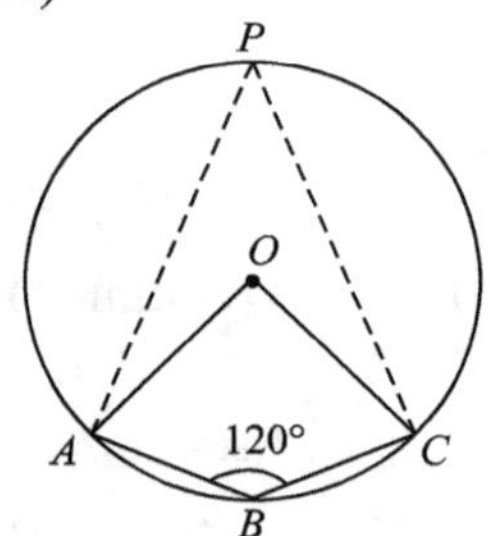

$\because ABCP$ is a cyclic quadrilateral.
$$\therefore \qquad \angle B + \angle P = 180°$$
$$\Rightarrow \angle P = 180° - 120° = 60°$$
$$\angle AOC = 2\,\angle P = 2 \times 60° = 120°$$
$$\therefore \quad \frac{\widehat{ABC}}{circumference} = \frac{120°}{360°} = 1:3$$

12.(D)

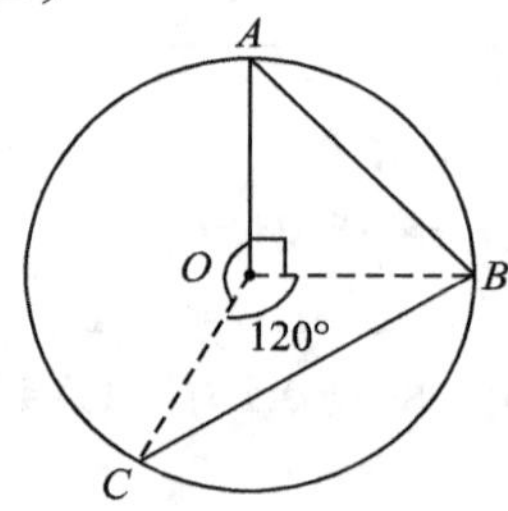

Reflex $\angle AOC = 360° - (90° + 120°) = 150°$
$$\therefore \angle ABC = \frac{reflex\angle AOC}{2} = \frac{150°}{2} = 75°$$

13.(C)

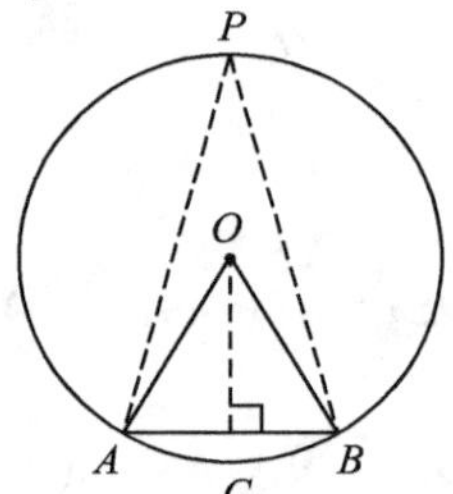

$$\because \qquad AB = r$$

OLYMPIAD WORKBOOK (IMO) CLASS— 9

And, $\qquad OA = OB = r$

$\therefore$ In ΔOAB,

$\qquad AB = OA = OB = r$

$\therefore \Delta OAB$ is an equilateral Δ.

$\therefore \angle OAB = \angle OBA = \angle AOB = 60°$

$\therefore \angle APB = \dfrac{60°}{2} = 30°$

$\because ACBP$ is a cyclic quadrilateral.

$\therefore \angle C + \angle P = 180°$

$\Rightarrow \qquad \angle C = 180° - 30°$

$\qquad\qquad = 150°$

14.(B)

In ΔACD,

$\angle ADC = 90°$ [$\because \angle ADC$ is angle in semicircle]

$\therefore AC^2 = DA^2 + DC^2$

$\Rightarrow (30)^2 = \left(10\sqrt{5}\right)^2 + DC^2$

$\Rightarrow DC^2 = 900 - 500$

$\Rightarrow DC = \sqrt{400} = 20$ cm.

15.(B)

In ΔOAB,

$\qquad OA = OB$

$\therefore \qquad \angle OAB = \angle OBA \qquad$ ...(i)

$\because \angle OBC + \angle OBA = \angle ABC$

$\Rightarrow \angle OBC + \angle BAO = \angle ABC$

$\Rightarrow \angle OBC + \angle BAC = 90°$

$\qquad\qquad$ [$\because \angle ABC$ is the angle in semicircle]

16.(D)

$\because ABCD$ is a cyclic quadrilateral.

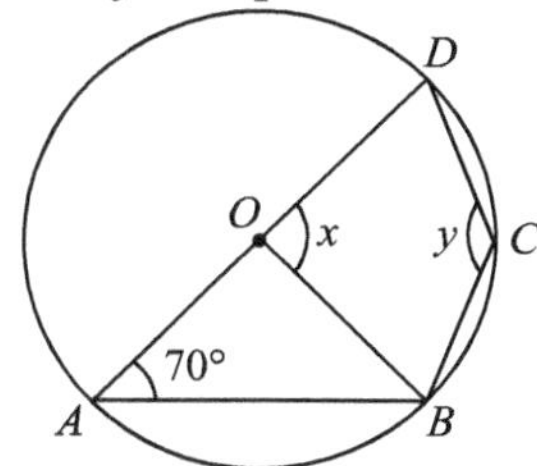

$\therefore \qquad \angle A + \angle C = 180°$

$\Rightarrow \qquad 70° + y = 180°$

$\Rightarrow \qquad\qquad y = 110°$

Now, in ΔOAB,

$\qquad OA = OB$

$\therefore \qquad \angle OAB = \angle OBA = 70°$

$\therefore \angle BOD$ is an exterior angle for ΔOAB.

$\therefore \angle OAB + \angle OBA = x$

$\Rightarrow \qquad\qquad x = 70° + 70°$

$\qquad\qquad\quad = 140°$

$\therefore \qquad x + y = 140° + 110°$

$\qquad\qquad\quad = 250°$

17.(B)

$\because AB = AC$

$\therefore \angle ABC = \angle ACB = 64°$

$\therefore \angle BAC = 180° - 64° \times 2 = 52°$

$\therefore ABCD$ is a cyclic quadrilateral.

$\therefore \quad \angle A + \angle E = 180°$

$\Rightarrow \qquad \angle E = 180° - 52°$

$\qquad\qquad\quad = 128°$

18.(C)

The sum of the angles in the 4 segments of a cyclic quadrilateral $= 6 \times 90° = 540°$

19.(D)

Let $\angle CAB = x$,

$\therefore \qquad \angle ACD = x \qquad\qquad$ (Alternate $\angle S$)

In ΔACD,

$\qquad \angle D = 180° - (30° + x)$

$\qquad\qquad = 150° - x$

$\because ABCD$ is a cyclic quadrilateral.

$\therefore \qquad \angle D + \angle B = 180°$

$\Rightarrow 150° - x + 65° = 180°$

$\Rightarrow \qquad\qquad x = 35°$

20.(D)

$\angle A + \angle C = 180°$

$\Rightarrow \qquad \angle C = 180° - 60° = 120°$

$\qquad \angle CBQ = 180 - \angle CBA$

$\qquad\qquad\quad = 180° - 80° = 100°$

$\because \angle DCB$ is an exterior angle for ΔBCQ

$\therefore \angle BQC + \angle CBQ = \angle DCB$

$\Rightarrow \angle BQC = 120° - \angle CBQ$

$\qquad\qquad = 120° - 100° = 20°$

| 21. (B) | 22. (A) | 23. (C) | 24. (D) | 25. (C) |

11. CONSTRUCTIONS

Answer Key

| 1. (C) | 2. (B) | 3. (B) | 4. (C) | 5. (A) | 6. (C) | 7. (C) | 8. (D) | 9. (A) | 10. (D) |
| 11. (B) | 12. (C) | 13. (B) | 14. (A) | 15. (B) | 16. (A) | 17. (B) | 18. (B) | 19. (A) | 20. (A) |

HOTS (ACHIEVERS SECTION)

| 21. (B) | 22. (B) | 23. (D) | 24. (C) | 25. (D) |

12. HERON'S FORMULA

Answer Key

| 1. (C) | 2. (C) | 3. (C) | 4. (B) | 5. (C) | 6. (A) | 7. (A) | 8. (B) | 9. (B) | 10. (D) |
| 11. (B) | 12. (B) | 13. (B) | 14. (C) | 15. (D) | 16. (C) | 17. (C) | 18. (C) | 19. (C) | 20. (A) |

1.(C)

Length of median of equilateral

$$\text{triangle} = \frac{\sqrt{3}a}{2} = 2\sqrt{3} \text{ cm.}$$

$$\Rightarrow \quad a = \frac{2\sqrt{3} \times 2}{\sqrt{3}} \text{ cm} = 4 \text{ cm.}$$

2.(C)

Length of median of equilateral triangle

$$= \frac{\sqrt{3}a}{2} = \sqrt{3}$$

$$\Rightarrow \quad a = 2 \text{ cm.}$$

∴ Area of triangle

$$= \frac{\sqrt{3}a^2}{4} = \frac{\sqrt{3} \times (2)^2}{4} = \sqrt{3} \text{ cm}^2$$

3.(C)

$$BC = \sqrt{AC^2 - AB^2}$$

$$= \sqrt{(13)^2 - (5)^2} = 12 \text{cm.}$$

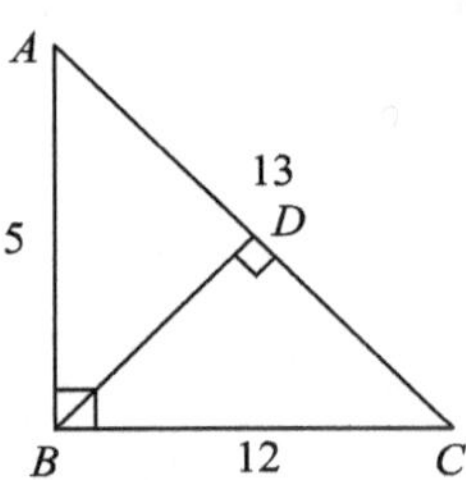

$$\text{Area of } \Delta = \frac{1}{2} \times AC \times BD = \frac{1}{2} \times AB \times BC$$

$$\Rightarrow AC \times BD = AB \times BC$$

$$\Rightarrow 13 \times BD = 5 \times 12$$

$$\Rightarrow \quad BD = \frac{60}{13} \text{ cm}$$

4.(B)

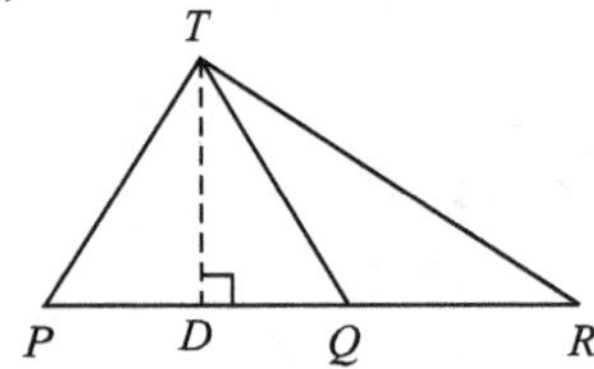

$$\frac{Ar(\Delta PQT)}{Ar(\Delta PRT)} = \frac{\frac{1}{2} \times TD \times PQ}{\frac{1}{2} \times TD \times PR}$$

$$\Rightarrow \quad \frac{Ar(\Delta PQT)}{40} = \frac{3}{3+2} = \frac{3}{5}$$

$\Rightarrow \quad$ ar $(\Delta PQT) = 24$ cm²

$\therefore$ area $(\Delta TQR) =$ ar $(\Delta PRT) -$ ar (ΔPQT)

$$= 40 - 24 = 16 \text{cm}^2$$

5.(C)

In $\Delta DOC,$

$$OD^2 + OC^2 = DC^2$$

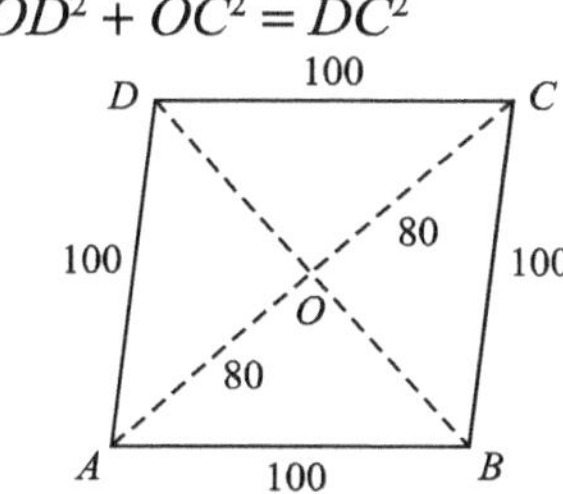

$$\Rightarrow OD = \sqrt{DC^2 - OC^2}$$

$$= \sqrt{(100)^2 - (80)^2} = 60 \text{ cm.}$$

$\therefore \quad DB = 2 \times OD = 2 \times 60 = 120$ cm.

$$\text{Area of rhombus} = \frac{1}{2} \times d_1 \times d_2 = \frac{1}{2} \times 160 \times 120$$

$$= 9600 \text{ cm}^2$$

6.(A)

$$BD = 2 \times OD = 2 \times 60 = 120 \text{ cm}$$

7.(A)

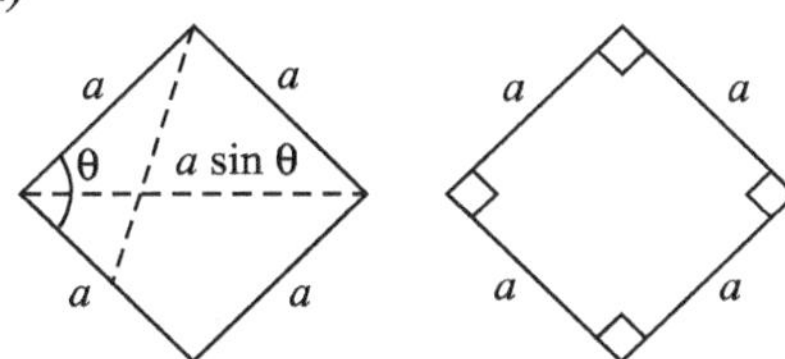

Area of square $= a^2$

Area of rhombus $= a^2 \sin \theta$

$\because \qquad \sin \theta < 1$

$\therefore \qquad a^2 > a^2 \sin \theta$

ar (square) > ar (rhombus)

$\Rightarrow \qquad S > R$

8.(B)

Perimeter of square

$= $ Perimeter of equilateral $\Delta = x.$

$\therefore$ length of side of square $= \dfrac{x}{4}$

Length of side of equilateral $\Delta = \dfrac{x}{3}$

$$A_1 = \left(\frac{x}{4}\right)^2, \quad A_2 = \frac{\sqrt{3}\left(\frac{x}{3}\right)^2}{4} = \frac{\sqrt{3}x^2}{36}$$

Clearly, $A_1 > A_2$

9.(B)

Area of square $ABCD = \dfrac{1}{2} \times AC \times BD$

$$= \frac{1}{2} \times 32 \times 32$$

$$= 16 \times 32 \text{ cm}^2$$

$$= 512 \text{ cm}^2$$

Here $s = \dfrac{6+6+8}{2} = \dfrac{20}{2} = 10$

$\therefore$ Area (ΔDEF)

$$= \sqrt{\left(\frac{6+6+8}{2}\right)(10-6)(10-6)(10-8)}$$

$$= \sqrt{10 \times 4 \times 4 \times 2}$$

$$= 8\sqrt{5} \text{ cm}^2 = 17.84 \text{ cm}^2$$

$\therefore$ Total area $= 512 + 17.84 = 529.84$ cm²

10.(D)

$AE = x,$ FB $= (17 - x)$ cm.

In ΔAED and ΔCFB

$$CF^2 = DE^2$$

$\Rightarrow \quad (26)^2 - (17-x)^2 = (25)^2 - (x)^2$

$\Rightarrow \quad (26)^2 - (25)^2 = (17-x)^2 - (x)^2$

$\Rightarrow (26-25)(26+25) = (17-x+x)$
$$(17-x-x)$$

$\Rightarrow \quad 51 = 17(17-2x)$

$\Rightarrow \quad 17 - 2x = 3$

$\Rightarrow \quad 2x = 14 \Rightarrow x = 7 \text{cm}.$

$\Rightarrow CF = DE = \sqrt{(25)^2 - (7)^2} = 24 \text{cm}.$

$\therefore \text{ area} = \dfrac{1}{2} \times (60+77) \times 24 \text{ cm}^2$

$\qquad = 137 \times 12 \text{ cm}^2 = 1644 \text{ cm}^2$

11.(B)

Area of $\triangle ACD$ = area of $\triangle ACB$

$= \dfrac{1}{2}$ (Area of ||gm $ABCD$)

$\Rightarrow$ area of $\triangle ACD = \sqrt{s(s-a)(s-b)(s-c)}$

$$\left\{ s = \frac{34+20+42}{2} = 48 \text{ cm} \right\}$$

$= \sqrt{48 \times (48-34) \times (48-20) \times (48-42)}$

$= \sqrt{48 \times 14 \times 28 \times 6}$

$= 4 \times 6 \times 7 \times 2$

$= 4 \times 84 = 336 \text{ cm}^2$

$\therefore$ area of ||gm $= 2 \times ar(\triangle ACD)$

$\qquad = 2 \times 336 \text{ cm}^2$

$\qquad = 672 \text{ cm}^2$

12.(B)

Side of rhombus $= \dfrac{80}{4} = 20 \text{ m}.$

$\therefore$ Length of other diagonal

$= 2 \times \sqrt{(20)^2 - \left(\dfrac{24}{2}\right)^2}$

$= 2 \times \sqrt{400 - 144}$

$= 2 \times 16 = 32 \text{ m}.$

$\therefore \text{Area} = \dfrac{1}{2} \times 32 \times 24$

$\qquad = 16 \times 24 \text{ m}^2 = 384 \text{ m}^2$

13.(B)

In $\triangle AOB$,

$$AB = \sqrt{OB^2 + OA^2}$$

$$= \sqrt{(16)^2 + (12)^2}$$

$$= 20 \text{ cm}.$$

$\therefore ar(\triangle AOB) = \dfrac{1}{2} \times 12 \times 16 = 96 \text{ cm}^2$

For $\triangle ABC$,

$$s = \frac{52+48+20}{2} = 60 \text{ cm}.$$

$\therefore ar(\triangle ABC) = \sqrt{s(s-a)(s-b)(s-c)}$

$= \sqrt{60 \times (60-52)(60-48)(60-20)}$

$= \sqrt{60 \times 8 \times 12 \times 40}$

$= 480 \text{ cm}^2$

$\therefore$ Area of shaded region

$\qquad = 480 - 96$

$\qquad = 384 \text{ cm}^2$

14.(C)

$$BD = \sqrt{AD^2 + AB^2}$$

$$= \sqrt{(9)^2 + (40)^2} = 41 \text{ m}$$

$\therefore$ For $\triangle DBC$,

$$s = \frac{28+15+41}{2} = 42 \text{ m}$$

$\therefore ar(\triangle DBC) = \sqrt{s(s-a)(s-b)(s-c)}$

$= \sqrt{42 \times (42-28) \times (42-41) \times (42-15)}$

$= \sqrt{42 \times 14 \times 1 \times 27}$

$= 14 \times 3 \times 3$

$= 126 \text{ m}^2$

$$\text{Ar}(\Delta ABD) = \frac{1}{2} \times 9 \times 40$$

$$= 180 \text{ m}^2$$

$\therefore$ Total area $= (126 + 180)$ m^2

$$= 306 \text{ m}^2$$

15.(D)

Length of equilateral triangle $= \dfrac{x}{3}$ cm

Length of side of square $= \dfrac{x}{4}$ cm.

Length of side of square

$$= \frac{\text{length of diagonal}}{\sqrt{2}}$$

$$= 12 \text{ cm.}$$

$\therefore$ area of $\Delta = \dfrac{\sqrt{3}}{4}\left(\dfrac{x}{3}\right)^2 = \dfrac{\sqrt{3}}{4}\times\left(\dfrac{48}{3}\right)^2$

$$= \frac{\sqrt{3}}{4}\times 16 \times 16 = 64\sqrt{3} \text{ cm}^2$$

16.(C)

Let the length of the third side be x.

$\therefore s = \dfrac{11+6+x}{2} = \dfrac{17+x}{2}$, and,

Area =

$$20\sqrt{2} = \sqrt{\left(\frac{17+x}{2}\right)\left(\frac{x-5}{2}\right)\left(\frac{x+5}{2}\right)\left(\frac{17-x}{2}\right)}$$

$$\Rightarrow \quad 800 = \frac{1}{16}\,(x^2 - 25)\,(289 - x^2)$$

$$\Rightarrow 800 \times 16 = (x^2 - 25)\,(289 - x^2)$$

$$\Rightarrow \quad x = 15\text{m.}$$

$\therefore$ cost of fencing $= (11 + 6 + 15) \times 10$

$$= ₹\ 320$$

17.(C)

Let the length of third side be x.

$$\therefore \quad s = \frac{54+x}{2} = 27 + \frac{x}{2}$$

Area

$$= \sqrt{\left(27+\frac{x}{2}\right)\left(27+\frac{x}{2}-26\right)\left(27+\frac{x}{2}-28\right)\left(27-\frac{x}{2}\right)}$$

$$= \sqrt{\left(729 - \frac{x^2}{4}\right)\left(\frac{x^2}{4}-1\right)}$$

$$= 336 \text{ cm}^2$$

$$\Rightarrow x = 30 \text{ cm.}$$

$\therefore$ Third side $= 30$ cm.

18.(C)

In ΔAED,

$$DE = \sqrt{AD^2 - AE^2} = \sqrt{(15)^2 - (6)^2}$$

$$= \sqrt{189} \text{ cm}$$

$$= 3\sqrt{21} \text{ cm.}$$

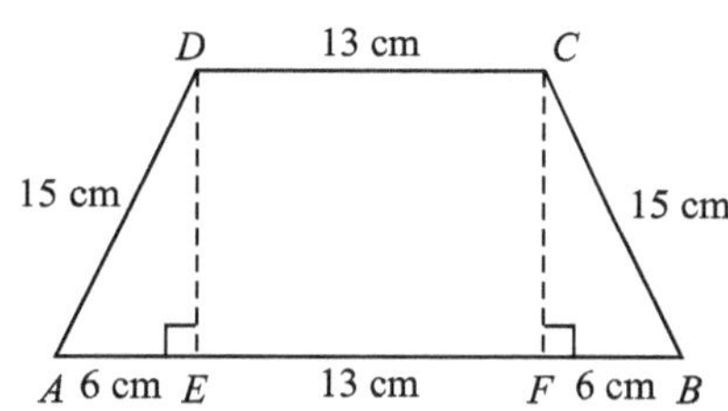

$\therefore$ area $= \dfrac{1}{2} \times$ (sum of $\parallel$ sides) $\times$ DE

$$= \frac{1}{2} \times (13 + 25) \times 3\sqrt{21}$$

$$= 19 \times 3\sqrt{21} = 57\sqrt{21} \text{ cm}^2$$

19.(C)

Lengths of sides of triangle

$$= 3\left(\frac{144}{3+4+5}\right),\left(\frac{144}{3+4+5}\right)4,\left(\frac{144}{3+4+5}\right)5$$

$$= 36,\ 48,\ 60$$

$\therefore$ Area

$$= \sqrt{72 \times (72-36) \times (72-48) \times (72-60)}$$

$$= \sqrt{72 \times 36 \times 24 \times 12}$$

$$= 12 \times 12 \times 3 \times 2$$

$$= 144 \times 6 \ cm^2$$

$\therefore$ Height corresponding to the longest side

$$= \frac{2 \times 144 \times 6}{60} = 28.8 \ cm$$

20.(A)

The two parts of ||gm are congruent.

$\therefore$ they have equal area.

<table><tr><td colspan="5" align="center">HOTS (ACHIEVERS SECTION)</td></tr><tr><td>21. (C)</td><td>22. (D)</td><td>23. (D)</td><td>24. (B)</td><td>25. (A)</td></tr></table>

21. (C)

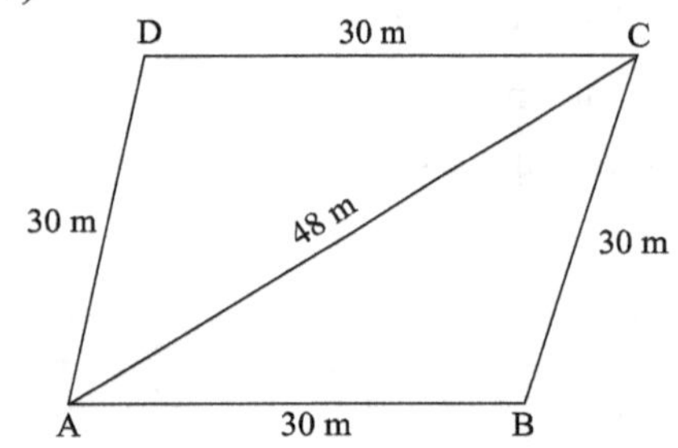

$\triangle ABC \cong \triangle ADC$

Area $\triangle ABC$ = area $\triangle ADC$

For $\triangle ABC$,

$$5 = \frac{48+30+30}{2} = 54$$

Area $\triangle ABC =$

$$\sqrt{54(54-48)(54-30)(54-30)} = 432 \, m^2$$

Area of rhombus ABCD = $2 \times 432 = 864 \ m^2$

Area of grass field for each cow = $\dfrac{864}{18}$

$$= 48 \ m^2$$

22. (B)

Let r be the radius of the base of the cone and h be the height.

r = radius of hemisphere

Volume of cone = volume of hemisphere

$$\frac{1}{3} \pi r^2 h = \frac{2}{3} \pi r^3$$

$$h = 2r$$

$$h:r = \frac{2r}{r} = 2:1$$

13. SURFACE AREA AND VOLUME

Answer Key

1. (B)	2. (A)	3. (B)	4. (A)	5. (B)	6. (A)	7. (A)	8. (B)	9. (C)	10. (C)
11. (B)	12. (A)	13. (D)	14. (C)	15. (A)	16. (B)	17. (A)	18. (B)	19. (B)	20. (D)

1.(B)

Volume of the water accumulated in the reservoir in 18 hours = $(120 \times 75 \times 2.4) \ m^3$

Let speed of water = v km/hour.

The width of cuboid = $b = \dfrac{20}{100} = \dfrac{1}{5} m$

Height = $h = \dfrac{20}{100} = \dfrac{1}{5} m$

Length of water cuboid formed in 18 hours

$$= 18\,v \text{ km} = 18 \times 1000\,v \text{ m}$$
$$= 18000\,v \text{ m}$$

Volume of the water accumulated in reservoir in 18 hours

$$= 18000v \times \frac{1}{5} \times \frac{1}{5} = 720\,v \text{ m}^3$$

$$\Rightarrow 720v = 120 \times 75 \times 2.4$$

$$\Rightarrow \quad v = \frac{70°}{2} = 30 \text{ km/hour}$$

2.(A)

Curved surface area of the roller $= 2\pi r h$

$$= 2 \times \frac{22}{7} \times 150 \times \frac{84}{2}$$

$$= 44 \times 150 \times 6$$

Area covered by roller in 100 revolutions

$$= \frac{44 \times 150 \times 6 \times 100}{100 \times 100} \text{ m}^2$$

Cost of leveling the playground

$$= \frac{44 \times 150 \times 6}{100} \times \frac{50}{100} = 11 \times 6 \times 3$$

$$= ₹\, 198$$

3.(B)

Let r be the inner radius of the cylinder.

$$r = 12 \text{cm}$$

Outer radius $= R = 12 + 2 = 14$cm

$$h = 35 \text{cm}$$

Volume of wood $= \pi\,(R^2 - r^2)\,h$

$$= \frac{22}{7}\,(14^2 - 12^2)\,35$$

$$= \frac{22}{7} \times 2 \times 26 \times 35$$

$$= 44 \times 130 = 5720 \text{ cm}^3$$

4.(A)

Volume of the cylinder $= 448\pi$

$$\Rightarrow \qquad \pi r^2 h = 448\pi$$

$$\Rightarrow \qquad r^2 h = 448$$

$$\Rightarrow \qquad r^2 = \frac{448}{h} = \frac{448}{7} = 64$$

$$\Rightarrow \qquad r = 8 \text{ cm}$$

Lateral surface area $= 2\pi r h$

$$= 2 \times \frac{22}{7} \times 8 \times 7$$

$$= 22 \times 16 = 352 \text{ cm}^2$$

5.(B)

Curved surface area

$$= \frac{1}{3} \times \text{total surface area}$$

$$= \frac{1}{3} \times 462 = 154$$

$$\Rightarrow \qquad 2\pi r h = 154 \qquad\qquad \dots(1)$$

Total surface area $= 462$

$$\Rightarrow \quad 2\pi r h + 2\pi r^2 = 462$$

$$\Rightarrow \quad 154 + 2\pi r^2 = 462$$

$$\Rightarrow \qquad 2\pi r^2 = 308$$

$$\Rightarrow \qquad r^2 = \frac{308 \times 7}{2 \times 22} = 49$$

$$\Rightarrow \qquad r = 7 \text{ cm}$$

Putting this value in (i), we get

$$2\pi r h = 154$$

$$h = \frac{154 \times 7}{2 \times 22 \times 7} = \frac{7}{2} \text{ cm}$$

$\therefore$ Volume of cylinder $= \pi r^2 h = \dfrac{22}{7} \times 7^2 \times \dfrac{7}{2}$

$$= 11 \times 49 = 539 \text{ cm}^3$$

6.(A)

Let the number of glasses be n.

$\therefore$ Total volume in the vessel

$$= \text{volume of juice in glasses}$$

$$\Rightarrow \qquad \pi R^2 H = n \times \pi r^2 h$$

$$\Rightarrow \qquad R^2 H = n r^2 h$$

$$\Rightarrow \quad (15)^2 \times 32 = n \times (3)^2 \times 8$$

$$\Rightarrow \qquad n = 5 \times 5 \times 4 = 100$$

7.(A)

$h = 10.5$ m.

Let the area of each circular face be A m²

∴ According to question,

$$3(A + A) = 2 \times 2\pi rh$$
$$\Rightarrow \quad 3 \times 2\pi r^2 = 4\pi rh$$
$$\Rightarrow \quad 6\pi r^2 = 4\pi rh$$
$$\Rightarrow \quad 3r = 2h$$
$$\Rightarrow r = \frac{2}{3}h = \frac{2}{3} \times 10.5\text{m} = 7 \text{ m}$$

∴ Volume of the cylinder $= \pi r^2 h$

$$= \frac{22}{7} \times 7 \times 7 \times 10.5 \text{ m}^3$$
$$= 154 \times 10.5\text{m}^3 = 1617 \text{ m}^3$$

8.(B)

$$l = \sqrt{r^2 + h^2} = \sqrt{7^2 + 24^2} = \sqrt{49 + 576}$$
$$= \sqrt{625} = 25 \text{ m}$$

Curved surface area $= \pi rl = \dfrac{22}{7} \times 7 \times 25$

$= 550 \text{ m}^2$

Length of canvas used

$$= \frac{\text{Area}}{\text{Width}} = \frac{550}{5} = 110 \text{ m}$$

9.(C)

Radius of sphere = 3 cm.

Volume of sphere $= \dfrac{4}{3}\pi r^3$

$$= \frac{4}{3} \times \frac{22}{7} \times 3 \times 3 \times 3$$
$$= \frac{88 \times 9}{7}$$

Radius of cylindrical wire $= \dfrac{0.2}{2} = 0.1$ cm

Volume of wire $= \pi r^2 h$

$$= \frac{22}{7} \times (0.1)^2 \times h$$

$$= \frac{22}{7} \times \frac{1}{10} \times \frac{1}{10} \times h = \frac{88 \times 9}{7}$$
$$\Rightarrow \quad h = \frac{88 \times 9 \times 10 \times 10}{22} = 3600 \text{ cm}$$
$$\Rightarrow \quad h = \frac{3600}{100} = 36 \text{ m}$$

10.(C)

Let the diameter of earth be x m.

∴ Diameter of moon $= \dfrac{x}{4}$ m

$$\frac{\text{volume of moon}}{\text{volume of earth}} = \frac{\dfrac{4}{3}\pi\left(\dfrac{x}{4}\right)^3}{\dfrac{4}{3}\pi x^3} = \left(\frac{1}{4}\right)^3 = \frac{1}{64}$$

11.(B)

$$\text{No. of planks} = \frac{\text{volume of wooden block}}{\text{volume of each plank}}$$
$$= \frac{600 \times 15 \times 40}{200 \times 2.5 \times 4} = 180$$

12.(A)

Volume of water in the tank

$$= 150 \times 100 \times 3 = 45000 \text{ m}^3$$

Area of cross − section of the pipe

$$= 2\text{dm} \times 1.5\text{dm}$$
$$= \frac{2}{10} \times \frac{1.5}{10} = \frac{3}{100} \text{ m}^2$$

Let the time taken be t hours.

Volume of water that flows into the tank in t hours.

$$= \frac{3}{100} \times 15 \text{ km/}h \times t \text{ m}^3$$
$$= \frac{3}{100} \times 15 \times 1000 \times t \text{ m}^3$$
$$= 450\, t \text{ m}^3$$
$$\Rightarrow 450t = 45000$$

$$\Rightarrow \quad t = \frac{45000}{450} = 100 \text{ hours}$$

13.(D)

Length of diagonal of a cube

$$= \sqrt{3}\,(Edge)$$

$$= \sqrt{3} \times 20 \text{cm}$$

$$= 1.732 \times 20 \text{cm}$$

$$= 34.64 \text{ cm}$$

14.(C)

Volume of water

$$= 2 \times 10000 \times \frac{5}{100} = 1000 \text{ m}^3$$

15.(A)

Total surface area of a cube = 486

$$\Rightarrow \quad 6a^2 = 486$$

$$\Rightarrow \quad a^2 = 81$$

$$\Rightarrow \quad a = 9 \text{cm}$$

Lateral surface area of cube $= 4a^2$

$$= 4 \times 81$$

$$= 324 \text{ cm}^2$$

16.(B)

Curved surface area of pillar = 264

$$\Rightarrow \quad 2\pi rh = 264$$

Volume of pillar = 396

$$\Rightarrow \quad \pi r^2 h = 396$$

$$\therefore \quad \frac{\pi r^2 h}{2\pi rh} = \frac{396}{264}$$

$$r = \frac{2 \times 396}{264} = 3 \text{ m}$$

$$\therefore \quad 2\pi rh = 264$$

Now

$$h = \frac{264}{2\pi r}$$

$$= \frac{264 \times 7}{2 \times 22 \times 3} = 14 \text{ m}$$

17.(A)

Radius of coin $= \dfrac{1.5}{2} = 0.75$ cm

Thickness of coin = 0.2 cm

Volume of each coin $= \pi r^2 h$

$$= \pi \times 0.75 \times 0.75 \times 0.2$$

Radius of new cylinder $= \dfrac{4.5}{2} = 2.25$ cm

Height of new cylinder = 5 cm

Volume of new cylinder $= \pi\,(2.25)^2 \times 5$

$$\text{No. of coins} = \frac{\text{volume of new cylinder}}{\text{volume of each coin}}$$

$$= \frac{\pi \times 2.25 \times 2.25 \times 5}{\pi \times 0.75 \times 0.75 \times 0.2}$$

$$= \frac{225 \times 225 \times 5 \times 10}{75 \times 75 \times 2}$$

$$= 3 \times 3 \times 5 \times 5$$

$$= 225$$

18.(B)

Volume of the cone = 1232

$$\Rightarrow \quad \frac{1}{3}\pi r^2 h = 1232$$

$$\Rightarrow \quad \frac{1}{3} \times \frac{22}{7} \times \left(\frac{14}{2}\right)^2 \times h = 1232$$

$$\Rightarrow \quad h = \frac{1232 \times 3 \times 7}{22 \times 7 \times 7}$$

$$= 24 \text{ cm}$$

Slant height $= l$

$$= \sqrt{h^2 + r^2} = \sqrt{576 + 49} = \sqrt{625}$$

$$l = 25 \text{cm}$$

19.(B)

Length of longest rod = length of diagonal

$$= \sqrt{l^2 + b^2 + h^2}$$

$$= \sqrt{(10)^2 + (10)^2 + (5)^2}$$

$$= \sqrt{225} = 15 \text{m}$$

20.(D)

Let radius be r and height be h.

New radius be $\dfrac{r}{3}$ and height H.

$\therefore \qquad \pi r^2 h = \pi\left(\dfrac{r}{3}\right)^2 H$

$\Rightarrow \qquad r^2 h = \dfrac{r^2 H}{9}$

$\Rightarrow \qquad H = 9h$

Length will become 9 times.

HOTS (ACHIEVERS SECTION)

21. (B)	22. (D)	23. (B)	24. (A)	25. (C)

21. (B)

Let $BD : DC = 3x : 2x$

Area of $\triangle ABC$

$= \dfrac{1}{2} \times (3x + 2x) \times h = 40 \ cm^2$

$\Rightarrow = 5x \times h = 80$

$\Rightarrow = h = \dfrac{80}{5x}$

$\Rightarrow = h = \dfrac{16}{x}$

Area of $\triangle ABD$

$= \dfrac{1}{2} \times \dfrac{16}{x} \times 3x = 24 \ cm^2$

Area of ADC $= (40 - 24) \ cm^2 = 16 \ cm^2$

22. (B)

Curved surface area of cylinder

$= \dfrac{1}{3} \times$ total surface area of cylinder

$2\pi rh = \dfrac{1}{3} \times 462$

$2\pi rh = 154 \ \dots\dots\dots\dots\dots\dots (1)$

Total surface area $= 462$

$2\pi rh + 2\pi r^2 = 462$

$154 + 2\pi r^2 = 462 \Rightarrow 2\pi r^2 = 462 - 154$

$r^2 = \dfrac{308 \times 7}{2 \times 22} = 49$

$r = 7 \ cm$

$2\pi rh = 154 \Rightarrow h = \dfrac{154 \times 7}{2 \times 22 \times 7} = \dfrac{7}{2}$

Volume of cylinder $= \pi r^2 h$

$= \dfrac{22}{7} \times 7^2 \times \dfrac{7}{2}$

$= 11 \times 49 = 539 \ cm^3$

23. (A)

Surface area of sphere $= 5544$

$4\pi r^2 = 5544 \ \Rightarrow r^2 = \dfrac{5544 \times 7}{4 \times 22} = 441$

$r = 21$

Volume of the sphere $= \dfrac{4}{3}\pi r^3$

$= \dfrac{4}{3} \times \dfrac{22}{7} \times 21^3$

$= \dfrac{4}{3} \times \dfrac{22}{7} \times 21 \times 21 \times 21$

$= 88 \times 441 = 38808 \ cm^3$

24. (C)

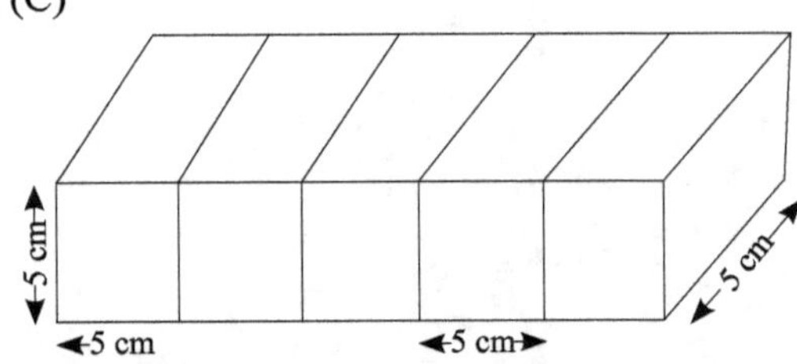

Length of cuboid $= 5 \times 5 = 25$ cm

Breadth $= 5$ cm; height $= 5$ cm

Surface area of cuboid $= 2(lb + bh + lh)$

$= 2(25 \times 5 + 5 \times 5 + 25 \times 5) = 2 \ (125 + 25 + 125)$

$= 2 \times 275 = 550 \ cm^2$

OLYMPIAD WORKBOOK (IMO) CLASS— 9

14. STATISTICS

Answer Key

1. (B)	2. (B)	3. (B)	4. (B)	5. (A)	6. (C)	7. (A)	8. (A)	9. (C)	10. (A)
11. (C)	12. (C)	13. (A)	14. (B)	15. (C)	16. (B)	17. (D)	18. (C)	19. (A)	20. (B)

1.(B)

Tallys are usually marked in a bunch of 5.

2.(B)

$$m = \frac{l+u}{2} \Rightarrow 2\,m = l+u \Rightarrow 4 = 2\,m - l$$

3.(B)

$$\text{Upper limit} = \text{mid value} + \frac{\text{class size}}{2}$$

$$47 = 41 + \frac{\text{class size}}{2}$$

$$\therefore \text{ Class size} = (47 - 41) \times 2$$

$$= 12$$

4.(B)

$$\text{Lower limit} = \text{mid-value} - \frac{\text{class size}}{2}$$

$$= 14 - \frac{2}{2} = 13$$

5.(A)

X-axis represents class interval,

Y-axis represents frequency.

6.(C)

Mid-value is always considered for frequency polygon construction.

7.(A)

The lower limit of the concerned class interval is used for 'more than' type of ogive.

8.(A)

Ogives represent cumulative frequency.

9.(C)

$\because$ the class interval $30 - 40$ has highest peak.

$\therefore$ it has highest frequency.

10.(A)

Total number of students

$$= 4 + 10 + 16 + 20 + 16$$

$$= 66$$

11.(C)

$$\frac{x_1 + x_2 + x_3 + x_4 ..... + x_n}{n} = \overline{X}$$

$$\Rightarrow x_1 + x_2 + x_3 + x_4 .... + x_n = n\,\overline{X}$$

$$\Rightarrow x_1 + x_2 + x_3 ...... + x_n$$

$$= \overline{X} + \overline{X} + \overline{X} ...... n \text{ times}$$

$$\Rightarrow (x_1 - \overline{X}) + (x_2 - \overline{X}) + (x_3 - \overline{X})$$

$$..... + (x_n - \overline{X}) = 0$$

12.(C)

Given $\dfrac{x_1 + x_2 + x_3 + x_4 ..... + x_n}{n} = \overline{X}$

$\Rightarrow$ if 5 is added to every number, then,

$$\frac{(x_1 + 5) + (x_2 + 5) + (x_3 + 5) .... + (x_n + 5)}{n}$$

$$= \frac{x_1 + x_2 + x_3 + x_4 ..... + x_n + 5n}{n} = \overline{X} + 5$$

13.(A)

Given $\dfrac{x_1 + x_2 + x_3 + x_4 ..... + x_n}{n} = \overline{X}$

$$\Rightarrow \frac{kx_1 + kx_2 + kx_3 + ... + kx_n}{n}$$

$$= k\frac{(x_1 + x_2 ..... + x_n)}{n} = k\overline{X}$$

14.(B)

$$\frac{x_1 + x_2 + x_3 \ldots\ldots + x_{10}}{10} = 16$$

$$\Rightarrow \quad x_1 + x_2 \ldots\ldots + x_{10} = 160 \quad \ldots\ldots \text{(i)}$$

Let x_2 and x_3 are removed, then,

$$\frac{x_1 + x_4 \ldots\ldots + x_{10}}{8} = 18$$

$$\Rightarrow \quad x_1 + x_4 + \ldots\ldots + x_{10} = 144 \quad \ldots\ldots\text{(ii)}$$

Now, eq. (i) $-$ eq (ii)

$$x_2 + x_3 = 160 - 144 = 16$$

15.(C)

$$\sum_{i=1}^{n} x_i - 2\sum_{i=1}^{n} 1 = \sum_{i=1}^{n} x_i - 2n = 110 \quad \ldots\text{(i)}$$

$$\sum_{i=1}^{n} x_i - 5\sum_{i=1}^{n} 1 = \sum_{i=1}^{n} x_i - 5n = 20 \quad \ldots\text{(ii)}$$

Subtracting eq (ii) from eq (i), we have,

$$3n = 90 \Rightarrow n = 30$$

$$\therefore \text{mean} = \frac{\sum\limits_{i=1}^{n} x_i}{n} = \frac{110 + 2n}{n} = \frac{110 + 60}{30} = \frac{17}{3}$$

16.(B)

$$\sum_{i=1}^{n}(x_i - 50) = -10 \Rightarrow \sum_{i=1}^{n} x_i - 50n = -10$$

$$\ldots\text{(i)}$$

$$\sum_{i=1}^{n}(x_i - 46) = 70 \Rightarrow \sum_{i=1}^{n} x_i - 46n = 70$$

$$\ldots\text{(ii)}$$

Subtracting eq. (i), from eq. (ii),

$$-46n - (-50\,n) = 70 - (-10)$$

$$\Rightarrow \qquad 4n = 80$$

$$\Rightarrow \qquad n = 20$$

17.(D)

Sum of marks of 10 students $= 10 \times 43$

$$= 430$$

Correct summation of marks

$$= (430 - 40) + 30$$

$$= 420$$

$$\therefore \text{correct mean} = \frac{420}{10} = 42$$

18.(C)

$$\text{Mean} = \frac{\sum\limits_{i=1}^{5} f_i x_i}{\sum\limits_{i=1}^{n} f_i}$$

$$= \frac{10 \times 7 + 30 \times 8 + 50 \times 10 + 70 \times 15 + 89 \times 10}{7 + 8 + 10 + 15 + 10}$$

$$= \frac{70 + 240 + 500 + 1050 + 890}{50} = 55$$

19.(A)

$$\text{Mean} = \frac{\sum f_i x_i}{\sum f_i}$$

$$\Rightarrow 20 = \frac{15 \times 2 + 17 \times 3 + 19 \times 4 + 5p(20 + p) + 23 \times 6}{2 + 3 + 4 + 5p + 6}$$

$$\Rightarrow 20\,(15 + 5p) = 30 + 51 + 76 + 100p + 5p^2 + 138$$

$$\Rightarrow 300 + 100p = 295 + 100p + 5p^2$$

$$\Rightarrow \qquad 5p^2 = 5$$

$$\Rightarrow \qquad p = 1$$

20.(B)

$$f_1 + f_2 + 17 + 32 + 19 = 120$$

$$\Rightarrow \qquad f_1 + f_2 = 52 \qquad \ldots\text{(i)}$$

Mean

$$= \frac{10 \times 17 + 30f_1 + 70f_2 + 50 \times 32 + 90 \times 19}{120}$$

$$\Rightarrow 50 \times 120 = 170 + 1600 + 1710 + 30f_1 + 70f_2$$

$$\Rightarrow \qquad 30f_1 + 70f_2 = 2520$$

$$\Rightarrow \qquad 3f_1 + 7f_2 = 252 \qquad \ldots\ldots\text{(ii)}$$

From eq (i) and eq (ii).

$$f_1 = 28, f_2 = 24$$

21. (B)	22. (D)	23. (A)	24. (B)	25. (B)

21. (B)

$$\frac{x_1 + x_2 + \ldots\ldots\ldots\ldots x_{16}}{16} = 8$$

$$x_1 + x_2 + x_3 \ldots\ldots\ldots\ldots + x_{16} = 16 \times 8 = 128$$

New Mean =

$$\frac{(x_1 + 2) + (x_2 + 2) + \ldots\ldots\ldots + (x_{16} + 2)}{16}$$

$$= \frac{(x_1 + x_2 + \ldots\ldots\ldots\ldots x_{16}) + 2 \times 16}{16}$$

$$= \frac{128 + 32}{16} = \frac{160}{16} = 10$$

15. PROBABILITY

Answer Key

1. (B)	2. (C)	3. (A)	4. (C)	5. (A)	6. (C)	7. (A)	8. (C)	9. (A)	10. (B)
11. (B)	12. (B)	13. (B)	14. (C)	15. (C)	16. (C)	17. (B)	18. (C)	19. (B)	20. (B)
21. (C)	22. (C)	23. (D)	24. (A)	25. (D)					

1.(B)

P (composite number)

$$= \frac{100 + 100}{600} = \frac{200}{600} = \frac{1}{3}$$

$$\{\because \text{composite numbers are 4 and 6}\}$$

2.(C)

P (drawing sum as even number)

$$= \frac{18}{36} = \frac{1}{2}$$

3.(A)

Prime numbers are 2, 3, 5, 7.

$\therefore$ Sum of frequencies $= 23 + 20 + 11 + 30$
$$= 84$$

$\therefore$ Required probability $= \dfrac{84}{200} = \dfrac{42}{100} = 0.42$

4.(C)

1, 3, 5, 7 and 9 are odd numbers.

$\therefore$ Required probability

$$= \frac{26 + 20 + 11 + 30 + 20}{200} = \frac{107}{200}$$

5.(A)

Prime numbers which can be got as a sum of the numbers on dice are 2, 3, 5, 7, 11.

$\therefore$ Required probability $= \dfrac{1 + 2 + 4 + 6 + 2}{36}$

$$= \frac{15}{36} = \frac{5}{12}$$

6.(C)

Tail is obtained $\left(\dfrac{3}{8} \times 1000\right)$ times $= 375$ times.

$\therefore$ Head is obtained $(1000 - 375) = 625$ times.

7.(A)

$$P \text{ (getting tail)} = \frac{545}{1000} = \frac{109}{200}$$

8.(C)

P (student getting 40 or more marks)

$$= \frac{23+20}{90} = \frac{43}{90}$$

9.(A)

Outcomes are HH, TT, TH, HT

$$P \text{ (getting at least 1 tail)} = \frac{3}{4}$$

10.(B)

$$P \text{ (getting a red card)} = \frac{26}{52} = \frac{1}{2}$$

11.(B)

$$P \text{ (getting a king)} = \frac{4}{52} = \frac{1}{13}$$

12.(B)

$$P \text{ (student chosen is girl)} = \frac{36-20}{36}$$
$$= \frac{16}{36} = \frac{4}{9}$$

13.(B)

Outcomes are HHH, HHT, HTH, HTT, THT, TTH, TTT, THH.

$$P \text{ (getting exactly 2 heads)} = \frac{3}{8}$$

14.(C)

(1, 1), (2, 2), (3, 3), (4, 4), (5, 5), (6, 6) are the doublets.

$$\therefore P \text{ (getting a doublet)} = \frac{6}{36} = \frac{1}{6}$$

15.(C)

Multiples of 8 are 8, 16, 24 and 32.

$$\therefore P \text{ (getting a multiple of 8)} = \frac{4}{35}$$

16.(C)

P (neither white nor black ball)
$$= P(\text{red or green ball})$$
$$= \frac{6+5}{6+8+5+3} = \frac{11}{22} = \frac{1}{2}$$

17.(B)

Remaining cards $= 52 - 2 \times 4$
$$= 52 - 8 = 44$$

$$\therefore P \text{ (drawing a black king)} = \frac{2}{44} = \frac{1}{22}$$

18.(C)

Let the number of black balls in the bag be x.

$$\therefore \quad 3 \times \frac{5}{5+x} = \left(\frac{x}{5+x} \right)$$
$$\Rightarrow \quad x = 15$$

19.(B)

1987 is non-leap year.

$\therefore$ Number of days = 365

$\therefore P$ (birthday will fall on different days)
$$= 1 - P(\text{birthday on same day})$$
$$= 1 - \frac{1}{365} = \frac{364}{365}$$

20.(B)

P (getting a non – defective bulb)
$$= \frac{200-20}{200}$$
$$= \frac{180}{200} = \frac{9}{10}$$

21.(C)

Leap year has 366 days, i.e.,
$$\frac{364}{7} = 52 \text{ weeks and 2 days.}$$

The 2 days can either be MT, TW, WTH, ThF, FS, SS, SM.

$\because$ Thursday–Friday and Friday–Saturday are 2 favourable outcomes.

$$\therefore \text{ Required probability} = \frac{2}{7}$$

22.(C)

P (occurrence of a event) $+ P$ (non- occurrence of event) = total probability = 1

23.(D)

Number of multiples of $5 = \dfrac{100-50}{5} = 10$

$\therefore$ Required probability $= 1 - \dfrac{10}{50} = 1 - \dfrac{1}{5} = \dfrac{4}{5}$

24.(A)

King, queen and jack are known as face cards.

Number of red face cards $= 2 \times 3 = 6$

$\therefore$ Required probability $= \dfrac{6}{52} = \dfrac{3}{26}$

25.(D)

The outcomes are:

$(1, 1)\ (1, 2)\ (1, 3)\ (1, 4)\ (1, 5)\ (1, 6)$
$(2, 1)\ (2, 2)\ (2, 3)\ (2, 4)\ (2, 5)\ (2, 6)$
$(3, 1)\ (3, 2)\ (3, 3)\ (3, 4)\ (3, 5)\ (3, 6)$
$(4, 1)\ (4, 2)\ (4, 3)\ (4, 4)\ (5, 5)\ (5, 6)$
$(5, 1)\ (5, 2)\ (5, 3)\ (5, 4)\ (5, 5)\ (5, 6)$
$(6, 1)\ (6, 2)\ (6, 3)\ (6, 4)\ (6, 5)\ (6, 6)$

Even $\times$ odd = even and odd $\times$ odd = odd.

$\therefore$ For product to be odd, both numbers should be odd.

$\therefore$ Required probability $= \dfrac{9}{36} = \dfrac{1}{4}$

HOTS (ACHIEVERS SECTION)

26. (A)	27. (A)	28. (B)	29. (C)	30. (D)

16. LOGICAL REASONING

Answer Key

1. (B)	2. (C)	3. (D)	4. (A)	5. (C)	6. (C)	7. (A)	8. (C)	9. (B)	10. (C)
11. (C)	12. (C)	13. (A)	14. (B)	15. (B)	16. (B)	17. (B)	18. (D)	19. (B)	20. (A)
21. (D)	22. (C)	23. (A)	24. (B)	25. (C)	26. (A)	27. (A)	28. (A)	29. (A)	30. (C)
31. (A)	32. (C)	33. (E)	34. (A)	35. (C)	36. (C)	37. (B)	38. (C)	39. (A)	40. (C)
41. (A)	42. (D)	43. (C)	44. (B)	45. (B)					

1.(B)

First word is hatred for the second word.

2.(C)

The word in each pair are synonyms of each other.

3.(D)

The second word is more intense form of first word.

4.(A)

Except pallete, all words are parts of a gun.

5.(C)

Except explosion, all words are natural calamites.

6.(C)

Except groundnut, all are type of spices.

7.(A)

The given numbers are in the set of three numbers which are Pythagorean triplet.

$$3^2 + 4^2 = 5^2, \quad 5^2 + 12^2 = 13^2,$$
$$7^2 + 24^2 = 25^2, \quad 9^2 + 40^2 = 41^2.$$

8.(C)

The pattern of the given series is

$$3 - 1 = 2; \quad 6 - 3 = 3; \quad 10 - 6 = 4;$$
$$15 - 10 = 5; \quad 21 - 15 = 6;$$
$$\therefore \quad 21 + 7 = 28$$

HINTS AND SOLUTIONS

9.(B)

The pattern of the given series is
$$3^2 + 1 = 10; \quad 4^2 + 1 = 17; \quad 5^2 + 1 = 26;$$
$$6^2 + 1 = 37; \quad 7^2 + 1 = 50;$$
$$\therefore \ 8^2 + 1 = 65.$$

10.(C)

Taking $Z = 2$, $Y = 3$, …… $N = 14$,

$B = 26$, $A = 27$

$\therefore \ \text{ZIP} = (2 + 19 + 12) \times 6 = 33 \times 6 = 198$

and $\text{VIP} = (V + I + P) \times 6 = (6 + 19 + 12) \times 6$
$$= 37 \times 6 = 222$$

Hence $\text{ZAP} = (Z + A + P) \times 6$
$$= (2 + 27 + 12) \times 6$$
$$= 41 \times 6 = 246$$

11.(C)

Here STATEMENT $\rightarrow$ TNEMETATS

Then POLITICAL $\rightarrow$ LACITILOP

12.(C)

Given $134 \rightarrow$ good and tasty.

$478 \rightarrow$ see good pictures

$428 \rightarrow$ pictures are good.

Hence $4 \rightarrow$ Good and $8 \rightarrow$ Pictures

13.(A)

When Pankaj shifts 3 places towards Raju his position is 15th from right and 10th from left.

$\therefore$ No. of students $= 15 + 10 - 1 = 24$ students.

14.(B)

Day after tomorrow is Saturday, means today is Thursday. Yesterday was Wednesday, three days before Wednesday was Sunday.

15.(B)

1st November is Wednesday.

31st October is Tuesday.

29th, 22th, 15th, 8th, 1st October were Sundays.

16.(B)

As per question

Z Y X W V U T S R Q P O N M L K J I H G F E D C B A
13th   4th

17.(B)

A B C D P O N M L K J I H G F E Q R S T U V W X Y Z
7th   14th

$\therefore$ J is the required letter.

18.(D)

According to the question AZ, BY, CX, DW, EV, FU, GT, HS, IR, JQ, KP, LO, MN.

19.(B)

Meena's mother's son = Meena's brother

Rajan is son of Meena's brother.

So, Meena is Rajan's aunt.

20.(A)

Sarita's father's only daughter means Sarita.

Rekha is Sarita's daughter.

21.(D)

Sulekha's father's only son = Sulekha's brother.

Kanchan is son of Sulekha's brother.

Kanchan's mother is wife of Sulekha's brother.

So, Kanchan's mother is Sulekha's sister in law.

22.(C)

We have 4 P 10 Q 6 R 3 S 8
$$= 4 + 10 \times 6 \div 3 - 8$$
$$= 4 + 10 \times 2 - 8$$
$$= 4 + 20 - 8$$
$$= 24 - 8 = 16$$

23.(A)

Here 14 A 6 B 8 C 2 D 12
$$= 14 \times 6 + 8 \div 2 - 12$$
$$= 14 \times 6 + 4 - 12$$
$$= 84 + 4 - 12$$
$$= 88 - 12 \qquad\qquad = 76$$

24.(B)

Here 27 J 15 K 2 M 18 L 3
$$= 27 - 15 \times 2 + 18 \div 3$$
$$= 27 - 15 \times 2 + 6$$
$$= 27 - 30 + 6$$
$$= 33 - 30 = 3$$

25.(C)

Let the no. of horses be x

Then no. of men $= x$

$\therefore$ total number of legs $= 4x + 2 \times \dfrac{x}{2} = 70$

$\Rightarrow \qquad 5x = 70 \Rightarrow x = 14$

26.(A)

Let Ram's age $= x$, Mohan's age $= y$

Lokesh's age $= z$

$\therefore \qquad\qquad x = 3y \qquad\qquad\qquad \dots(1)$

and $\qquad z - 4 = 2\,(x - 4)$

$\qquad\qquad z = 2x - 8 + 4 = 2x - 4 \qquad \dots(2)$

$\qquad\qquad x + 4 = 31 \Rightarrow x = 27$

$\qquad\qquad 3y = 27 \Rightarrow y = 9$

Using eqn. (2) $z = 2x - 4 = 2 \times 27 - 4 = 50$

Hence $\quad z - y = 50 - 9 = 41$

27.(A)

Let Mukesh's present age be x years.

$\therefore \qquad x + 1 = 2\,(x - 12)$

$\qquad\qquad x + 1 = 2x - 24$

$\Rightarrow \qquad\qquad x = 25$ years

Mukesh's age 5 years ago $= 25 - 5 = 20$ years

28.(A)

Here $\left(\sqrt{1} + \sqrt{9} + \sqrt{25} + \sqrt{81}\right)^2$

$\qquad = (1 + 3 + 5 + 9)^2 = (18)^2 = 324$

and $\left(\sqrt{64} + \sqrt{4} + \sqrt{9} + \sqrt{16}\right)^2$

$\qquad = (8 + 2 + 3 + 4)^2 = (17)^2 = 289$

$\therefore \ ? = \left(\sqrt{16} + \sqrt{25} + \sqrt{1} + \sqrt{81}\right)^2$

$\qquad = (4 + 5 + 1 + 9)^2 = 361$

29.(A)

Here $4 \times 2 \times 8 \times 6 = 384$

$\qquad\qquad 3 \times 3 \times 4 \times 6 = 216$

$\therefore \qquad 6 \times 8 \times 7 \times 4 = 1344$

30.(C)

Here $(3^2 + 6^2) - (2^2 + 4^2) = 45 - 20 = 25$

and $(11^2 + 7^2) - (6^2 + 8^2) = 170 - 100 = 70$

$\therefore \qquad (x^2 + 3^2) - (2^2 + 7^2) = x^2 + 9 - 53 = 20$

$\qquad\qquad \Rightarrow x^2 - 44 = 20$

$\qquad\qquad \Rightarrow x^2 = 64 \Rightarrow x = 8$

31.(A)

Two and three half-leaves are added to the figure alternately. The addition of half-leaves takes place in an ACW direction.

32.(C)

The two elements together move two spaces (each space is equal to half-a-side of the square boundary) and three space ACW alternately. Also, in one step, the two elements interchange positions and together rotate 90° CW and in the next step, the two elements interchange positions and together rotate through 180°.

33.(E)

The arrow moves one, two, three, four, ... spaces ACW sequentially. The arrowhead changes in the sequence: circle $\rightarrow$ arc $\rightarrow$ triangle $\rightarrow$ circle $\rightarrow$ ....

34.(C)

In this figure, there is 1 column having 3 cubes, 7 columns containing 2 cubes and 13 columns containing 1 cube.

$\therefore$ Total number of cubes

$\qquad = 1 \times 3 + 7 \times 2 + 13 \times 1$

$\qquad = 3 + 14 + 13 = 30$

35.(B)

In this figure, there are 23 columns having 3 cubes each, 8 columns having 2 cubes each and 3 columns having 1 cube each.

$\therefore$ Total no. of cubes $= 23 \times 3 + 8 \times 2 + 3 \times 1$

$\qquad\qquad = 69 + 16 + 3 = 88$

36.(B)

In the figure, there are 48 columns having 3 cubes each and 12 columns having 2 cubes each.

$\therefore$ Total no. of cubes $= 48 \times 3 + 12 \times 2$

$\qquad\qquad = 144 + 24 = 168$

Answer Key

1. (C)	2. (B)	3. (A)	4. (A)	5. (B)	6. (A)	7. (C)	8. (C)	9. (B)	10. (B)
11. (D)	12. (A)	13. (A)	14. (B)	15. (D)	16. (A)	17. (B)	18. (D)	19. (A)	20. (B)
21. (D)	22. (A)	23. (D)	24. (A)	25. (D)	26. (A)	27. (C)	28. (A)	29. (A)	30. (B)
31. (B)	32. (B)	33. (A)	34. (B)	35. (D)	36. (B)	37. (A)	38. (B)	39. (C)	40. (A)
41. (B)	42. (B)	43. (A)	44. (D)	45. (D)	46. (D)	47. (A)	48. (B)	49. (C)	50. (A)

SAMPLE OMR ANSWER SHEET

1. STUDENT NAME (IN ENGLISH CAPITAL LETTERS ONLY)

Students must write and darken the respective circles completely using HB Pencil only. Othewise their Answer Sheets will not be evaluated.

PERSONAL DETAILS

2. SCHOOL CODE

3. CLASS

4. SECTION

5. ROLL NO.

6. QUESTION PAPER SET

A ○ B ○ C ○ D ○

MARK YOUR ANSWERS

1.	A B C D	26.	A B C D
2.	A B C D	27.	A B C D
3.	A B C D	28.	A B C D
4.	A B C D	29.	A B C D
5.	A B C D	30.	A B C D
6.	A B C D	31.	A B C D
7.	A B C D	32.	A B C D
8.	A B C D	33.	A B C D
9.	A B C D	34.	A B C D
10.	A B C D	35.	A B C D
11.	A B C D	36.	A B C D
12.	A B C D	37.	A B C D
13.	A B C D	38.	A B C D
14.	A B C D	39.	A B C D
15.	A B C D	40.	A B C D
16.	A B C D	41.	A B C D
17.	A B C D	42.	A B C D
18.	A B C D	43.	A B C D
19.	A B C D	44.	A B C D
20.	A B C D	45.	A B C D
21.	A B C D	46.	A B C D
22.	A B C D	47.	A B C D
23.	A B C D	48.	A B C D
24.	A B C D	49.	A B C D
25.	A B C D	50.	A B C D

7. MOBILE NUMBER

8. GENDER

MALE ○

FEMALE ○

9. STREAM

(Only for Class XI and XII Students)

MATHEMATICS ○
BIOLOGY ○
OTHERS ○

Signature of the Student & Date of Examination	Signature of the Invigilator & Date of Examination

www.ingramcontent.com/pod-product-compliance
Lightning Source LLC
LaVergne TN
LVHW060354200726
843506LV00003B/218